WHATEVER THE ODDS

KUSHAL PAL SINGH, popularly known as K.P. Singh, has been the chairman of DLF Ltd for several decades and is a trustee and member of the governing boards of various educational and philanthropic institutions. He was conferred the Padma Bhushan by the President of India in 2010 in recognition of his outstanding achievements.

RAMESH MENON is a journalist with thirty-seven years of experience in print, television and new media. He won the prestigious Ramnath Goenka Award for Excellence in Journalism in 2005. He is presently Managing Editor of *India Legal*, the country's first politico-legal magazine. He is also the author of *Modi Demystified: The Making of a Prime Minister* (HarperCollins, 2014).

RAMAN SWAMY is a Delhi-based journalist and writer. He has worked with the *Times of India*, the *Economic Times*, *India Today* and *Sunday Observer*. He has been editor of *This Fortnight*, *Surya India* and *Now Magazine*. He is the co-author of *The Other India at Work*, a coffee-table book published by the ILO.

PRAISE FOR *Whatever the Odds*

'Singh takes us to the tales behind DLF, Gurgaon and countless others in his autobiography. *Whatever the Odds* is a fascinating account of [his] journey.'—*Free Press Journal*

'The book celebrates the harmony of close-knit extended families, the loyalty, trust and affection invested in hard-to-come-by friendships and a happy union of business ethics and personal beliefs.'—*Business World*

'The book is punctuated with gripping anecdotes on the deciding moments in Singh's life and the turning points both on his professional and personal fronts. [It] documents the journey of DLF, its early setbacks, the happy milestones and the constant battle for survival.'—*Business Line*

'A fascinating account it is, smoothly racing from his childhood as a "village lad" to his polo-playing days and eventually to "grappling with a labyrinth of archaic laws" in his effort to convince farmers, field by field, it seems, to let him develop Gurgaon to better their futures.'—*TimeOut*

WHATEVER THE ODDS

The Incredible Story behind DLF

K.P. Singh

with

Ramesh Menon and Raman Swamy

HarperCollins *Publishers* India

First published in India by
HarperCollins *Publishers* in 2011
An imprint of HarperCollins Publishers
HarperCollins *Publishers* India, Cyber City, Building 10-A, Gurugram, Haryana-122002, India
www.harpercollins.co.in

2 4 6 8 10 9 7 5 3

P-ISBN: 9789351160373
E-ISBN: 9789351160977

Typeset in 12/16 Aldine401 BT at
SÜRYA

Printed and bound at
Manipal Technologies Limited, Manipal

*

HarperCollins *Publishers*, Macken House, 39/40 Mayor Street Upper, Dublin 1, D01 C9W8, Ireland

Dedicated to all young men and women who have a burning desire to build a better India

CONTENTS

PREFACE

IT HAD NEVER really occurred to me to write a book about myself till a few years ago when some of my friends began to persuade me to pen down my autobiography. Mohan Primlani, the managing director of Oxford & IBH, planted the idea in my mind that perhaps the story of my life was worth writing about. Aroon Purie, the India Today group chairman, not only urged me to write but also offered to get it published by HarperCollins India, which too he heads.

I owe my thanks to both of them, and to many others who convinced me that my experiences could be of interest to the public at large and especially useful to budding entrepreneurs and business management students alike.

It is a different matter that nobody warned me just what I was getting into. I soon discovered that conjuring up old memories of people and places, revisiting half-forgotten episodes and encounters and trying to piece together the high points of my life, spanning eight decades, would take many months of very hard work and evoke strong emotions by bringing alive once more the joys and sorrows of years gone by.

Indeed, this book could not have been written without the meticulous and painstaking research by senior journalist Ramesh

Menon, who worked tirelessly for long hours with me for nearly two years, helping sift through mounds of information and transforming my thoughts into the written word. As a matter of fact, we started working on an authorized biography, but my publishers pushed me to agree to an autobiography as they felt my story would be more evocative if told in the first person. Hence, I was forced to use the pronoun 'I'. This made me a bit uncomfortable, as on my own, I would never have achieved all that I did. All through my life's journey, it was the collective effort of my family, friends and colleagues which helped and guided me. So, wherever in this book you see 'I', especially with regard to my effort to revive DLF, please take it to mean many others who were with me. Among those who provided invaluable information and details were my late sister Vikramdevi Singh, Sridevi Sundarajan, Ranjit Cheema, Brigadier A.P. Singh, Akash Ohri, Rajeev Talwar, Rajiv Malhotra, R. Hariharan, K. Swarup, Subhash Setia, A.P. Garg, Amritlal Jain, Saroop Chand Ansal, K.C. Katoch and Chaudhary Rajpal Singh and his grandson Dhananjay Tevathia. Special thanks are due to Rakeysh Omprakash Mehra and his creative team of film makers for capturing the spirit of the book on celluloid.

Once the first draft of the book was ready, we went through a tireless process of many, many rewrites to add value to the narrative and bring to life the dramatic twists and turns, anecdotes and incidents that have marked my life. This is where co-author Raman Swamy, who probably understands both me and DLF as few others do, came in. He critiqued the chapters, gave invaluable advice and helped to make the book as readable as possible with his practised pen. I also owe very special thanks to seasoned writer Dilip Bobb, who made a significant contribution with his uncanny knack of capturing the mood and flavour of my life.

Critical comments by my dear friend Maharajakrishna Rasgotra, the distinguished former bureaucrat, helped me see some parts of the book in a new light. I would like to place on record my grateful thanks to him for the time he has spent in poring through each page, line by line, of the draft manuscript. Despite her busy life in London, Mala found the time to provide many perceptive comments and imaginative inputs. Vinayak Venkatraman made some useful suggestions. I am also indebted to Jaquine and Bob Arnold, Henry Dallal, Michael Menezes, Col. Prithvi Nath, Vipin Khanna, and Barbara and Hira Sehgal and their daughter Romilla for their suggestions and contributions.

I had no penchant for preserving photographs though thousands of them had been taken. I did not even know where they were. But Chhote Lal Maurya, who has been working with me for over three decades, rummaged through old trunks and discovered vintage pictures that I did not know existed. I was delighted to find pictures of Marthe Wadalia that her daughter Tara found for me. Sanjey Roy along with his colleagues, Divya Puri and Binayak Bhattacharjee, then spent many hours for weeks trying to bunch the right photographs together and providing catchy captions. Hari Gopalakrishnan worked on new visuals, exploring different angles with great patience. Senior photographers Saibal Das, Hardev Singh and Pervez came up with evocative images. Debashish Gupta of HT Burda tirelessly showed me numerous design options. I am grateful to the Commandant of the Indian Military Academy (IMA), Lt Gen R.S. Sujlana, for providing access to the academy archives. And I am thankful to Goyal Studios, the official photographers of the IMA, who retrieved old albums and were able to ferret out photographs of me.

My personal staff also played an important role. Sethumadhavan K.C., my executive assistant, who is a retired honorary captain of the Indian Army, toiled for many months patiently helping with numerous corrections as we worked on rewrites and revisions. He also travelled to Dehra Dun to dig out the documents and photographs pertaining to my training at the academy. General

Manager V.K. Bhatia, who has spent over three decades with me, made several visits to the offices of the Faridabad Industrial Association, PHD Chamber of Commerce and Industry and ASSOCHAM to obtain useful information. S.K. Mukhi travelled to various places like Haridwar, my birthplace Abupur, Khandera, Ghaziabad, and other places to help in tracing my roots. Aruna de Souza, with her extraordinary charm and efficiency, set up important meetings and interviews with a variety of personalities like my old army colleagues, foreign dignitaries and other government officials. Special thanks are due to Manjit Kaur, who took such good care of Indira's medical and emotional needs during the writing of this book that I was able to spend long hours over many months with a free mind, secure in the knowledge that someone who has almost become a part of our family would always be at my wife's side. A word of appreciation to Nathu Singh and Dalbir Singh, without whose dedicated services I would not have been able to sit for long hours late into the night working on this autobiography.

Krishan Chopra, Chief Editor and Publisher at HarperCollins, helped me to objectively look at the material we had. His suggestions were useful in helping us meet deadlines and in guiding us through the process of taking the manuscript to publication. I also appreciate the fine teamwork at HarperCollins all through from Shantanu Ray Chaudhuri, Shuka Jain, Amrita Chakravorty, Amit Sharma, Rajeev Sethi and others in providing editorial, design and production support for the book. I also specially thank Rajinder Ganju of SÜRYA for his invaluable help in typesetting the text for production.

A very special word of thanks is due to my wife Indira, who has stood by me during my toughest years, for inspiring and encouraging me to write my life story. I am also deeply indebted to all the members of my family for their moral support and critical comments.

There are so many more friends and associates to thank and I may please be forgiven if I have inadvertently missed mentioning anyone. They must know that I am grateful for everything they did to make this book a reality. A big thank you to all of you!

1

THE MYSTERIES OF FATE

I HAVE CHEATED death on five occasions, switched almost overnight from the rural backwaters of Uttar Pradesh to being chauffeured around in a Rolls-Royce, rubbed shoulders with English high society and almost married into it, but fate intervened and sent me back to India and a cavalry regiment of the Indian Army. From the polo fields of Rajasthan to an armoured tank on the Punjab border, I was thrown into the world of business without any management background, hovered on the edge of bankruptcy, faced personal tragedy and been the target of a powerful politician's ire. I have shared a meal with impoverished farmers by day and been in the company of the cream of Indian society by night, and along the way, met some truly remarkable people who helped guide my life.

Through most of my life and career, there have been moments when I have arrived at the crossroads of a momentous decision. I could have taken any of the radial roads; there were soft options and hard ones, a life of leisure or one of struggle, hard work and perhaps failure, a comfortable, familiar environment or a plunge into the unknown.

Today, when the media writes about my status as one of India's richest men and the biggest real estate entrepreneur, of how I led DLF to becoming the country's most valuable real estate company, and the high honours and awards that have come my way, they are telling only one part of the story. What they do not speak about are the incredible twists and turns in my life and career path, the long years of struggle, the hundreds of hours I spent under the burning sun, trying to persuade villagers that giving up their relatively small piece of land would guarantee their children and grandchildren a better life.

Each stage was a learning experience, a springboard to reach the next level. My years in England taught me sophistication, self-confidence and also the value of relationships. My nine years as a cavalry officer taught me discipline and courage, as well as ethical behaviour and values. In the early stages of my real estate career, it was my rural and army background that allowed me to be accepted by the farmers whose land I was trying to buy. My involvement with horse-breeding and polo gave me access to people of influence and social mobility in India and abroad. My corporate involvement provided key lessons in management, leadership and networking, while marriage led me, unexpectedly, to the birth of a business empire.

Chance meetings and unplanned events sometimes affect our lives in ways we can never imagine. As a callow, wide-eyed youngster fresh from a semi-rural existence in a small town like Bulandshahr, I was visiting my uncle who was in charge of the stables at the Viceregal Lodge, now Rashtrapati Bhavan, when the viceroy, Lord Wavell, walked in. I could have been arrested or thrown out, but instead he encouraged me to take up riding. That act of kindness and his unscheduled visit opened many doors. The love of riding I acquired in those stables changed my life. It gave me a passion for horses that was to take me to new adventures and experiences.

My father sent me to England at great personal sacrifice, hiding from me the debt he had to incur to get me there. In England, the riding skills learnt at the viceregal stables gave me access to high society and led to a romantic relationship that showed me a different side of life. Playing polo near Windsor, I met an officer of the Indian Army who tried to convince me that my future lay in India, and in a cavalry unit of the Indian Army. It was an excruciating dilemma; of perhaps marriage and settling down in England to embrace a privileged existence or returning to India to undergo a regimented military life and a career I wasn't sure I wanted. Again, fate intervened and brought me to another turning point. I was given permission to sit for the entrance examination for the IMA – Indian Military Academy – in England, the first time such a concession was granted. I passed with excellent grades, but life in the UK still exerted a strong pull, as did a young lady I had become attached to. Then another rare concession added a twist in the tale: the government agreed to pay my fare back to India. The pressure was mounting. I sought advice from people whose opinion I valued and finally decided to return and join the IMA, a heart-wrenching move but one that, in hindsight, proved the right one. It put me on the road to an incredible journey.

That was not so apparent during my introduction to the academy. It was so regimented after the liberated, happy-go-lucky life I had led until then that I actually hatched a naïve and foolish plan to run away and catch a train home. The battalion commander became aware of my plans and it could have resulted in my being labelled a deserter and my life would have been ruined. Instead, he threw away the rule book and his astute advice and guidance convinced me to carry on with my army career. It proved to be another fateful decision. Army life turned out to be exciting, adventurous and rewarding, but it also brought me an unexpected bonus: an introduction to the woman who would become my wife and the rock in what was till then a turbulent existence.

Those days, the image of a dashing cavalry officer and the fact that my seniors felt I had the potential to reach high rank gave me the status of a most eligible bachelor. My commanding officer became matchmaker and approached his friend, an honorary colonel with another cavalry unit, to set up a meeting between his daughter, Indira, and me. We met, courted, fell in love and married. Another fascinating journey had started, one that was destined to teach me a lot about sacrifice, humility, love, dedication, togetherness and support. She was to become my most reliable anchor and strength in the years to come. Indeed, her advice and encouragement enabled me to chase dreams that seemed unachievable at first sight. In most traditional business families in India, the wife is rarely consulted on business matters. With Indira, it was different. I respected her advice and instinct and her ability to push me beyond the boundaries I had erected for myself. On numerous occasions when I was in doubt, her words: 'You can do it,' were enough for me to go further and higher. What I am today in the world of business is largely due to her instinctive understanding of my ambitions and goals and my entrepreneurial abilities. Often, in the heady rush of achievement and success, one forgets to give credit where it is due. Indira was the wind beneath my wings.

I quit the army but maintained my romance with horses by setting up a stud farm on a barren, rocky piece of land with my father-in-law. He happened to be the founder of a real estate company called DLF. From a comfortable but hectic life in the army, I found myself thrown into the world of business. It was like diving into the deep end without knowing how to swim, but it gave me invaluable experience in dealing with red tape and negotiating the bureaucratic labyrinth of land acquisitions and obtaining clearances. At first, it was difficult to tear myself away from the heady, jet-set world of polo and horse-breeding and its attendant social merry-go-round. My wife and I were partying almost every night with the elite of Delhi and international celebrities, often returning home when my father-in-law was going out for his morning walk. It was on one of these occasions that he brought me down to earth by reminding me that I had business responsibilities as well. Not used to being admonished by him, I resented what he had said. But reflecting on it later, I realized I had to now make changes in my life, tear myself away from my night parties and focus on a business career. Indira was understanding and supportive. It became another of those turning points, the start of another chapter in my life. More importantly, it laid the foundation of a real estate empire and an enduring legacy.

I entered the corporate world with little knowledge of its inner workings but again, I was fortunate enough to meet stalwarts who would mentor and inspire me to aim for greater heights. I became close to two corporate legends, one of them being George Hoddy, founder of Universal Electric Co. in the United States. He taught me a lot about leadership, teamwork, management and business strategy, elements that would prove indispensable when I set out on my own to try and revive DLF and build it into one of India's biggest brands. The other was Jack Welch, then the head of GE and one of the world's most celebrated business leaders. My association with him helped me to think big and aim to be number one. It was a time of enormous struggle that called for patience and perseverance, but also a time of immense successes. All those hours of sitting on charpoys in the middle of a dusty field drinking endless glasses of buttermilk would sow the seeds of a burgeoning business, while, at the same time, I was rubbing shoulders with senior political leaders, corporate gurus, top bureaucrats, and social celebrities. Whatever fate may have in store, in the end, you have to write your own destiny. Mine was written in a township, later a boom city called Gurgaon.

Gurgaon was then a typical small town of Haryana. In 1972, my father-in-law retired from DLF. He had almost closed it down after private developers were forced out of the business of urban land development by obstructive government regulations. Three years later, DLF almost shut down for lack of finance. In those days, banks were barred from giving loans to the real estate sector. It was a high-risk gamble, but I took another momentous decision – to leave the manufacturing sector and try and revive DLF armed with nothing more than the credibility of my father-in-law's image as a builder. DLF was then Delhi's most admired real estate company, having built some of the most coveted colonies in the capital, including Greater Kailash, South Extension and Hauz Khas, standing proof of high standards of construction and clean financial transactions. Haryana was a different proposition. Farmers here were emotionally attached to their land. Using my own rural background, I set out to convince them of the benefits of the partnership model we proposed. We also offered a unique business plan for compensation which established trust and transparency. It worked and DLF was on its way to becoming a corporate legend while Gurgaon set out to earn the title of Millennium City.

Today, when in Gurgaon, I sometimes take the elevator to a rooftop of one of DLF's highrises and look out over the sprawling, ever-evolving city. Despite its infrastructural drawbacks, it is the most modern-looking city in India with its glittering malls, gated condominiums, neatly divided sectors, contemporary skyscrapers housing some of the world's best-known multinational corporations, and exciting nightlife. It is a heady but also a humbling experience to examine my role in all this. Building colonies in Delhi is what gave DLF its name and reputation, building the foundations of what would become a dynamic, thriving city in nearby Haryana took it to an altogether new level.

A meeting in Gurgaon one afternoon with a young man driving

an all-terrain vehicle had much to do with this. His vehicle had stalled because of an overheating radiator. I happened to be near by and arranged for water to cool the radiator. He asked me what I was doing out in the wilderness and heard with great interest about my plans and how archaic laws and policies were stifling real estate development. Not long after, he became the prime minister of the country and was instrumental in ushering the private sector back into urban development. Those reforms would revolutionize the real estate sector and also allow DLF to expand at a scorching pace. There was chance, too, at work in my encounter with the militant union leader who had shut down my business by getting the workers to strike and damage equipment and offices. I dropped in unannounced to meet him and introduced myself. It turned out my father had helped him in a time of dire need. Not only was the strike called off but I was permitted to sack four hundred employees who had violated the rules and indulged in violence. Then, there was the long-haired barefooted man I helped during a train journey many years ago, a painter of hoardings and an artist. On a whim, I offered him a job in DLF. He would repay that act of kindness by gifting me paintings of my favourite subject: horses. It also was the start of a close friendship. And those paintings that hang on the walls of my residence in Delhi are today worth a fortune.

The pages that follow attempt to capture and recreate some of the people, events and encounters that helped shape and enrich my life. I share these chronicles with my readers in the hope that young people may find the story inspiring and perhaps even worthy of emulation in their own lives. Also, it might perhaps provide some useful ideas to those young men and women who rise to positions where they can take or influence decisions that affect millions of lives.

2

CHASING RAINBOWS

MY EARLIEST MEMORIES are of happy, carefree days running barefoot through the wheat fields and mango groves that surrounded the village where I was born, playing rustic games like gilli-danda with other children, climbing on to the backs of buffaloes and catching the bright fireflies that filled the air after the sun had set.

I remember, as a little boy, how I loved to chase butterflies across the fields. Often, as the yellow butterflies dodged and weaved in the air, I would trip and stumble and fall into dark brown puddles, bruising my knees on the stones that lay scattered on the ground. The bruises would turn into an angry red, which would soon mellow into a deep purple. My mother would scold me for my foolishness and would warn me never again to run after butterflies, that it was a waste of time and energy, and that I would only end up getting hurt.

But that very night, I would again venture out with my sister, this time to catch fireflies in the dark. We would fill our hands with the star-like twinkles of bright light. We would look up in wonder and longing at the trees lining the canal, illuminated by hundreds of twinkling fireflies.

Another fascination, as for any child, was the rainbow. During the rainy season, as the sunlight filtered through the heavy clouds, at the first hint of violet and pink, I used to sprint across the courtyard. Out through the huge iron gate, towards the miracle of colours in the sky, skipping over the slush and ignoring the reprimands of elders.

It was simply the exhilaration of the chase, of course, because the rainbow stayed as far away as ever.

When I look back today at my youth and early childhood, I feel that even after all these years, butterflies and fireflies and rainbows are still a part of my existence. I sometimes feel that I have been chasing rainbows all my life.

Many people who meet me today assume that I must have been born with a silver spoon in my mouth, enjoyed a privileged childhood in some elite big-city school and been very good in studies. The reality was quite different. I grew up in a small village, travelled in bullock-carts and my playgrounds were open fields which were dry and dusty in summer and turned wet and muddy during the rainy season. My first school was the local madrasa where I used to walk barefoot to attend classes. It was only later that I switched to an English-medium school, but the truth is that I was never really interested in classrooms and books. I spent as much time as I could outdoors, playing all kinds of games and sports, and even though I always tried to win, I know that what I liked most of all was the sheer thrill of competing and doing my best.

My parents were proud and hard-working people who gave me every opportunity they could afford to encourage my growth and prospects. I was their only surviving son. My elder brother, Rajendar, had died very young of pneumonia. We lived in a village called Khandera and the nearest medical centre was quite some distance away in the city of Bulandshahr.

I was born a few years after my parents lost Rajendar and the celebrations that followed my birth were an indication of the hopes that my parents, Rampyari Devi and Chaudhry Mukhtar Singh, had of me. Their expectation that I would enhance the family name and reputation made me strive harder for success. I was fortunate to have a great motivator and role model: my father. He was a self-made man. He obtained a law degree and started practice in Bulandshahr. He soon acquired a reputation as a strong, upright, no-nonsense personality and commanded considerable respect in judicial circles and civil society.

As he was a strict disciplinarian even in his personal life, I did not have much interaction with him since, like most people, I lived in awe of him; but for a youngster there is no better foundation in life, no matter where he is and in what financial situation, than a strict but fair-minded father and the strength, support and confidence that a close-knit extended family provides. My sister Vikramdevi, who passed away in March 2011 at the age of eighty-six, and my cousin, Chaudhry Rajpal Singh, who is now ninety-five, had between them a much better recollection of my earliest years and of life as it was then.

As per their recall, I had two different dates of birth. One was 19 November 1929, as written in the horoscope prepared by the well-known Pandit Udhav Dutt of Jasrana in Aligarh. However, in the local municipal records, it was registered as 15 August 1931. I suspect the earlier version is more accurate. It was a fairly common practice in India in those days, especially among salaried social classes, to deliberately lower their children's ages in official documents in order to give them a couple of extra earning years in government service before retirement. Moreover, as I was born in a village, there were no reliable birth records. I never celebrated my birthdays until much later in life, although I must admit that I did opt for 19 November as my date of birth and I more than made up for all the birthday parties I had missed!

I seem to have inherited my father's passion for sports. He was an outstanding sportsman who even represented Uttar Pradesh in inter-state tennis and hockey tournaments. Inspired and encouraged by him, I also took up tennis and hockey and excelled in sports during my college days, which later played a significant role in both my personal and professional life.

Despite our rural upbringing, we were quite comfortable as a joint family of landlords and lawyers and owned substantial farmland and mango orchards. We grew some of the most famed mangoes in the country and, as a kid, I loved going to the farm using every opportunity I got. As the land was extremely fertile, we grew sugarcane, wheat and gram. While my father was busy working hard to build his law practice, others in the family did the farming. My mother was from Abupur village near Modinagar, which is quite close to Delhi. I grew up there for the first four to five years of my life. She had two brothers, Chaudhry Bhaktavar Singh and Chaudhry Dilawar Singh.

Even as a child, I loved the atmosphere of the village and its close-knit community. One unforgettable image is of the canal just short of Modinagar called the Ganga Canal. I often went to its banks to play. Growing up in such tranquil surroundings, mostly under the open sky, was in itself an education.

Rural life makes you tough and robust mainly because of the lack of many of the conveniences and comforts that those living in towns and cities take for granted. It also forces you to spend a lot of time outdoors, leading an active life and imparting an awareness for exercise and health that I appreciate to this day. Even now, at the age of eighty, a 24-hour day still seems too little. If you love your chosen field of work, it adds an incredible amount of energy and enthusiasm to whatever you do, while an active outdoor life encourages longevity.

One outdoor activity I loved was horse-riding. My uncle Bhaktavar Singh would often ride his horse to the highway and then take a bus to his workplace. I used to beg him to let me ride with him. I was just five then and he used to let me sit in front of him. The ride to the highway used to be over pretty rough terrain and, according to my sister's recollections of the incident, on one occasion, the horse lost its footing and both of us fell. Uncle Bhaktavar escaped without any injuries, but I got a bad gash over my right eyebrow. It was only decades later during a routine MRI scan that doctors told me I had suffered an internal injury. It explained the occasional dizzy spells I used to have and ignore. The doctors told me I was lucky to have survived. It wasn't the first time.

I had another narrow escape in my early childhood. It was, I am told, a sweltering day at Khandera. In that part of Uttar Pradesh, temperatures can hit 45 degrees Celsius in the height of summer. Buddha, our family servant, was asked to draw water from the old well behind our house and pour bucketfuls of cool water on the floor. I was then about six years old. I followed Buddha to the well and was intrigued by the process of how the water was drawn via the bucket and the rope tied around the pulley. Curiosity took me to the very edge of the well, which was slippery with moss. I leaned over to get a better look, slipped and fell, hitting the water twenty feet below with a resounding splash.

I surfaced almost immediately, but not knowing how to swim, I flailed about in panic and was about to go down for a second time when my fingers brushed the side of the well, which too was slippery. Through a stroke of luck my fingers closed around a brick that was jutting a little bit out of the well wall. I was even luckier to find that this particular brick did not have moss on it and my fingers did not slip. It was only due to this brief reprieve and a villager called Tejpal, who was nearby, that I survived that day. He immediately jumped in and held me up till the rope could be lowered. It was a miracle that he was there and had the presence of mind to dive in after me. Buddha was in such a state of shock that he had been struck motionless. My mother was hysterical, thinking I had drowned. She had lost one son and could not bear the thought of losing another. Destiny, and a courageous villager with quick reflexes, had given me a new lease of life.

My father struggled with his education, which happened in fits and starts, because of circumstances at home. Finally, he obtained his law degree and started practice in Bulandshahr. Because of his growing reputation, my father was selected by the state government in 1945 as a revenue officer of the Uttar Pradesh Provincial Service. Soon after joining his new assignment, he got disillusioned and resigned from his secure government job to practise law again. Subsequently, he was selected again by the state government to become the public prosecutor at Bulandshahr, where I started my formal education. That is how I came to live in the bustling town.

My mother was a homemaker. She was a very soft-natured person who lived in awe of my father. One of the things that I remember most about her is that she loved to prepare those special dishes which I was most fond of. Every dish that she made had a special flavour of its own. She would never ask me any questions about my academic progress but used to be thrilled with my sporting achievements. I knew that, having lost one son, she was quite protective of me.

I'm still not sure why my father decided to send me to a madrasa when there were other good schools available. It may be because it just happened to be the educational institution nearest to our house. The madrasa was located on the first floor of a small building in a crowded area. It was run by a rigid maulvi who believed that the only way to discipline children was to beat them now and then. He was the caricature of the small-town maulvi, and his only interest lay in getting us to learn Urdu, Persian and the Quran. It was an entirely forgettable experience and I hated every minute. So did my close friend, Sheoraj Singh, as we both got caned for the flimsiest of reasons.

Sheoraj was the son of Than Singh, a lawyer who was a friend of my father. It was Than Singh who taught me some valuable lessons about pride and ancestry. When we complained to him about the maulvi beating us and that we both wanted to leave the madrasa, he gave us a stern lecture.

'How come you have been beaten by a maulvi?' he asked tauntingly. 'Since when have Jat youngsters become so meek? Jats do not get beaten by anybody. If they do, they fight back.'

Fired up by his words, we hatched a plan to take revenge on the maulvi but ultimately, better sense prevailed.

He then told his son that he did not need to go there any more. Encouraged, I asked my father if I could leave as well. To my surprise, he readily agreed. I never forgot that incident and what it taught: never accept something that is unjust and unfair, stand up for your rights and uphold the pride and reputation of your family and community.

In those days, the male members of the family were the ones you turned to for advice and support. Jats were fiercely proud of their ancestry of being a warrior race, which is why the community was male-dominated. Not having a brother and because my father's stern demeanour came in the way of camaraderie between us, I became very close to my sister, Vikramdevi. She looked after me in my younger days and later on, our bond became even stronger. She even helped me out financially during the toughest period of my life, when I was struggling to build a business. She spent her last years in Aralias, which overlooks the DLF Golf and Country Club where I play golf frequently and which also gave me an excuse to visit her. Even though she was very frail and her memory was getting weaker, she would muster up the energy every time I visited her in the months before she died to tell me some of the half-forgotten incidents of my earliest childhood.

She remembered, with some trepidation, the second time I flirted with death. While my father was shifting from Khandera village to Bulandshahr, I contracted diphtheria, which at that time was a near-fatal disease. I was eight years old and in a serious state as the infection was spreading. There were no medical facilities around, just local quacks who had given up on me. The fact that my elder brother had died of pneumonia because of lack of access to medical care made the situation worse. My father's brother, Giriraj Singh, decided to take me to Bulandshahr. It was a gruelling journey. We had to wait for hours for the next bus to arrive as public transport services were very poor. When an overcrowded bus finally arrived, my uncle had to bribe the conductor to get us on board.

By the time we reached Bulandshahr it was late in the evening and my condition was critical. I was rushed to Dr Berry, a well-known allopath. After examining me, he declared that it was too late and he could do nothing. By now, I was gasping for breath. My cousin, Rajpal Singh, remembers how I was taken to Dr Banerjee, a homoeopath who was known for his miraculous cures. At his clinic the doctor gave me some white-coloured pills which were repeated every few hours. By the next day there was marked improvement in my condition. Within a week, I was as good as normal. Everyone, including Dr Berry, felt it was a miracle. From that day, I gained an unusual inner strength, the feeling that some higher force had saved me because there were greater things written in my destiny. It was no coincidence that Giriraj Singh would also play a hidden role in my future.

I spent most of my childhood with him and his wife, Mohar Kaur. They pampered me a lot as they did not have any children. They invested a lot of time in me and I gladly lapped up the attention at both my uncle's home and my parental home being the only son in both families. Giriraj was married into a family from Saidpur village where nearly 90 per cent of the residents had something to do with the defence services, mainly the cavalry. Giriraj's brother-in-law, Raghubir Singh, had become a risaldar major of the 9th Royal Deccan Horse in the early 1940s. It was a regular cavalry regiment of the British Indian Army. I never envisaged my connection with Uncle Raghubir and cavalry horses would dramatically impact my life.

The truth is everyone in the family was extremely fond of me, but none of them ever thought I would amount to much. My sister once told a common friend: 'He was not the studious type at all. No one would have ever imagined that he would emerge as a big businessman. He became serious only after he went abroad to study. Then he started excelling in everything he did.'

She was right when she said I was not into academics. The school I was sent to next was part of the Dayanand Anglo-Vedic Schools System, better known as DAV. This was 1939, when it was the single largest non-governmental education society in India. It was based on the ideals of social reformer Swami Dayanand Saraswati. It was one of those English-medium schools that were scattered across the small towns of India. DAV had a reputation for being an excellent institution but academics had never fired my imagination. What did inspire me, though, was sports. In fact, my most durable memories of school are all to do with the sportsfield. My report card showed me as a mediocre student but I excelled in every sport I took part in, whether it was hockey, tennis, volleyball or athletics. No one was surprised when I was selected as captain of the school's hockey team.

As things turned out, sports played an even larger role in my life when I entered college. My father used to play tennis regularly at two clubs in Bulandshahr. One was the Mumford Club and the other was a government-run club patronized by senior officials. Aware of my aptitude for sports, he used to take me along. The clubs were well-maintained and attracted the more sophisticated Indians because of the facilities, which included tennis courts, billiards, card rooms and a club house. However, this being the backwaters, neither alcohol nor non-vegetarian food was served there.

My father would come back from court by about 4:30 in the evening and I used to look forward to his taking me thereafter to the tennis club. He would make a special effort to teach me the subtler aspects of the game. It was on such rare occasions that I felt close to him.

There were also several professionals playing in both clubs. Sometimes I used to be left in the care of Muzaffar Ali, who was one of the professional players. I learnt the game just by watching him and other professionals play and sometimes, even by playing with them. With their tips, training and encouragement, I became proficient at the game when I was barely ten years old.

After the game my father and I used to sit down on the terrace and I would look forward to a soothing, fragrant drink of *khus khus*. These experiences also exposed me to correct social etiquette as both clubs had gentrified members.

Apart from tennis, my father was an outstanding hockey player. He used to drop in at my school during hockey practice and would teach us the finer aspects of dribbling. I became known as a good player in the right-in position. Whenever we won in either tennis or hockey, my father would come and share in our joy.

Sports opened numerous windows for me, as did the social graces I had learnt at the clubs. Sports also taught me my first lessons in leadership as well as teamwork, both so essential for a successful career. Being on the playing field taught me how to get along with others, how to inspire others to perform, effective team building and the art of formulating strategy.

That career had its beginning in the stables of the Viceregal Lodge, now called Rashtrapati Bhavan. Bulandshahr is around 80 km from Delhi; so, as a youngster, I was able to go there often to visit Uncle Raghubir. In consideration of his outstanding services to the Indian cavalry, he had been awarded the honorary rank of captain and posted as the aide-de-camp (ADC) to Lord Wavell. Being from a cavalry regiment, he was put in charge of horses and stables in the viceroy's contingent. While in college in Meerut, I often visited my uncle's house in Delhi as I was fond of him and his family. But that was not the only reason. I also loved watching the magnificent, well-trained horses he commanded. Invariably, most of my vacations were spent at their house. I used to accompany my uncle when he went to the stables, which lay just behind his Willingdon Crescent residence. I would spend hours watching the horses being fed, groomed and trained by some of the best horsemen in India, mostly British. It was here that my fascination with horses began and the chance encounter with Lord Wavell came about.

Lord Wavell was an exceptional soldier and leader of men and was sent to India after achieving distinction on and off the battlefield. On one of those days when I followed my uncle into the stables, I was busy admiring the horses when suddenly I heard a commotion. The viceroy had made an unannounced visit to the stables. Seeing him enter, everyone sprang to attention. I froze in fear. The viceroy was held in awe because of the enormous powers he exercised. In the entire stable, I was the only one dressed in civilian clothes, all the rest were in uniform. I also happened to be just fifteen years old. Civilians were not allowed to enter the stable area and someone tried to hide me from his view, but my clothes made me stand out like a sore thumb.

As my uncle helped the viceroy dismount, a member of his entourage strode up to him.

'Who is this boy and what is he doing here?' he loudly demanded.

He then proceeded to give my uncle an earful for breach of discipline. My uncle could have lost his job for allowing me into the stables. Everyone was waiting for Lord Wavell's reaction. He walked up and inquired who I was.

'He is my nephew. I brought him here because he loves horses,' my uncle replied, hesitatingly.

I suddenly realized that everyone's attention had shifted to me. It was a tense moment. I waited agonizingly for the viceroy's reaction, knowing I would be responsible for costing my uncle his job. Instead, to my relief, Lord Wavell patted me on my shoulder and said, 'Young man, do you want to be a horseman?'

I could not understand his accented English and so my uncle translated for me.

'Yes,' I managed to mumble feebly.

Turning to my uncle, the viceroy said, 'Then, you should make him a good horseman by getting him trained by the best trainers we have.'

It was this unexpected order from the viceroy that allowed my uncle to give me access to the best British trainers. I was singularly lucky as this facility was not available to any Indian. Learning about horses from the very best trainers opened a new chapter in my life.

To begin with, we were taught how to understand horses and communicate with them. Horses respond to the touch and it all depends on how you are able to use it to communicate. I learnt the right way to mount and dismount. Most injuries happen as riders do not dismount in the proper way. All these details were fascinating for a fifteen-year-old. The toughest part was when we were made to ride without the saddle. We were taught how to grip the sides of the horse with our knees and maintain our balance as the horse started to walk, trot, canter or gallop. We were taught to fix the saddle, stirrups and mouth guards. After we learnt to ride and were comfortable with the horses, we were taken to the Ridge area where the horses and riders were put through a variety of obstacles.

Over a period of almost two years I often skipped college in Meerut to come to Delhi to take advantage of this structured training. Even today, images of those horses and riding expeditions are clearly etched in my mind. Unfortunately, I also had to overcome the obstacle course in my academic career. I had joined Meerut College, now known as Meerut University, in July 1945. I opted for science as it was considered 'intellectual'. Frankly, I had no particular affinity for science. In those days, there was no counselling and many students like me did not really know why they had opted for streams like science. Meerut College was packed with Jats who mostly came from agricultural families in western Uttar Pradesh. In the villages, boys used to start academics quite late and by the time they reached college level, they were much older than students like me. Some were even married and others older than their teachers. Their families were largely illiterate but realizing the importance of education, had started sending them to college. Many came from far away and had never experienced urban India.

In that sense, college was a huge disappointment. The campus was dominated by rustic Jats who were more interested in showing their clout and muscle power. They ran roughshod over everybody, including teachers. Studies were the last thing on their mind. Most were ruffians feared even by the professors. Teachers got beaten up routinely if they objected to anything the Jat gangs did. Meerut College was notorious for its political wrangles between these aggressive students. There were violent fights which used to be referred to as 'hockey fights' because of the free use of hockey sticks. The late prime minister Charan Singh, a rustic Jat himself, was from Meerut College, where he had his induction into the world of politics. For many students, the college was a stepping stone to a political career. Thankfully, I was not pulled into the vortex of that culture as their brand of aggressive and narrow-minded politics was abhorrent to my nature and upbringing.

Sheoraj Singh, who followed me from school, was one of my

closest friends. Another close friend was Ambuj Jain, who was studying history. He stood out for his academic brilliance, so much so that he was hired by the college as a teacher. We were not surprised when he became director general of audit, Central Revenue. We had great times together in college. His son, Anshu Jain, is one of the brightest non-resident Indians I know and has recently been appointed as the co-CEO of Deutsche Bank, one of the world's largest banks.

Those like Ambuj who seriously pursued studies did well. Those who excelled in sports like me also made a mark. If any laurels came my way, it was only through my performance in athletics, hockey and tennis. Otherwise, my college life was largely lacklustre. The only noteworthy activity I remember is how groups of very concerned and passionate young boys would gather together for clandestine meetings in support of the Quit India Movement. They moved around on bicycles given by the Congress party, the dominant political party of that time. They used to meet in secret to discuss ways to wage war against the British and gain independence.

One person who had a lasting influence on me was Vinod Gupta. He was a powerful speaker and excellent at motivating students to join the fight for freedom. I too was fired by his passion and sense of commitment. We used to play tennis together and were good friends. It was because of such bright, focused friends that college life became easier to bear. I graduated with fairly good marks and thereafter obtained admission in the University of Lucknow's M.Sc. (Chemistry) course.

I had only been at the university a few weeks when events took an unforeseen turn. Bopal Singh, a friend from Meerut, told me that he had got selected for the ground engineering course at the Air Service Training (AST) facility at Coventry in England. He had joined an earlier course that had started six months before.

Bopal Singh was the kind of person who loved helping friends, even without their asking. He sent in an application on my behalf for the same course and only after that wrote to tell me that he had done so. Even before I could give it serious thought, my application was processed and I received an official letter from the AST informing me that I had been granted admission.

I was thrilled. The very idea of going abroad to study was exciting. Apart from the chance to escape chemistry, for which I had no real flair or interest, this was the time just after Independence when getting an education abroad in either engineering or medicine was the ultimate ambition for any young Indian and indeed his parents. It was considered a passport to a successful career.

On the other hand, ground engineering in aviation held no special attraction for me. There was also the worrying problem of finding the money to pay for an expensive education abroad. With these conflicting thoughts in my mind I sought the advice of my sister. With some trepidation, I approached my father, with my sister beside me for support, and broke the news about being selected for training at the AST.

To my surprise, my father was overjoyed. He agreed immediately, probably with a sense of relief that his son had finally found the right focus and might be able to build a useful career. Moreover, there was a precedent in our family in the form of Uncle Surendra, who had gone to England for his graduation. He was at Peterhouse College in Cambridge University from 1936 to 1939.

It was only much later, after several decades, that I came to know just how much of a personal and financial sacrifice my father had to make to muster up the money to send me to Coventry.

I prepared for my trip in great excitement and when the day came for my departure, all the members of our entire joint family came up from Bulandshahr to see me off at the Delhi airport.

Every single thing that happened from then on for the next nine months was a new experience. Even boarding the plane was a novel exercise, because it was the first time I had ever set foot inside an aircraft. The journey itself was long and tiring because in those days there was no direct flight from Delhi to London; we had stopovers at Damascus and Istanbul before finally landing in London.

I arrived exhausted and jet-lagged but was looking forward eagerly to the adventure of life in a new country, one so different from my own. I was fascinated with every building, every store and every road in the great city of London, about which I had heard so much. I had never seen so many cars. Even the air was fresh and invigorating.

In England, when you say that someone has been 'sent to Coventry' it means that the person has been ostracized by society or family for some action that has caused offence or brought embarrassment to them. In my case, it was exactly the opposite. I was sent to Coventry to get trained as an aviation ground engineer and to ensure my future. I knew I had to do my best to make my family proud. This was one rainbow which would open up new horizons for me.

Little did I know that Coventry would change my life and transform my personality in the most unexpected ways. Far from becoming an expert ground engineer, I was drawn into the inner circle of the English upper class and fell in love with a beautiful girl who was a member of that class.

3

LIFE IN ENGLAND

IT WAS THE summer of 1949 and the English countryside was at its most beautiful. As I travelled by train from London to Coventry and then was driven down from the station to the Air Service Training campus in the tiny village of Ansty on the outskirts of the city, I was struck by the green everywhere, and the grassy meadows and thick woods that ran alongside my route.

The AST facility was near a village called Walsgrave-on-Sowe and close to a small airfield called Ansty Aerodrome, which had been an RAF base during the Second World War. The campus was neatly laid out and I was really excited at the prospect of spending the next few years here. I was allotted a small but clean en-suite room. It had a huge bay window from where I could get a breathtaking view of the West Midlands countryside. The residential area had a well-stocked library and a billiards room plus other recreational facilities. Among these were the tennis courts.

At that time, the only person I knew at Ansty was my friend and benefactor Bopal Singh. Had it not been for his spontaneous decision to submit my name for the course without even asking me, I would have still been languishing at Lucknow University. But he was not around on the day I arrived at Ansty. So I spent a few minutes just gazing out admiring the view. My eyes fell on the tennis courts on one side and my love for the game lured me outdoors to have a closer look. A young man and a girl were playing on one of the two courts, while another young woman, also in tennis whites, was sitting on a courtside bench.

As I approached hesitantly, the strikingly attractive girl on the bench gave me a friendly smile and said: 'Hello, my name is Julie. Do you play tennis?'

I was so surprised that a total stranger was speaking to me directly and even telling me her name that I found myself unable to reply. Back in Bulandshahr, I had never interacted with young women my own age because of strict social taboos. In both my school and college, there had only been boys.

This was the first time that someone from the opposite sex, who was not related to me in any way, had addressed me directly. I just stood there tongue-tied and embarrassed.

Noticing me standing there awkwardly, the young man stopped playing, walked across the court, introduced himself as Fakhruddin and repeated Julie's question: 'Can you play tennis?'

Getting my voice back, I answered: 'Yes, I can.'

'Then why don't you join us?' he asked, explaining that their regular doubles partner had not shown up and I could make it a foursome.

I readily agreed, but confessed I did not have a tennis racquet or shoes. Telling me not to worry, he dashed off somewhere and soon returned with a pair of shoes and a tennis racquet.

My years of learning the game stood me in good stead as I was a better player than they were. Julie was my doubles partner and when we won, she was so happy that she gave me a quick hug. I felt an electric shock. This was the first time any girl outside my close family circle had ever hugged me and my mind was in a whirl.

The three of them seemed to have taken an instant liking to me and they complimented me on my tennis skills. Fakhruddin asked if I would like to play tennis the coming weekend at Julie's place.

I nodded in bewilderment. I could not believe my luck. Here I was on my first day on campus in England, playing a game of tennis with three new friends, being hugged by a beautiful English girl and then being invited to her house.

The very next day, Fakhruddin, who I learnt was from an affluent Egyptian family, helped me to buy tennis whites and a racquet. I began looking forward eagerly to the weekend. I could not get Julie out of my mind, even though I knew nothing at all about her, except that she was not a student at AST.

That Saturday morning, I got some inkling of her background when a chauffeur-driven car came to pick us up. It was a gleaming Rolls-Royce. Julie, whose full name was Julie Rosemary Wells, lived in a sprawling country estate in the Midlands that was a thirty-minute drive from Ansty aerodrome. Her father, an Armoured Corps officer, had been killed in the Second World War and being the only child, she was taken in by her grandparents.

The house had ten spacious bedroom suites, each with a sitting room and attached bath. It boasted a lavish living room, library and a billiards room. There were numerous well-mannered liveried attendants. It was an eye-opening introduction to a way of life I had only read about in books or seen in the movies. During high tea following tennis, there was an array of delicious sandwiches, pastries and scones served by a succession of servants. I couldn't help marvelling at the transition from Bulandshahr to here, all thanks to tennis!

Another of my sporting passions would cement this newly formed connection even more. I had spotted some paddocks nearby with horses running around in them. Julie's grandfather was himself a good horseman despite his advanced age. He noticed me admiring the horses and invited me to the paddocks. Julie came along. Seeing me interact with the horses, Julie's grandfather judged I was a horseman and we started chatting animatedly. Learning of my involvement with horses, he invited me for a cross-country ride during the upcoming weekend with some of their friends. Unfortunately, as with the tennis outfit, I had no riding gear. I mentioned this to Julie, who passed it on to her grandfather. He was gracious enough to say that it was fine if I came normally dressed.

The following Saturday, Julie's car came on time to pick me up but I was a bit late in getting ready. By the time I reached the estate I noticed that almost all the other riders were in the process of mounting their horses. They all were from the upper echelons of British society, and dressed in appropriate riding gear. I remember one man named John who gave me a dirty look when he saw me dressed in normal clothes. I was also the only brown-skinned person in the group. Looking at this sophisticated crowd, I panicked, thinking that I would end up embarrassing Julie and her family.

John, who seemed to have taken a dislike to me, was in charge of allotting horses to the riders and he had deliberately given me a frisky horse. As I was mounting the chestnut I had been allotted, Julie intervened and asked the groom to bring me another horse. John, however, seemed determined to belittle me.

'He can either ride the horse I have given him or he can drop out,' he flatly declared.

'Please opt out,' Julie begged me, with concern in her voice. She was worried that I had been given a high-spirited horse and I might not be able to complete the ride.

The ride was to be cross-country, with natural obstacles like hedges and rivulets to be jumped over. A spirited horse can easily throw off a rider in such situations. It was a Hobson's choice. I could avoid embarrassment, even injury, by opting out of the ride. Or, I could take a risk and go ahead.

I suddenly realized that John was fond of Julie and was jealous because she was being protective of me. He wanted me to make a fool of myself in her presence, it seemed. Steeling myself, I decided to play the game and accepted the challenge. Julie was both pleased and worried, I could make out from her face.

Horses have an uncanny ability to sense a rider's confidence and skill. They either take over the rider or the rider controls the horse. I mounted and then steered the horse to clear the first obstacle, a medium-sized hedge. It did not take the jump smoothly and fluently, the way a good horse should, but I had enough training and experience to guide it and cajole it over the remaining obstacles. At the back of my mind were the riding lessons I had learnt from Uncle Raghubir. Had it not been for his rigorous training I would not have triumphed that day. And throughout the ride I was conscious that Julie was riding just behind me, afraid that my horse might get out of control. I felt I could not let her down.

When we stopped for brunch, Julie made no effort to hide her sheer delight with my performance. Some of the other riders praised my riding skills and asked where I had learnt to ride so well. I told them about Lord Wavell and how I had been trained by the best British trainers at the viceroy's stables. That established a rapport. It turned out that Julie's grandfather had known Lord Wavell personally.

My integration into British high society was smoothly established. I was accepted – thanks to an over-energetic horse! It was, however, quite a dramatic cultural shift, so radically different from India and the social restrictions I was used to at home. England was liberating and I was tasting new-found freedom and enjoying a developing friendship – that with Julie.

While the tennis matches continued with Fakhruddin and his girlfriend, Marie, Julie and I found ourselves growing closer to each other. A few days after the cross-country ride, she came to the campus unannounced, picked me up in her car and drove me to a tailoring shop in Coventry. It was a high-end establishment with an affluent clientele. She asked the master tailor to make two riding outfits for me. She also ordered other outfits, basically what the well-dressed young English gentlemen would wear: a Harris tweed jacket with beige corduroy trousers, a blue blazer and a dark grey suit. She picked the materials and selected the colours as if she had planned it all in her mind.

I was worried. All these clothes were obviously going to cost a lot of money. I had limited funds and my heart sank at the thought that I would not be able to afford the lifestyle Julie's status commanded. I did not know how to tell her.

I picked up courage and asked the tailor how much it would cost. Before he could answer, Julie clutched my arm, burst out laughing and asked, 'How does it matter?'

Deep down I was embarrassed. Once back at the AST campus, I confided in Bopal Singh. But he just shrugged off my worries and said: 'Don't worry, I will lend you the money. Pay it back when you can.'

I was greatly relieved. A week later, I returned to try on the new outfits. Julie insisted on accompanying me, saying she wanted to make sure of the new look she was sculpting for me.

Secure in the knowledge that Bopal Singh would help with the finances, I told her I would take care of the bill. 'You can't pay,' she replied firmly. 'These riding outfits are a gift from my grandfather.'

'What about the other clothes?' I persisted.

'For God's sake, it is a gift from my grandfather, accept it gracefully,' she said in exasperation. 'Besides, from now on please address my grandfather as Pa and my grandmother as Granny, as

I do,' she added, with a smile. It was clear that her growing affection for me was getting more serious than I had bargained for. It set me thinking, half in hope and half in despair.

But my confidence surged once I had tried out the new outfits. Being naturally tall and well-built, I felt the impeccably tailored clothes looked good on me. Even the master tailor expressed his admiration and kept nodding approvingly. I felt I was ready to face the world and take in my stride the rapid changes that were taking place in my life.

I began to like the life that Julie had introduced me to. But I still had much to learn before I could fit in fully into this lifestyle. I had never, for instance, learnt how to dance – there was no reason to back home – and suddenly I was invited to a grand ball. I was told that it was a black tie affair and I thought it literally meant wearing a black tie!

Once again, Julie took charge. She dragged me off to a shop that rented out formal wear for such occasions and it was only then that I understood what a black tie meant – I had to dress in a tuxedo and wear a bow tie.

The grand ball was an exclusive affair. When Julie asked me for a dance, I was really embarrassed and confessed that I did not know how to dance. She laughed, threw her arms around me and said, 'You are really sweet and I love you.'

The next day, she took me to a dancing school in Coventry. In college, I had never been exposed to Western music and here I was struggling to learn the foxtrot and other dance steps to unfamiliar rhythms. It felt odd to be told how to take dancing steps by the instructor without any feeling for the rhythm in me. Julie sat in a chair, smiling most of the time at my embarrassment. Finally she would hug me and make me dance. What the instructor could not teach me, I picked up from her in a couple of minutes! Once I got the hang of it I started enjoying going to dance parties with Julie. Thankfully, Julie did not drink, which made it easier for me to refuse: I had never touched a drop of alcohol in India.

By now, the two of us had become really close. Just being together with her gave me a kind of happiness that I had never known before. I looked forward to and enjoyed every excursion with her. But there was a downside to all this fun and frolic. I was neglecting my studies. I had gone all the way to England to be trained as an aviation ground engineer. Instead, I was skipping classes to play tennis, go horse-riding and attend dance classes. My fellow-pupils and the instructors at the AST had started to notice. How could they not, considering it was a Rolls-Royce that came to the campus regularly to pick me up? Some of my classmates were extremely jealous and one of my teachers told me that it was 'not the done thing' for a student to be driven around in a Rolls. When I informed Julie of the predicament, she immediately came out with an ingenious solution – she replaced the Rolls with an old Morris Minor belonging to her butler!

Julie had transformed my life and turned me into a sophisticated, well-attired young man increasingly at ease in high society. It helped that my English pronunciation wasn't too bad. She was also quite proud of the changes I had gone through and the growing acceptance of her family and friends. Before long, we became a sought-after couple and began to be invited to many parties. Even though classes at AST had begun in right earnest, my mind was always thinking about the weekends when I could be with Julie.

Ironically, my main involvement with the AST was playing hockey. The institute would occasionally send its hockey team in a bus to nearby places for friendly matches. My hockey skills got me into the team and it gave me a chance to see more of England. I didn't miss home much as I was so busy enjoying all the new activities and Julie's company. Apart from tennis, Julie loved riding and we often took the horses out together. Since I was visiting their house several times a week, Julie's grandfather offered me the exclusive use of a bedroom suite where I maintained a set of clothes. Julie was thrilled with this arrangement and the growing fondness of her grandparents towards me.

One of my enduring memories of England was a trip with Julie and her grandparents to their family friend's estate in Scotland for a pheasant shoot. Julie said that her family was keen for me to accompany them on this trip. As we took the train from Coventry to Edinburgh I recollected how I used to go with Uncle Raghubir for shooting partridges around the sugarcane fields in Khandera village. I was just fifteen then. He used to come with his British army colleagues when he was posted as ADC to Lord Wavell. It is here that I learnt to use a double-barrel Holland and Holland shotgun.

As I had never been to a pheasant shoot, I was wondering what it would be like. Selection of my clothing, including purchase of shooting gear items, was done by Julie, who knew exactly what I would be required to wear on each occasion. In England, one thing that struck me was that they did everything with great style. The butlers had packed our shooting gear, riding gear and formal wear that we would require depending on what we chose to do on the trip. It seemed such an elaborate affair as two cars carrying our household staff along with lots of baggage and equipment had been sent well in advance.

Getting off at Edinburgh, we were driven in a Rolls-Royce to their estate. It was a thickly wooded, picturesque place. The sky was so blue and the air so pure that it seemed a different world altogether. I was enraptured by the Scottish countryside, wild and lonely. Soon it was evening, and we got ready for a formal dinner. The next day after breakfast, we were driven to the area of the shoot. Those who were participating in the shoot were dressed in smart brown-and-olive-green jackets, trousers, caps and gumboot-like shoes. Part of the entourage were the retrievers with their handlers. Then, there were the beaters with their drums. We also had helpers who carried a second barrel as a replacement for when the double-barrelled gun we were using became hot after intermittent firing.

The game-master ensured that everything was in order before the shoot commenced by placing all the participants in strategic positions. As the drumming by the beaters rose in a crescendo, the pheasants shot out from the woods. The crackle of gunfire echoed in the countryside. The birds were easy game. As soon as the birds fell, the well-trained retriever dogs sprang to bring the birds to us. After the shoot, we were served steaming hot soup as it was bitterly cold. We then enjoyed a relaxed picnic-style lunch before we moved to another location to continue with our shoot. Returning before sunset, we freshened up to move into dinner. All of us were formally dressed, the men in black ties and the ladies in formal long dresses.

The next day, we again went for a shoot. On the third day, Julie and I opted for a ride while some others chose to play tennis. Those rides with Julie and her friends in the enchanting Scottish countryside have remained etched in my memory. The surprising treat that day was when Julie's cousin and her husband rode us to an idyllic location along a small river where they had organized salmon fishing. This was the first time I used a fishing tackle but after a few hiccups, I soon got the hang of it. Julie's cousin then treated us to freshly caught and grilled fish and white wine.

Each day was refreshingly different. The following day, we got down to playing tennis. After the game, in the evening, we headed to a pub for some traditional Scottish music and dancing, bagpipes and all, around a huge bonfire.

I was learning a great deal about the life of a gentleman. What was absent was AST! I was busy having the time of my life while my classmates were trying to learn the complicated jargon of ground engineering.

On another occasion, Julie's grandfather had taken us to Windsor. Initially I treated it as just a chance to see the areas around Windsor, which is close to the Mecca of polo, Cowdray Park. Thanks to Uncle Raghubir's training, I was adept at polo and soon Julie's uncle, Richard, who was based at Windsor, invited me to play. At one of the polo games I met an impressive Indian army officer, Brig. Mohinder Singh Wadalia. Being a cavalry officer, he was no mean polo player. He was military advisor at our high commission in London. That meeting would prove a major turning point in my life and draw me back to India and my ultimate destiny. It was an amazing series of coincidences. If I had not known Bopal Singh I would not have landed up in Coventry, met Julie, her grandfather and her uncle, and consequently, Brigadier Wadalia. Throughout my life, I've been reminded time and again of the value of relationships. You never know where they will take you.

As it turned out, Brigadier Wadalia being an Indian cavalry officer knew my uncle, Risaldar Major Raghubir Singh, and his nephew, Lt. Col. Sheodan Singh, who was a highly decorated soldier. The family connections established an instant camaraderie and a new friendship blossomed.

Julie's grandfather as well as her uncle also knew the Wadalias, who were regular guests at his Windsor tea parties. The brigadier asked me to drop in at his office or residence in London. Julie decided to take up his invitation and we went to see him at his residence.

After a few minutes of general conversation, he turned to me and asked curiously: 'Of all the things in life, why are you doing an engineering course? Do you have a flair for it or are you doing it for the heck of it? You are fond of horses and riding. Logically, you should be in the cavalry.'

I did not know what to say since Julie was opposed to my returning to India. Yet, his words kept echoing in my head. India had just gained Independence and being in the army was a highly rated profession, glamorous, active and patriotic with plenty of sports like riding thrown in. The only rival then was the Indian Civil Service. I continued to resist the idea since I loved life in England, but the brigadier convinced me that the least I could do was to appear for the entrance exam conducted by the defence ministry for the Indian Military Academy in Dehra Dun.

'As a special case, you could be permitted to appear for the written exam in London at my office at South Audley Street,' he added.

I had no intention of joining the army, but to humour him, I appeared for the test. I forgot about it once I was back in Coventry and immersed myself in academics and sports. All of a sudden, I got a call saying I had cleared the test and the next step was to appear before an interview board at the Officers Selection Board near Sandhurst. Again, as a special case, I was the only Indian allowed to take the interview abroad along with other candidates for service in the regular British Army.

Most Indians abroad would have grabbed the opportunity and the special dispensation, but I took it very casually. In fact, I saw it as an opportunity to see the southern part of England near Sandhurst. After all, the Government of India was paying for my travel there.

The interview, when it took place, was a grilling that lasted four days. There were numerous physical and mental tests to evaluate skills, leadership qualities and endurance levels. Many dropped out from sheer fatigue. I looked at it as just another challenge and enjoyed the experience thoroughly. At one point, they brought up subjects on which we were to speak extempore. The subject I was given was how India would be in tatters soon as the British had granted it freedom. I argued forcefully how India would use its freedom to rise and develop faster than any other British colony had done. I felt really good after I spoke so convincingly and confidently about the future of India. I am happy to see that all of what I spoke then is actually happening in India today, as the world watches an economic power emerge from its self-imposed shackles.

Meanwhile, back at Coventry, life continued and the interview was soon forgotten till I received a call a few weeks later from the military advisor's office in London informing me that I had been selected for the 8th course of the IMA and should report to Dehra Dun on 1 February 1950. I did not know what to do. There was no cause for celebration. I was not at all interested in an army career. Julie was vehemently opposed to my moving to India. When my classmates heard of my selection, they were unanimous in their reaction. They thought I was out of my mind to even consider joining the army. They repeatedly told me that it would be foolish to leave England and go back to India.

I was in an agonizing quandary. I was very happy in England. I had drifted away from my studies into an exciting social life. How could I now shift back to India? Julie kept pleading with me to stay. I decided to clear up the issue with the military advisor's office. I met a senior officer who told me not to take it lightly as I was the first Indian to have ever appeared for the IMA entrance abroad and made the grade. I was still not impressed and went to meet Brigadier Wadalia to thank him for having taken so much interest in my future.

I had made up my mind to tell him that I was grateful but not interested in an army career. The brigadier listened patiently and said, 'Look young man, I see you more as a cavalry officer than as an engineer. You will make a bigger name in the Indian Army than being an engineer repairing aircraft engines.'

While he was using logic and reason to sell me the idea of a career in the army, I was thinking about a trip to Switzerland scheduled during the Christmas–New Year break. A career in the army was the last thing on my mind.

'I can only join a few weeks later than the first of February and that too if my passage is paid for as I have made travel plans for Switzerland during the Christmas break,' I remarked to wriggle out of the situation.

I used this ruse confident that the Indian government would never accept such ridiculous conditions. My thoughts were fixed on a trip to St Moritz with Fakhruddin, Marie and Julie. St Moritz is where the rich and famous go for skiing in winter. It is the ultimate luxury skiing resort. Initially, Julie had wanted us to stay with some friends of her family but the rest of us wanted to go as students and rough it out on a tight budget. Finally, she relented and we stayed in a boarding house that offered basic amenities only.

After breakfast we would head for the snowy slopes. Since I had never skied before I had to undergo some training. It is amazing how the young can pick up skiing so quickly. The sport was fun but exhausting. In the evenings we used to have pleasant get-togethers and indulge in merrymaking. It was a hugely enjoyable two weeks in Switzerland and I completely forgot about the IMA.

Then, another of those twists of fate intervened. To my utter astonishment, the military advisor's office informed me that the defence ministry had agreed to my conditions of joining late and the Indian government was ready to pay the passage from UK to India. I was flummoxed. What was I to do now? The military advisor kept repeating that this was a very unusual decision by the Ministry of Defence. Brigadier Wadalia added to my predicament by pointing out that as I had obviously done exceedingly well in the interview and the evaluation by the world's best selection board it was a signal that I would do well in the army. It called for serious introspection. All my friends, including Julie, were dead against it. My parents were also against it. The War had resulted in a lot of casualties in Saidpur village where it was a tradition to join the army and where our family had a lot of relatives and friends. As I was the only son, my father did not want me to join the army.

At this point, Kanwar Surendra Pal Singh, who was my father's cousin and very close to him, dropped in to see me. Since he used to visit England often after his graduation from Cambridge, my father asked him to see how I had settled down. Julie and her grandfather knew that he was very close to me. They invited him to stay with them during his visit to Coventry to see me. Around the same time, Julie's grandparents had also invited the Wadalias for the weekend at their estate. While they were chatting, my predicament about the IMA was discussed. Julie and her grandfather wanted me to complete my engineering and stay back in England. Brigadier Wadalia and Uncle Surendra remained adamant that there was a better future for me in the cavalry and not in aviation engineering. After sensing the situation, my uncle observed that because of my growing relationship with Julie, I might decide to settle in England but it would be against my father's wishes.

When I told him that my father was against my joining the army, he said, 'Never mind, I will take care of that.' As he saw that I was still vacillating, he decided to delay his return to India.

A couple of days later, I got a note from Julie's grandfather asking me to join him for tea at their home as an urgent issue had to be discussed. The sudden invitation was a surprise as normally it would be Julie who called.

I vividly remember that afternoon as bitterly cold and windy. When I reached their house, the butler escorted me to the library, where Julie's grandparents were sitting. I felt something unusual was going on, more so since Julie wasn't around. Even the warmth that I was used to was lacking. I could sense uneasiness in the air. They started by saying that as they wanted to talk to me in private, they had requested Julie not to be present. Julie's grandfather, sounding quite emotional, told me not to be influenced by what my uncle or Brigadier Wadalia had advised. He then, quite literally in this case, got to the heart of the matter.

'Julie is deeply in love with you and I am aware of your feelings towards her. We lost our only son in the war. We now only have Julie and she is like our only daughter. It has been traumatic for us to see her like this in the last couple of days as she is totally broken-hearted at the thought of you returning to India. It will destroy our girl. If you do not like engineering, we will help you to do anything else you want. Julie cannot come to India with you as there is no one else to inherit our family estates and all that we have in England. You can help her to look after them. Both of you can live happily here as all our wealth is yours and hers.'

I glanced towards Julie's grandmother and saw tears welling in her eyes. We talked for almost two hours. It was the most emotionally draining moment of my life. I just did not know what to say. Uppermost in my mind was the thought that it made sense for me to stay back in England as life was so comfortable and organized.

I asked to speak to Julie and met her in another room. For the first time, the vitality and effervescence was missing from her face. She sat in a corner, sobbing. I could not bear to see her like this. I tried to comfort her. I held her in my arms and promised her that I had not yet taken a final decision and would not do so without talking to her. And that even if I did go to India, I would come back.

Knowing that she was depressed, I decided to stay back. As dinners were a formal affair in such families, I asked Julie to freshen up and we joined the grandparents for dinner. As we sat at the table together, they were very happy to see us. Next morning, after a late breakfast both of us went for a gentle ride in the estate on our favourite horses.

Returning to the AST campus, I discussed my dilemma with

Bopal Singh. He advised me against taking any hasty decision. He too was opposed to my going back to India and joining the army. Yet my mind was like a volcano. I decided to be objective about the issue and weigh the pros and cons.

Going back to India would mean returning to a life of hardship, while I could live like a lord in England for the rest of my years. While my mind was in turmoil, Uncle Surendra invited me to London. I went and Julie came along. We did this more than once. He knew I needed help to sort out my dilemma and was a great communicator. He took up each of the issues and gently but persuasively went through each one. Eventually, he even won over Julie who was bent on not letting me go back to India. He was very subtle and I never once felt he was persuading me to join the army.

Brigadier Wadalia had similar communication skills but was married to a foreigner. Marthe was a Belgian who had spent time in various army postings in India. She had loved the life of an army wife. During our occasional visits to London she had also grown close to Julie. She convinced her that after I completed my training in Dehra Dun, we could continue with our courtship and marry later. She told Julie how though she had met Brigadier Wadalia in 1931, they had only married about eight years later. Besides, she said, it was a normal practice in England for young men to join the army and marry later, after a few years of courtship. In retrospect, it was Marthe's influence and my uncle's delicate persuasion that were responsible for a change in Julie's attitude, I can make out.

My uncle had, both subtly and effectively in equal measure, made me think about my future more clearly and dispassionately. He had driven home the point that I was the only son among two families and my father had sacrificed a lot to finance my education in England. They had great expectations from me and my staying back would completely shatter them.

He then added the clincher: 'You can get the best of both worlds if you join the army and then arrange for Julie to come to India and marry her.' And then he added: 'I know that your parents are very conservative, but I will convince them to accept her.'

His argument made sense and gave me an option I had not considered before. We returned to Coventry and informed Julie's grandparents of the developments. Julie added that even if she joined me in India, she could always return to England later. Her grandfather hesitatingly said that if I still insisted on going, I had his blessings. I will never forget her grandmother's parting words: 'Son, we will live to see you again. Come back soon.'

Ultimately, my head ruled over my heart. Staying in England was the soft option. Joining the army in India was the tough one. It was a decision that could have gone either way. One major emotional tug that pulled me to India were recurring memories of my involvement with other students of Meerut College in the Quit India Movement and how it had ignited our dreams of a new India. The emergence of a newly liberated motherland excited me and I felt a surge of pride when I imagined myself in an army uniform.

Fate plays strange games with one's life and sometimes it is that one single decision that can make all the difference to one's future. In England, I would have been comfortable running an estate in the countryside, part of an aristocratic family. But I would be marrying into wealth, not creating it. Mahatma Gandhi once said: 'It only takes a single thought to move the world.' He said it in a different context, but in my case, it was a single decision that changed my world, and my future.

4

MARCHING TO THE ARMY BEAT

ON THE DAY of my departure, Julie and I bid each other goodbye with heavy hearts and deep foreboding. She had come to London airport to see me off before my flight to Delhi. Our two closest friends, Marie and Fakhruddin, were also there. As the moment of parting approached, it was difficult to hold back the tears or to control the emotions that welled up and choked our voices. Even as we hugged each other again and again, I knew in my heart that the happiest days of my youth had come to an end, and although I kept telling myself that I would soon return to England and be with Julie again, deep down inside me was the fear that perhaps this could be the last time I would see her and things might never be the same again.

My mind was in a whirl throughout the long flight and when the plane finally landed in Delhi, I realized with much misgivings that I was about to embark on a new phase in my life which I had not really prepared myself for. My nine months in the idyllic

Midlands, from the glorious summer of 1949 to the harsh winter of early 1950, had passed like a fairy tale and I had given little thought to life after returning home, especially to the rigours of becoming a soldier. The tennis, the hockey, the horse-riding and the dance parties had kept me physically fit but I wondered if the emotional scars would ever heal and whether my mind could ever focus on what lay before me.

I soon found myself on a train heading for Dehra Dun and experiencing, as if for the first time, all the chaos of Indian roads and the bustle of crowded bazaars. Dehra Dun was well known for its excellent schools and the presence of the IMA.

My orders were to report to the academy by 15 February 1950, which was fifteen days after the cadet training course had started. In the army, being even a minute late for anything was considered a serious breach of discipline and etiquette. And that wasn't all. I had arrived in a tonga, a common means of public transport in those days, looking exactly like I used to in England: elegantly tailored clothes and fashionably long hair. Not surprisingly, I was mistaken for a visitor rather than a cadet reporting for duty in the army. My mind was full of questions. Would I be able to adjust? Could I cope with the rigorous schedule? Would I fit into the new life that fate had chosen for me? What if army life didn't agree with me?

Some of the doubts and fears diminished as soon as I reached the imposing entrance to the IMA. The academy was splendid to look at, even awe-inspiring, and I was acutely aware of the fact that I was entering one of the premier military training institutions in the world. The Indian government had bent its rules and made unprecedented concessions, including paying my airfare from London to Delhi, to give me a chance to enter the IMA. I told myself that come what may, I should give it my best shot.

I showed my joining letter to the sentry at the gate, but in true army tradition he already knew I was scheduled to join on that day. Before I could ask for directions, a cadet on a bicycle materialized and asked if I was the new gentleman cadet Kushal Pal Singh.

When I said yes, he directed the tongawallah to follow him. We passed through a long tree-lined road towards the barracks. Everywhere I looked there was neatness – from the manicured lawns to the smart young men in olive green uniforms. Everything appeared clean and orderly and just as I began to feel the grandeur of being in the foremost military training institute in India, my escort suddenly stopped and asked me to remove the huge iron trunk containing my belongings from the tonga and place it in the middle of the road. It seemed odd but I did as I was told. He then paid off the tongawallah, turned to me and said with a perfectly straight face: 'If you turn right and take forty front rolls, you will reach the barrack you have to report to.'

I suspected that perhaps it was an initiation rite and asked what a front roll was. He stopped another gentleman cadet who was passing by and asked him to demonstrate a front roll. The other young man immediately squatted, rolled forward, sat up and rolled forward again.

'Do you now understand what a front roll means?' he asked me gruffly.

Frankly, I was appalled. If this was how my army life was going to start, I wanted no part of it. I would never fit in. I soon realized the joke was on me because an orderly arrived, picked up my heavy trunk and escorted me to the barracks.

I still looked decidedly odd compared to the other gentlemen cadets, especially when I met my coursemates for the first time at lunch. Hundreds of eyes swivelled my way, as they tried to figure out what this civilian guest was doing in their mess hall. My long hair and stylish clothes made me look like an alien. It didn't last. Immediately after lunch, I was marched off to the campus barber and given a military-style crew-cut. Olive green uniforms, boots, and other official gear completed the transformation. It was a symbolic moment, shedding my old skin and taking on a new identity. More would follow. Till then, I only knew the glamour of army life from the outside – the pomp and ceremony. Now, I was experiencing it from within.

It was not an easy transition. The days seemed endless, packed with activity right from the time we woke up every morning to the time we hit our beds at night, drained of energy. Every day would start with physical training and endurance tests followed by academics. Ragging, which was supposed to toughen you up, only made it worse. Since I had joined late and had come straight from England, I was the focus of unwanted attention and a prime target. My fellow-cadets seemed to go out of their way to make my life miserable, asking me to describe life in England in embarrassing detail and why I had been given the singular privilege of joining late. They enjoyed making me squirm. They would frighten me with exaggerated stories about army life and how I, the 'anglicized sahib', would not last long in the IMA.

However, after those agonizing first few days, the ragging became less as the others saw how good I was in sports and how quick I was to step forward whenever anybody needed any help. I began to make friends and one of my batchmates, Ved Prakash Gupta, who went on to become a lieutenant-general, claims that I was one of the most popular cadets at the IMA.

Perhaps my lifestyle in England had given me a greater degree of sophistication and self-confidence than the other cadets but inwardly I was unhappy. I started missing my English friends and yearning to see Julie again. I suffered from pangs of regret for having left all the love and comfort behind and I had recurring memories of the pampered life I had led. In contrast, life at the IMA was tough and demanding. There was very little time to call one's own and virtually no entertainment.

I began to seriously think of running away. I imagined myself slipping out of the campus without telling anyone, catching a train to Delhi and taking a flight to England to resume my course at the AST and re-unite with Julie and my other friends there. The idea of escape became so overpowering that I wrote a long letter to Julie telling her in detail about my plans. I sealed the envelope and dropped the letter into the letter box at the campus post office. The very thought of getting back to England filled me with excitement and a sense of daring.

But I had not fathomed how the army works. A few hours after I had posted the letter, I was summoned by the battalion commander, Lt. Col. Baljit Singh. I was escorted to his office by a sergeant who warned me to behave formally and to keep standing in his presence.

I was terrified, as any cadet would be when suddenly summoned by the battalion commander. At the back of my mind was the fear that he might have somehow found out about my plans to escape. It was a serious offence and the punishment would be severe. I expected the worst. My knees felt weak at the thought of the disgrace it would bring to the family name.

I was taken aback when Colonel Singh asked me to sit down. In typical military style, he came straight to the point.

'I believe you want to run away from the IMA?' were his first words.

I was too shocked to make a coherent reply. 'No, sir,' I managed to stutter.

He then pulled out my letter addressed to Julie and laid it on his desk. I realized the game was up – my letter had been opened and read by my superiors. I blurted out the truth. I admitted that I had planned to catch the night train to Delhi, fly back to England and resume my ground engineering course.

The battalion commander listened to my confession without any expression. Then he said: 'Your plan is foolish. Don't you know that we have military police posted at Dehra Dun railway station to catch deserters? If they arrest you, I will have no option but to punish you most severely.'

Then he said the strangest thing. 'No, let's do it another way. I will help you escape. I will take you in my car to the railway station at Haridwar around 50 km away from Dehra Dun, where there will be no military police. You can thereafter take a train to Delhi without anybody stopping you.'

I was struck dumb. I did not know whether he was being sarcastic or trying to trap me.

After a pause, he spoke again: 'By the way, what are your plans after you finish your course in England? Will you stay on to work in England or come back to India?'

'I would prefer to come back to India if there were a job opportunity,' I replied.

Leaning forward, his voice suddenly stern, he said, 'If you stay back in England, you will live like a nobody in a foreign country and go unnoticed. On the contrary, if you return to India, you will be known as a *bhagora*.'

I asked what *bhagora* meant. He said it meant a weakling who had run away from a challenge.

'You will be seen as a coward who ran away despite being from a family with a lot of highly decorated army officers. If you do not mind this stigma, I will help you run away. If not, think it over.'

In silence, I sat and thought. Did I want to be known as a coward and a deserter? I imagined how my parents and my uncle Raghubir Singh would feel if I was branded a *bhagora*. All my relatives in the army would hang their heads in shame.

The battalion commander continued, 'By the way, let me tell you another thing. We were all surprised when you were given permission to join late. I believe you were given one of the highest grades by the British Service Selection Board in the UK and the government also agreed to make an exception to pay your passage to India so that you would be able to join the IMA. It is very unusual for any cadet to get such special concessions and favours. Don't you think it would be foolish of you to throw this golden opportunity away and to be labelled forever as a deserter?'

It was my first real lesson in brilliant man-management. Had he reprimanded me sternly in the typical army way and threatened me with dire consequences, I would have probably quit. Instead, he used warmth and advice to get me to think the way he wanted me to.

Colonel Singh advised me to think about it and in the meantime not to talk to anyone about the conversation. If it leaked, he said, he would not be able to help me. However, I just couldn't keep it to myself. I related the incident to Pawittar Singh Thakkar, a fellow cadet who had become a close friend. His advice was logical. He said it would be foolhardy to leave now. 'Finish the first semester,' he suggested. 'If you still do not like it here, you can run away during the mid-term break after completion of the first semester.'

I thought it was a sensible option and I agreed to postpone my escape plan. It gave me time for introspection and as it turned out, I changed my mind. By the time the first semester ended, I had decided to stay and become a cadet that the IMA could be proud of.

Having resolved the inner dilemma, I quickly adjusted to the IMA routine. I began to work really hard to catch up with my peers to make up for the two weeks of academic work I had missed by joining late. By the time the first break was announced after six months, I was quite at home at the IMA. Every day was a challenge but I was determined to prove myself. A typical day at IMA used to start at 5 a.m., before first light, for physical training. It was rigorous but also full of adventure. It would last an hour with what was sometimes called 'Road Walk and Run', which, as the name suggests, was a combination of brisk walking and running. A regime of this kind was designed to toughen the cadets physically while other outdoor exercises were aimed at teaching us how to tackle unexpectedly rough conditions and situations.

Since I was physically fit and strong and enjoyed all kinds of outdoor activities, I was often among the top performers. Our instructors kept making the exercises tougher by the day. Eventually, the road walk and run routine was extended to ten miles (16 km), followed by climbing, jumping and crossing ditches and elevated terrain. We frequently went out on training camps. In one camp near Rishikesh, they made us swim against the current in the Ganga with a full backpack and a rifle. After the morning exercises, we would break for breakfast and then attend classes in geography, history, science and liberal arts to give us a broader perspective.

The post-lunch period was devoted to sports – tennis, hockey and riding, all three of which I was specially good at. The evenings were more formal and ceremonial, a get-together in our uniforms culminating in an elegantly laid-out dinner. I made a large number of friends at the IMA, and many of those friendships have lasted a lifetime. The IMA course was designed to create a strong bond. It is gratifying to look back at those eventful years as a great learning experience. Nowhere in the world would I have learnt so well, as I did at the IMA, the importance of discipline, endurance, patience, stress-management, courage and camaraderie.

As the months passed, the IMA grew on me. I loved the grandeur and expanse of the 1,400-acre campus. Large trees lined the roads and the flowers at the immaculately tended crossings and junctions were always in bloom. The buildings were a mix of colonial and modern architecture. The Chetwode Building, the academics hub, was named after Field Marshal Sir Phillip Chetwode, the founder of the academy. Maj. Gen. K.S. Thimayya was the commandant of the IMA at that time. He made sure that the IMA was maintained to the highest standards. He was one of the most decorated soldiers in the Indian Army and later became Chief of the Army Staff.

I was inducted into the Sangro Company at the IMA, named after the battle of Sangro, a river in Italy, where Indian troops had valiantly fought the Nazis in the Second World War. I worked very hard and was thrilled when during my last semester I was appointed as senior under officer with responsibility to command the Sangro Company.

There was a seven-day exercise called Camp Chinditis. We were thrown into the wilderness to manage on our own. The terrain was heavily wooded and rocky. It was full of narrow ravines, with no discernible track. We had to find our own route while at the same time keep alert for mock attacks. The aim of the camp was to toughen us up. Every day we would start out at first light and keep going till sundown, when we would pitch our tents and then get down to cooking in 'mess tins' – typical multipurpose utensils used in the army. Prizes were given for the tastiest meal. Cadet (now Major General) Mohinder Singh and I once got the prize for the best rice-and-mutton dish.

We learnt to survive the hardships cheerfully. I do believe that the army training has stood me in good stead throughout the rest of my life and moulded me to face the most difficult challenges and toughest of times even in my corporate career.

I must have done extremely well at the IMA because in my final term, whenever any dignitary visited, I was given the singular honour of commanding the parade, which was considered the ultimate acknowledgement of a cadet's performance in the last semester.

The passing-out parade of the 8th Course was held on 30 December 1951. Among the audience were my proud parents and equally proud Lt. Col. Sheodan Singh and Maj. Gen. Wadalia, to both of whom I owe an immense debt of gratitude for steering my life in the right direction. Coincidentally, Maj. Gen. Wadalia took over as commandant of IMA a few days before the parade.

The very next day, on 31 December, I was commissioned as a second lieutenant in Deccan Horse, the legendary cavalry regiment of the Indian Army. This regiment was raised in 1790. It had a proud record of service and had won many battle honours. It was known as Asaf Jah's Irregular Cavalry. The Nizam-ul-Mulk of Hyderabad had raised the unit with 10,000 men, then the largest cavalry regiment in the world, to bring order to the lawless regions of the Deccan. Horses had, since then, given way to tanks and modern weaponry, but it gave us an ancient and inspiring tradition to follow.

Around the same time, Maj. Gen. Wadalia was also given the honour of being appointed as the colonel commandant of Deccan Horse. The role of colonel commandant of a regiment is essentially to act as a custodian and guardian of the high traditions and values of the regiment. Such an honour is normally given to a senior and most respected officer of the army.

Life in the cavalry was a mix of hard work, adventure and fun. It was not an easy life but what I loved was the excitement and unpredictability. One of my early postings was at Jandiala Guru between Jalandhar and Amritsar. The army here was positioned in a combat zone near the Pakistan border. Since it was an operational area, we were in war-readiness all the time. It could pose some unexpected hazards.

It was standard practice to dig deep trenches around your tent to stop snakes from entering. Despite the precautions as I once reached for my boots in a dimly lit tent I saw a venomous snake crawl out of one!

Every unit in the army has its traditions. Deccan Horse was also jokingly referred to as Drunken Horse. One of the rituals a new officer had to go through was called Dining In. It was basically to test how many drinks a young officer could imbibe and still report for duty the next morning. The first peg of whisky would have everyone cheering the new officer. The moment his glass was empty, there would be officers rushing to fill it. It would go on till the officer was too drunk to stand on his feet. He would then be picked up and carried to his barracks by orderlies. The next morning, he was supposed to report at 5.30 and participate in the five-mile (eight-kilometre) run. It was a test not many officers managed to pass. When my turn came, I had a plan ready. Not being much of a drinker, I knew I had to keep a sober head.

Fortunately, the area was dark with plenty of shrubbery around. I picked one of the densest bushes and stood next to it with my glass of whisky. When no one was watching, I quickly tipped the contents into the bush. I did it each time my glass was full and everybody's attention was elsewhere. After almost an entire bottle of whisky had been emptied, I pretended to be sloshed. I was laid on the table and then carried away by the orderlies, who tucked me into bed. I slept like a log and the next morning, at 5.30, everyone was struck dumb when I reported for the morning run looking very energetic and fit.

All this time, I still had Julie in my thoughts and we had often discussed marriage once I was commissioned. So it was something of a shock when, after I had completed about nine months in Deccan Horse, Lt. Gen. Wadalia (he had been promoted) during a visit to the regiment, summoned me to meet him and Lt. Col. Sheodan Singh, the commanding officer, in the officers' mess. As Lt. Gen. Wadalia and Julie's grandfather had become well-acquainted in England, they were constantly in touch. Very gently and in a dignified manner, he told me that it would be in my interest to forget Julie as I would not be able to marry her. The army, he said, had recently come out with strict regulations that forbade army personnel from marrying foreigners. It was a rule that was not there earlier as Lt. Gen. Wadalia himself had married a Belgian. I still remember his words.

'KP, be a gentleman and make a clean break with Julie so that she can also get on with her life. The IMA has taught you that a gentleman cadet grows to become a gentleman officer. The qualities of a gentleman must be visible in all that you do in life.'

I knew Lt. Gen. Wadalia was fond of Julie and he must have thought about this long and hard and decided it was in her, and our, best interests. When I walked out of the room, I was shattered. It had come like a bolt from the blue and the immediate emotions were anger, resentment and a growing sense of rebellion. My first instinct was to resign from the army and go back to England, no matter what anybody said or thought.

After a couple of days of simmering in righteous indignation, I picked up the courage to go to the residence of Lt. Col. Sheodan Singh as he was my commanding officer and also a close relative. Without uttering a word, I handed over my letter of resignation. He said he had expected me to do something like this.

'I can understand your feelings, but you should also look at the ground realities. Permission to marry a foreigner will not be given. Your resignation will never be accepted by the government. You cannot run away from the army now and be declared a deserter, bringing shame to your family. Besides, you have always had an outstanding record. Why do you want to spoil it? Be pragmatic,' he firmly said and tore up my resignation letter. I went back confused and feeling trapped.

Lt. Col. Singh realized my mental state and arranged for me to be sent on an ongoing army exercise aimed at testing the battle-worthiness of participating army units. It was being held in the desolate areas of Punjab and, as such exercises simulate war, they are very strenuous and one has to be alert all the time because of mock attacks by the 'enemy' all through the day and night. Lt. Col. Singh had clearly done this so I would not get time to think about anything else. He had also informed my squadron commander for the exercise, Maj. Khusru Yar Jung, a soft-spoken officer from Hyderabad, to keep an eye on me. He kept me constantly occupied and as soon as the exercise was over, invited me to his house.

His wife, Nafisa, was a refined woman who went out of her way to make me feel at home. Over several dinners in the following days she gently urged me to face the facts and reconcile myself to the way things had turned out. There were some things we could not fight. After a gruelling fortnight of tough field army exercises, I found her gentle yet firm approach soothing and it helped me take stock of the situation more calmly and clearly. It dawned on me that in the new circumstances, it would be cruel for both Julie and me to wait for something that seemed destined not to happen. I went through a process of deep introspection, trying to look at all sides of the matter. It was heart-wrenching but, once again, I forced myself to think with my head rather than my heart. I had started enjoying army life and knew that settling down in England was now out of the question. With a heavy heart, I decided that the chapter of my life with Julie had to close.

Sometimes, it is important to use our head rather than our heart while taking decisions as the choices we make can impact life in ways we do not imagine. It was tempting to go back to Julie and the easy life that England offered, but I clinically thought of what my seniors had told me. Perhaps there is something in this for youngsters, who nowadays get easily carried away by infatuation and decide with the heart rather than good sense. Being in a relationship is very different from being in a marriage as it takes a lot of effort and maturity to make a marriage work and evolve into a partnership where both grow together. One has to be realistic and not dreamy. I realized this and decided on the tough option of saying goodbye to Julie.

Too many lives were involved on both sides. The dilemma was how to communicate my decision to Julie and her grandparents who had become very fond of me. To all intents and purposes, I had become part of their family circle. I could not muster the courage to talk to Julie on the telephone and decided to write to her. I must have composed several drafts. Finally, I wrote three letters – to Julie, her grandfather and grandmother. I got a response from Julie which was full of disappointment and hurt but it was also very dignified and I could see a reluctant understanding of my predicament. She ended the letter saying, 'It is not easy to wipe out memories. The only way you can help me to do it is by never trying to contact me again.'

But I would belie that expectation and go and personally meet her some years later. It was the gentlemanly thing to do. I felt I just had to explain the circumstances that led to my decision in person.

I managed to do so in 1966. Travelling abroad for Indian citizens had become very difficult after the government had imposed rigorous restrictions on foreign travel. Permission was given only in special cases and circumstances. I finally obtained government approval to travel to Owosso in the US for a training programme with Universal Electric Co. At Owosso, I met one Mr Johnson, who was then a sales agent for the company's products in England and was based in Woking near London. Not having been able to explain to Julie in person why I had taken the decision to stay back in India still weighed on my conscience. I happened to mention this dilemma to Johnson, who managed through his contacts in England to find out that Julie's grandparents had both passed away and that she had moved to Manchester after getting married. I was given the contact numbers of Julie's husband, a businessman. On my return journey to India, I took a detour via Manchester. They were living in the countryside, about twenty minutes from the city. Her husband answered the phone. When I introduced myself, he said Julie had told him all about me. I was surprised at the warmth he exuded over the phone. He insisted that I move out of the hotel and stay with them. I was hesitant but he was very persistent. He greeted me cordially when I reached their house. He appeared to be a mature, dignified person, much older than Julie. When she came into the living room, I immediately sensed hostility.

'Why have you come here?' she demanded, without mincing words.

Her husband interrupted to say that he had invited me over. She looked upset and took time to calm down. We eventually had a pleasant evening and chatted late into the night. She talked a lot about her grandparents and how much they had missed me and how life had changed after they were gone.

Time had been kind to her and she looked as appealing as ever. What was missing was the vibrancy and ebullience. The next morning her husband said he had to attend an urgent business meeting and left. Maybe he wanted us to get each other out of our systems.

When we were alone, she started sobbing. 'Why have you come? Didn't I tell you never to see me again? Why have you broken your promise? How can you be so cruel?' she asked through tears.

I did not know what to say. I tried to explain that I thought it was the right thing to do, to meet her one last time to tell her how sad I was about the way things had turned out, for letting her down. I just wanted her to know the reasons why. The last thing I wanted was to hurt her in any way.

It took her awhile to regain her composure. She said that she had made peace with life but with me visiting her, all the old memories had come rushing back. I said I was sorry and would go back to London at once. She insisted on driving me to the Manchester railway station. She remained very formal when we shook hands. We did not even hug each other. With tears in her eyes, she pleaded, 'Please, I beg of you, don't ever try to see me again. Let me live in peace. Let me die in peace.'

It was almost twenty years later, when I visited another old friend from Coventry, Bopal Singh, who had moved to Toronto, that I learnt that Julie had died. Bopal had been in touch with her off and on over the years. He said that she had eventually moved to Africa to settle down there. She had even told him how upset she had been when I suddenly landed up at her home in Manchester. Then Bopal turned to me and with a great deal of sadness in his voice said: 'I do not know how to say it, but I must – Julie had breast cancer, she passed away last year.'

It came as a terrible shock. Even though I had made no attempt to contact her after 1966, which was what she had made me promise, even though I kept my word to stay away from her, somehow Julie was always a part of me. I felt a deep sense of loss, as if something deep inside me had also died. My instinct was to go to Africa and visit her grave. But her words kept coming back to me and I resolved never to disturb her again. I did not visit her grave. Besides I did not want to be disloyal to my wife.

Bopal Singh had another shock in store for me. He said: 'This could be the last time we see each other. I have prostate cancer. Advanced stage. It won't be long now.'

So it was that he passed away a few years later. I had lost one more link to the past. Had it not been for him I would never have gone to Coventry in the first place. I would never have met Julie. Those happy and life-changing times would never have happened. A sense of yearning took hold of me and I decided that I should make one last trip to Coventry to relive the memories of those wonderful days.

There had been an opportunity in 1973, during one of my visits to London. I was a guest of India's acting high commissioner in the UK, Maharajakrishna Rasgotra, an outstanding career diplomat who later had another stint as high commissioner and would become the foreign secretary. He and his attractive wife Choti were a popular and highly admired couple in the diplomatic corps and wonderful hosts, with whom I have often stayed during my visits abroad.

During this particular trip he offered me his car to enable me to drive down memory lane, towards the outskirts of Coventry, hoping to see the Ansty aerodrome and my AST campus after almost twenty-five years. Sadly, nothing was as I remembered it. The area had been developed beyond recognition. The idyllic countryside had vanished. So had the campus and the aerodrome. New expressways crisscrossed the entire area. Even the area where Julie had lived with her grandparents had completely changed. The manor had disappeared. Rapid urbanization had taken its toll. I felt as if every vestige of that part of my life had been wiped out, as if it had never been.

5

TAKING ON NEW RESPONSIBILITIES

FEROZ SHAH KOTLA is a famous sports stadium in Delhi where major cricket matches are played. But for me, it has a very special significance as the venue of the most important match in my life – my first meeting with Indira. Even though chance encounters have often played an important role in my life and led to enduring friendships and relationships, my meeting with my future wife was not quite accidental or unplanned. Two very senior army officers had secretly conspired with Uncle Surendra to arrange our meeting.

Normally, one would not expect senior army officers to indulge in matchmaking. But that is exactly what happened. My commanding officer, Lt. Col. Sheodan Singh, who also happened to be related to me, had, it seems, talked about my future with his friend and colleague, Lt. Col. Qadam Singh, the erstwhile commandant of 17 Poona Horse Regiment, and my uncle. The three of them apparently agreed that as a dashing young cavalry officer with a bright career ahead of me, it was time for me to get married and settle down. They figured that the ideal match for me would be the strikingly attractive daughter of Chaudhry Raghvendra Singh, an honorary lieutenant colonel in the army, who was well known in Delhi's business and social circles. Uncle Surendra also knew Raghvendra Singh well. As my father was reticent by nature, my uncle took it upon himself to take charge of my marital future with the consent of my parents. This was in 1953, when society still frowned on young men and women meeting publicly. Fortunately, both our families were fairly progressive and felt we should meet before any decision on our engagement was taken. They managed to arrange a meeting at a cricket Test match at Feroz Shah Kotla, where it would not be out of place for us to sit in those more conventional times. Indira, however, was unaware of the arrangement or the purpose. She had come to watch the match with a group of her friends and relatives.

The moment I was introduced to her, I was struck by her bubbly personality. She, of course, had no idea it was a matchmaking exercise and was furious with her father when he told her about it that evening. She protested that she was too young, at seventeen, to think about marriage and claimed that she was not interested in me in any case. Yet, when one of her friends said she would not mind getting to know me, Indira immediately flared up and told her friend to stay away from me!

We met again soon and began seeing each other regularly and discovered that we enjoyed each other's company. Before long love blossomed. I was twenty-three, but in those days that was considered the right age to get married. The only problem was she was in Delhi and mine was a nomadic army existence. The opportunity came some months later when I was selected to lead the Deccan Horse tank contingent at the Republic Day parade in Delhi. It was a great honour; in addition, it also gave me a chance to meet Indira more often. I stayed with our close family friends from Bulandshahr, Lt. Col. Nepal Singh, who was then posted in the Delhi Area Headquarters. His wife, Amir Kaur, always made an effort to ensure that Indira and I met. Courtship went hand in hand with practice for the parade. It gave us an opportunity to get to know each other better to the point where marriage seemed the most natural outcome. We were married on 6 March 1954, a few months after that first meeting at a cricket match. My wedding was performed in traditional Indian style. The baraat – bridegroom's party – consisting of around a hundred people made its way from Bulandshahr to Delhi. The function was spread over three days and was full of festivities. The marriage took place at Pusa Road where my father-in-law was staying at that time.

The army teaches one how to adjust to every situation, but here, it was Indira who had to do all the adjusting. She was used to a life of comfort and large houses, and now here we were, posted in Jalandhar, and sharing a tiny room in the Jubilee Hotel where most married officers of the regiment stayed. Jalandhar is a well-known army cantonment almost halfway between Chandigarh and Amritsar. When an area is declared as an operational area, hotels are usually taken over by the army for accommodation. Jubilee Hotel, an old dilapidated building, was one such.

It was hardly suited for married couples, but we had no choice. We had just got married and had to make do. For Indira it would not have been easy at all but she neither complained nor showed any reluctance. She adjusted effortlessly to her new life. Till a few weeks before, she had a separate living room, bedroom and kitchen. Now, they were all in one room. Luxuries can spoil us, but Indira showed no sign of it and took on the hardships, including snakes slithering around the tiny bathtub, with equanimity. I guess we were too much in love with each other to bother about the negatives. We both saw it as a new way of life. I was only apprehensive about how my father-in-law would react, seeing his daughter having to rough it out. He made a surprise visit to Jalandhar along with his friend, Pratap Singh Kairon, who later became the chief minister of Punjab. One day, he came up to our room and was a bit embarrassed to find Indira starting her married life like this. However, as she was so happy and full of life, he soon saw merit in our new lifestyle, as the process of coping with a little hardship would help a young, newly married couple to get closer to each other.

What helped us adapt to our situation was the Deccan Horse. Indira and I made good friends. Even though we had to work hard and live in tough conditions, we managed to enjoy moments of fun and excitement. My stints at Ahmednagar, a centre where Armoured Corps officers were trained in various courses, were also enjoyable as we had to learn how to drive heavy-duty motor vehicles which took us out into the countryside. Indira and I used to look forward to our postings to Ahmednagar. During one such course, Indira learnt horse-riding, which gave us another common interest. Soon, both of us were riding together around Ahmednagar, which at that time had excellent open areas. Sadly, on one of these rides, she fell from a galloping horse. She was unhurt but it shook her confidence so much that she never rode again. Yet, there were still plenty of other activities and we had a great time. We used to play tennis, watch movies in the open air and despite the noisy projectors, it was an enjoyable experience for all the army families gathered there.

The Ahmednagar courses were a serious business and meant to rate your abilities as an army officer for higher training. My field reports must have been excellent because I was summoned to Army Headquarters for selection to undergo specialized training abroad. The course I was selected for would take me back to England and was designed for Armoured Corps officers to learn about advances in tank technology. I was very excited and so was Indira, who was to accompany me. I was also a little apprehensive. I had not told Indira about Julie as I felt she was too young. It was only much later in our marriage that I told her about my friendship with Julie. I need not have worried, since I had entered marriage without any emotional baggage and the experience with Julie actually helped build my relationship with Indira.

However, things turned out quite differently. A week before we were to sail from Bombay in October 1956, we were told the trip had been cancelled as the Suez Canal crisis had erupted following Egypt's decision to nationalize the canal.

My destiny took me instead to Udhampur, near Jammu. Lt. Gen. Wadalia had become general officer commanding (GOC) of XV Corps at Udhampur and he had picked me to be his ADC. It seemed that our lives were intertwined. Since Lt. Gen. Wadalia was the overall commander of the Jammu and Kashmir area, his principal residence was in Udhampur. However, as his work involved frequent travel to Srinagar, the government had given him another residence there, as a special courtesy. As his ADC, I had to accompany him on his travels and I enjoyed moving around both these places. So did Indira, who had found a ready friend in Marthe. Another benefit of being the ADC was that I was also given a houseboat on the Jhelum river.

Needless to say, it was a welcome change of scene for both of us. Wherever we went the army facilities were superb. As we were recently married, Mrs Wadalia was like a mother hen. The Wadalias had known Julie's family during their London days and Marthe had become very fond of Julie. However, she never brought up Julie's name when Indira was around. We travelled to all the beautiful tourist spots of Kashmir. Lt. Gen. Wadalia was usually busy in Udhampur and, as his ADC, it was left to me to look after his wife, so we could travel a lot in Kashmir. It was a memorable assignment. Indira loved it too.

In the late 1950s, I built a lovely small house there. So did many other officers. These houses, called *bhashas*, had thatched roofs with walls of rough brick. We also had a polo ground nearby. Indira was taking to the army life extremely well. She became close to other officers' wives and was very popular. It was like a closely knit family. Brig. Suresh Kochar and his wife, Shuli, would invariably come with us on weekend picnics. We converted Udhampur into an enjoyable place to be, more like a family station than a forward posting. Maj. Gen. Mohinder Singh Chadha was one officer who visited us at the *bhasha* in Udhampur. He still remembers the excellent dinner Indira served him on his return from an exercise on the border. Our married life was idyllic but I still had a lot to learn about being an officer with responsibilities.

In Udhampur, the layout of the office building ensured that any officer wishing to meet the general had to pass through my room. One day, he handed me a list of a few select officers of XV Corps located in different areas of Jammu and Kashmir. He told me that he would like to meet each one of them at specific intervals. This list was only known to the corps commander, the then brigadier general staff (BGS) of XV Corps, Brig. Joginder Singh, and myself. These were the brightest officers of the corps. They would arrive with typical army swagger and would pass through my room full of confidence. When they left, their body language was totally different, almost like that of schoolchildren after being admonished. I wondered why.

One day, I ventured to ask the corps commander what went on in his office. He gave me an important lesson, one of many I received from the general. He explained to me that one of the important ingredients of success while running a large military or civil organization was to, first, identify your key commanders and thereafter ensure that they always remained competent in their jobs commensurate with their designation and positions. Often, when such key identified officials get promoted to higher ranks they became egoistic unless they were constantly checked and counselled. The ability and the courage with which this task was performed by the top commander would determine the continued good performances of such officials and the organization.

Lt. Gen. Wadalia's strategy was to identify the levels where such officers would tend to become egoistic and slacken off. He would ensure that they remained on their toes by his periodic meetings with them. Some needed to be hauled up every month, some after two months and some others after three. His strategy of such counselling produced immediate results in terms of their improved performance. I observed that Lt. Gen. Wadalia devoted a lot of his personal time in such counselling sessions. He always believed that this responsibility must be carried out effectively by the top commander of any organization to achieve successful results. When I view this in the commercial world today I find that such counselling sessions are invariably conducted by the HRD managers only. Such counselling is rarely done by the top leaders. It is a practice that I put to use in business to great effect.

The Kashmir posting was one of the best times I had in the army. There was adventure at every step and a lot of learning. Lt. Gen. Wadalia was fond of visiting inaccessible outposts to raise the morale of the troops. So, we mostly walked or went on horseback.

One day, the general decided to inspect outposts high up in the hills of Gurez, Kargil and Drass that border Pakistan. The only way to go up the steep slopes was either to climb up or ride on sure-footed mountain artillery horses that were specially trained. Lt. Gen. Wadalia decided to visit these outposts on horseback. Consequently, the brigade commander of this area selected sure-footed horses for this trip. As part of this convoy, there were several horses in front of me. My horse was uncomfortable with the steep climb. I could feel it all along. But we were halfway up and there was nothing one could do except move onwards and upwards. The trail was narrow and the gorges were steep and deadly. As the height increased, the path became narrower and fell away to disappear several thousand feet below. A fall from here would be fatal. Suddenly, at around 10,000 feet, my worst fears came true. My horse slipped. In such a situation, the rider would have inevitably gone down with the horse as both feet are normally clamped in the stirrups. My early training with horses gave me a split second of reflex action to yank my feet free of the stirrups, grab a branch of a tree on the hillside and hang on for dear life even as my horse slipped down several thousand feet. It was my third and closest encounter yet with death.

I consider it a miracle to have survived. I still get the chills whenever I look at the scars on my hands, which were fractured in that incident. It was a huge ordeal for the army team to rescue me while I was precariously clinging on to a branch about thirty feet below the path they were on. Since the tree was located on an inaccessible incline, it took considerable time for the army team to re-group and pull me out from my position.

It was a rude reminder that for all its natural beauty, Kashmir was also a hazardous place for army personnel. Jammu and Kashmir, however, had its compensations. I once flew from Srinagar to Leh accompanying the GOC-in-C of Western Command – Lt. Gen. Kulwant Singh. On the day we were to fly back, bad weather interfered and the flight captain said he needed to reduce the load to take off. I, along with another captain, was asked to deplane as we were the juniormost officers. The weather continued to be bad for another twenty days but it meant an enjoyable stay in the Leh region, discovering its stunning landscape.

The Kashmir posting, however, could not last forever. Lt. Gen. Wadalia was promoted as deputy chief of army staff in January 1959 and I moved with him to Delhi as his staff officer at Army Headquarters. I entered a new role in New Delhi in a completely different environment. It was quite an experience as I got to see how the top echelons of the army and the defence ministry interacted. Even as I was settling down, my return to Delhi prompted a dramatic change in the course of my life and career.

My father-in-law began asking me to leave the army and help in the family business. He had started a real estate company called Delhi Land and Finance (DLF) way back in 1946 and was looking to diversify into new industrial ventures. Land development and construction, which was the core of his business, had come to a halt as the government had handed over all urban land development work to the state-owned Delhi Development Authority (DDA). Chaudhry Saheb did not have a son and wanted me to quit the army to aggressively pursue the diversification plan of DLF along with Indira's brother-in-law, Shamsher Singh.

I thought about it long and hard and finally decided to resign from the army and take the plunge into business. It was a tough decision as I would be leaving a life I was thoroughly enjoying. My seniors had told me often enough that I had a great future in the army and would rise to the top. But here was one of those opportunities that come knocking when you least expect them. I decided on taking up the new challenge and see where it would lead me. I wrote out my resignation but with enormous regret. After eight years, the army had become a part of my life.

In those days, resignations in the army were unheard-of. I was only a captain but even then, my resignation had to be cleared by the defence minister, V.K. Krishna Menon. He was known to be quite temperamental. I knew it was going to be a real battle to get his approval. H.C. Sarin, the joint secretary in the defence ministry who dealt with resignations, was a great buddy of Uncle Surendra since their days together at Cambridge during the late 1930s. Despite Sarin's best efforts, he could not prevail upon Menon to accept the resignation. Sure enough, my resignation was rejected on the grounds that a lot of money had been spent on my training. Moreover, the excellent reports in all my postings were actually working against me.

Fate intervened in the form of Lt. Gen. B.M. Kaul, chief of the general staff, who was known to be close to Menon but was also a stickler for rules and propriety. As I had developed a good relationship with him earlier as staff officer to Lt. Gen. Wadalia, I was quite frank and told him that I wished to quit the army not because I did not like it, but because I was needed to run the family business. He asked for my file and a couple of days later, he called me.

'Damn it, you have screwed your own case,' he thundered. 'All throughout your career, you have maintained an outstanding record. How do I convince the defence minister to let someone who is doing so well be allowed to leave?'

Lt. Gen. Kaul was known to have an ego so I decided to play to that.

'If you cannot do it, sir, no one can,' I pleaded.

My ploy worked. He assured me that it would be done in a week and he kept his word.

A satisfying and adventurous life in the army had come to an end. Yet, I will always remember what the army gave me. Not just the values, discipline, endurance and courage to take on overwhelming challenges, but also the many friends I made with whom I still remain close. Maj. Gen. K.M.K.S. Waraich, 81, is one. He is always in touch and travelled all the way with his wife to Delhi on 31 March 2010 when I was awarded the Padma Bhushan by the President of India, Pratibha Devisingh Patil. I was quite touched by his gesture. Sitting in the lawns of my house that evening at a felicitation ceremony that my children had organized, he held forth on the values the army had instilled in us that made us give priority to work over wealth. He was absolutely right. I would not have been what I am today had it not been for the training I received from the army.

6

LEARNING THE ROPES

IT WAS TIME to start another chapter in my life. I was about to enter the world of business, about which at that time I knew nothing at all. Even though I had a few friends and relatives who were businessmen I had never taken any real interest in their activities or asked about the problems and challenges of running a business venture. It is one of life's ironies that today, decades later, I am often invited to address the bright students of some of the best B-schools in the world, including Harvard and Wharton, the ISB and the IIMs, even though I have never had any formal management education. I am often asked about the secret of the success of DLF, which many see as quite spectacular. My answer, invariably, is to confess that I learnt the ropes the hard way, through a process of trial and error, but that in the early years it was my army background that gave me the confidence and the qualities needed to confront the challenges of running a business – the army culture of sharing and teamwork, the ability to think fast, analyse problems quickly and come out with innovative, out-of-the-box solutions. Above all, army life had inculcated in me a dogged determination never to give up, whatever the odds.

All these attributes and attitudes helped me immensely when I took the first tentative steps into the unfamiliar and complex world of business. I learnt many more things along the way in later years from personal experience and from certain incredibly dynamic individuals I had the good fortune to come in touch with, but I knew one thing for sure: if I did manage to achieve something in life, the army would have to be given a great deal of the credit.

As coincidence would have it, shortly after I left the army and plunged into business, Lt. Gen. Wadalia retired after a long and distinguished career. Being the livewire he was, he had no intention of leading a relaxed retired life but was toying with the idea of launching into business himself. He discussed his post-retirement options with my father-in-law. He was keen to set up an industrial venture but was wondering in what area it should be.

'What are you best at?' Chaudhry Saheb asked him.

'Horses,' Lt. Gen. Wadalia replied, looking at me with a twinkle in his eye.

Whenever he visited his friend Fali Wadia's Yervada Stud Farm in Pune, he would come back with the conviction that this was what he would like to do after retirement. The problem was that he did not know how to acquire land for it and felt I could help him as I was familiar with the real estate business and above all, shared his passion for horses.

Chaudhry Saheb was taken up with the idea of starting a stud farm near Delhi and got down to exploring possibilities. They identified a site in the Gadaipur–Chhattarpur area in Mehrauli on the outskirts of Delhi. I was a bit sceptical of starting a stud farm in the middle of nowhere. Chhattarpur was in those days a godforsaken place with no habitation, no roads and no civic amenities. Both of them were sold on the idea and I was pulled into this new venture reluctantly. We had to traverse the uneven terrain on a tractor as there were no roads. It was an uninhabitable wilderness, with mounds of irregular size and littered with stones. Brushing aside my apprehensions, Chaudhry Saheb predicted that one day this area would be worth its weight in gold. He was absolutely right. Today, the area is not only prohibitively expensive, it also has some of the capital's most influential people living in elegant and imposing farmhouses. As events proved, it was his vision that eased me into the world of business.

My first task was to develop the stud farm and supervise its day-to-day management. Lt. Gen. Wadalia took over as a managing partner. Apart from me, there were two other partners in the venture: Kamal Singh, the maharaja of Dumraon, and Chaudhry Saheb. The conversion of agricultural land into a stud farm required special approval from the Municipal Corporation of Delhi (MCD). I got busy with the thankless job of getting numerous government clearances. I had to grapple with endless red tape and ran from pillar to post to get the papers cleared by multiple departments even though they were in perfect order. Back then, it was extremely irritating and frustrating, but when I look back, I realize that it was a valuable learning opportunity. All the networking with officials for clearances helped me in later years when I had to deal with numerous land acquisitions and permissions for DLF.

Working on the stud farm was an education as well, as I was tasked with converting the rough, barren terrain into a level, grassy stud farm. My experience with horses in the cavalry proved invaluable as I had to deal with bloodstock, from yearlings to fully grown horses. I learnt about the kind of grass required to be planted, how to build stables, transport bloodstock, get the best nutrition for the horses and so on. Lt. Gen. Wadalia was a great help; he taught me how to select the bloodline from stallions and broodmares, mostly from England. He had an intimate knowledge about the performance of racing horses around the world. Getting these horses from abroad and transporting them to India was aided by his brother-in-law in Belgium as there were tight foreign exchange regulations in those days governing import of bloodstock into India.

I worked steadily on levelling the land and soon Lt. Gen. Wadalia was ready with his Qutab Stud and Agriculture Farm. It was an exciting new field and I was soon tending to over seventy horses. Breeding was a new area for me. Picking up the right stallion was the key to making money and it was a bit of a gamble. Two of the horses we imported, Asopo and Young Lochinvar, belonged to two of the best stallion breeds in England. Asopo performed well in India while Young Lochinvar did not. Yet, the uncertainty added to the appeal. Each day, when I drove to the farm I felt lucky to be doing something I enjoyed and also getting paid for it. One of the first business lessons I learnt was of being able to do things that others felt might not succeed. Everyone thought we were insane trying to build a stud farm business on such a useless piece of land. The fact that I was able to convert a remote and arid piece of land into a green, productive farm gave me the knowledge and the confidence that would prove extremely useful when I was rebuilding DLF.

The DLF business group at that time included DLF Housing and Construction Pvt. Ltd, which was involved in the real estate and construction business, Delhi Land and Finance Pvt. Ltd, which dealt with financial services, and Raisina Cold Storage Pvt. Ltd, which dealt with storage of frozen food items. In 1969, the three entities merged to become DLF United Limited. At the time of the merger, the company had a very small capital base. Prior to that, the shareholding of DLF United was held primarily by my wife, Indira, her sister, Prem Mohini, Sardar Hari Singh of Dabra, and Kanwar Giriraj Singh of Sahanpur. The rest of the shares were held by hundreds of public shareholders. In its early years, DLF had done well, developing numerous residential colonies in Delhi. After Partition, the influx of refugees had almost doubled the capital's population and there was acute shortage of residential accommodation. At that time, DLF was the most prominent private builder in Delhi. Under Chaudhry Raghvendra Singh, it developed its first residential colonies on some 5,800 acres of land soon after Independence. These included Hauz Khas, Greater Kailash I and II, Kailash Colony, South Extension, Shivaji Park, Model Town, and Rajouri Garden.

Over time, it had built up a rock-solid reputation because of the high quality of its buildings and construction work and fair and transparent dealings with its customers. All that changed in 1957 when the government set up the Birla Committee to recommend measures for a better-planned capital city. The committee suggested the creation of a single authority to deal with urban land development and housing. This gave birth to the DDA. Its conception basically ensured that private developers were kept out of urban land development in Delhi henceforth.

Prime Minister Jawaharlal Nehru wanted to ensure that urban housing was available to the middle and lower middle class at reasonable prices. He also wanted farmers whose land was acquired to be fairly compensated. The stated aim was to allow Delhi to grow in a planned way. His intentions were noble but the inevitable happened due to the inability of the DDA to cope with the demand for urban land and housing. Unauthorized construction erupted and fly-by-night developers started looking for loopholes to evade the law. This became the pattern all over India and very soon, urban land development in the capital was firmly in the hands of an unscrupulous mafia. Aesthetics and planning were thrown out of the window.

In 1960, in one sweeping move, an ill-conceived government

order banned the development of urban land by the private sector. The business of reputable private builders, including the then-prosperous DLF, came to a grinding halt. The future growth and development of the capital would now be in the hands of the DDA and unauthorized developers. In the changed scenario, DLF could have done the same but Chaudhry Saheb took a decision that in many ways defined what DLF stood for: he said that he would rather stay out of business than do anything underhand or illegal.

The real estate business of DLF was thus put in cold storage and he decided to diversify into other businesses. He focused on manufacturing. I was still involved in the stud farm, but DLF's entry into the manufacturing sector would have a huge impact on my life and future career. It would bring me in contact with an extraordinary man who would become my mentor in life and business, and an inspirational figure for his values, business ethics and his humanity.

His name was George Warren Hoddy, an American entrepreneur who was looking to invest in India. The reason he wanted to invest offered a clue to his personality. He had read a report in an American newspaper about poverty in India and the swelling ranks of the unemployed. He was a businessman but also a humanitarian.

Hoddy decided to invest in India to create additional job opportunities also because the report had mentioned that many technically trained and skilled young men in India were unemployed. His company, based in Michigan, manufactured precision electric motors. Coincidentally, a budding young Indian entrepreneur, Vimal Kochhar, was also scouting for a foreign partner to set up a plant in India to manufacture similar products. Kochhar had graduated from an American university and his search led him to Universal Electric, the company owned by Hoddy. When Kochhar met Hoddy to explore the possibility of a business partnership in India, the latter jumped at the idea and said he would love to do something in India if he got a good and reliable Indian partner. Kochhar had the right partner in America but lacked the backing of a reliable and established Indian company. He returned to India where he met a family friend, the well-known ENT specialist Dr H.S. Trehan (father of leading cardiologist Dr Naresh Trehan) and asked him if he could recommend a reliable partner for Universal Electric. Dr Trehan suggested Chaudhry Raghvendra Singh, who, he knew, was looking to diversify.

Hoddy flew to Delhi, met up with Chaudhry Saheb, and they hit it off instantly. In a very short time, in July 1963, they decided to set up a joint venture company to manufacture fractional horsepower precision electric motors and named it American Universal Electric India Ltd. The factory was set up at Faridabad, on the outskirts of Delhi. Chaudhry Saheb's family held a 49 per cent share, Dr Trehan held two per cent and 49 per cent was held by the Michigan-based Universal Electric.

I became its managing director not because of any merit or expertise but because my father-in-law was a major partner. The chairman of American Universal at that time was Hoddy's brother, Gerald. Although officially I was the managing director, I was still not serious about business, preferring to breed horses at the stud farm. Part of the attraction was also the glittering social life that revolved around horse breeding, racing and polo. Indira and I were part of a sophisticated, well-heeled crowd, Delhi's social elite, who believed in living life to the fullest. We used to be invited to parties that would extend into the early hours of the morning. This happened every second day. Late nights almost became routine till the day Indira and I came home at 5.30 a.m. and met my parents-in-law going out for their morning walk.

'Some time, you might also want to get more serious about your work and the business,' my father-in-law remarked as he passed me.

It was a rude jolt. His comment kept replaying in my mind. It was the wake-up call I needed. That day, I reassessed what I was doing and realized I was nearing mid-life and needed to get serious with my business career. Having fun was important, but working hard to prove myself was more important. It marked another turning point in my life. It would lay the foundation for the building of a business empire. For that, I must give credit to my father-in-law for the wake-up call, and Hoddy for steering me in the right direction. By this time, Hoddy had taken over as chairman of the company but I still had no inkling of the lasting influence that he would have on my life.

If Hoddy was an icon for me, it was with good reason. Not only was he a colourful personality, he also taught me many valuable lessons in the twenty years that I worked with him. Having become serious about my position in the company, I carefully watched his style of dealing with employees, the meticulous detail he went into before formulating any business strategy and his way of micro-managing problems or complications. He treated me like his son, constantly guiding and mentoring me. I can safely say that I owe a lot that I have achieved in business to him. I felt truly blessed to have worked with such a man.

Hoddy had studied electrical and mechanical engineering at the Ohio State University and was an entrepreneur at heart. He thought of developing a small electric motor after he saw his mother's washing machine using a heavy cast iron-frame electric motor. He started work on building one and was hired by General Motors and later by A. Redmond & Co., where he worked on the development and manufacture of small electric motors to operate windshield wipers and fans in the automotive field.

Hoddy, however, had his own entrepreneurial dreams and quit the job to start Universal Electric. By then, he had developed a special motor for military aircraft and bagged his first contracts from the US Defence Department. That proved the start of his business empire and, thanks to the Second World War, Universal Electric would go on to make millions. His fractional horsepower motors were used on ships, aircraft and top secret projects like radar instruments. By the end of the War, Universal Electric had moved into domestic home appliances and become a leader in the field of precision motors. Hoddy attributed his company's success to working hard, treating employees as family, ensuring quality management and giving consumers what they wanted. It was something that I later adopted and practised at DLF.

My stint at American Universal was a great learning experience and sharpened my skills as a professional manager. I had acquired the experience of managing people but lacked the overall qualities required to be a business leader. Hoddy would turn me into one. Learning the nuts and bolts of business from someone like him was a stroke of great luck. He gave me the hunger to succeed as a businessman and the tools to ensure I got there. Yet, our initial enterprise was not a roaring success. The motors we made were not in great demand as they were mainly used in air-conditioners and other such high-priced appliances which had a very limited market in India in those days. I was managing the commercial side of the business and though I did not have a business management degree, my stint in the army had given me enough skills to succeed. And there was Hoddy. Every year, he would come to India to spend a month at the Faridabad factory. Alternatively, I would spend a month at Hoddy's factory at Michigan. He got me to work on the shop floor. At the time, I resented the menial tasks I had to do but I later realized it was Hoddy's way of getting me to understand the importance of hard work and the dignity of labour.

He taught me several other important lessons too. The factory at Faridabad used to open at 8 a.m. At exactly 7 a.m., Hoddy's car would arrive to pick me up. He insisted that both of us should be in the plant before the workers arrived. It would increase their regard for the management and it also taught me that punctuality earned its own respect. The greatest lesson he taught me, however, was business ethics. It has been the moving force in my life and career. Hoddy once told me that it was so tempting to lose sight of ethics as India's archaic laws and bureaucracy made it almost impossible for business to flourish. His solution was not to break or evade laws, but to lobby to change them. I learnt that there is no right way to do a wrong job. This was something I consciously followed in business deals in the years to follow. He had a knack of surrounding himself with talented people and I learnt from him that to be an effective corporate leader you have to acquire exhaustive knowledge of a particular subject, then figure out macro objectives and thereafter get into micro-management. I later used Hoddy's technique of combining micro- and macro-management not just in business strategies but even in handling personal problems.

Hoddy went on to make a fortune selling his shares and merging Universal Electric with ESB (Electric Storage Batteries) Inc., which was a leading manufacturer of storage batteries in the United States with ownership of brands like Exide, Willard and Ray-o-Vac. Even at the peak of his success, he was never wasteful or extravagant. The aspect of India that fascinated Hoddy the most was how a lot of business in India was transacted with very low overheads. I recall an incident on the way to our Faridabad factory when Hoddy suddenly stopped the car, jumped out with his camera and started taking pictures of a wayside barber who ran his shop with just a chair and a mirror nailed to a tree. He was intrigued with the idea of people in India earning money with so little infrastructure.

That roadside barber even had an impact in Michigan! I had gone there a few months later. My hair needed trimming and so

I walked into a haircutting salon and sat in one of the vacant chairs. I was taken aback when the owner rushed towards me asking which country I was from. I proudly told him I was from India.

'Sorry, no haircut for any Indian,' he said, waving his hand angrily.

I was bewildered by his insulting attitude and demanded an explanation. The owner quietly produced the picture of the Faridabad barber and said that Hoddy had shown the picture to his clients saying there was no basis in charging $10 for a haircut in Michigan while an Indian barber charged just a few cents to do the same job! After this, he complained, no one wanted to pay $10 any more.

'Hoddy has ruined my business by showcasing this example and I will not entertain any Indian,' he vowed angrily.

I could not help bursting into laughter. Hoddy was like that. Tight overheads was his style of business.

He taught me the virtues of humility and austerity even in times of plenty. I never forgot what he once told me: 'Practising austerity in the time of prosperity is the biggest wisdom of a business leader.' It was largely his inspiration that helped us keep DLF insured against the severe effects of the global meltdown around 2009. We did lose billions of rupees during that period when the real estate market took a beating. I remember a *Forbes* magazine cover story on me at the peak of the recession when DLF's market capitalization was down by 90 per cent. DLF's share price at an all-time high in January 2008 was Rs. 1,225 which worked out to a market capitalization of Rs. 2,088 billion – about US $50 billion. That is how bad it was. Hoddy's lessons on austerity during prosperity which we had followed at DLF helped us minimize our losses and deal with the recession. It was a tough time for everybody and I believe it was my army training which had prepared me for adversity and unexpected challenges that helped me lead DLF out of the crisis stronger, leaner and fitter. I went through hell but I learnt a crucial lesson: that there are other things more valuable than money. Friends, family, colleagues, non-business activity, these are all priceless assets.

As we developed a close relationship, Hoddy naturally grew fond of my family. At that time, Rajiv, my son, was studying at Delhi's Modern School.

'What are his future plans?' he asked me.

I replied that Rajiv was thinking of pursuing an engineering course in a good college.

'If Rajiv has to emerge as a good business leader he needs to be exposed to education abroad as it will give him a wider worldview,' he told me.

He suggested that Rajiv should try to get into the Massachusetts Institute of Technology (MIT) at Boston, but before that it would be beneficial if he went to a good American school and got used to the educational system there. He mentioned Hillsdale School in Michigan and said he would offer to be his local guardian.

'What I could not do for my children I want to do for Rajiv,' he said.

True to his word, he got Rajiv admitted at Hillsdale which was about 110 km from Owosso and Detroit. He also made arrangements for Rajiv to work in his factory and earn some pocket money. He ensured that he was just paid the bare minimum so that he would learn to value money. He used other occasions to hammer home that message. He once took Rajiv out for dinner and Rajiv asked for a second helping. Hoddy told him that the extra money would be cut from his pocket money. I am eternally grateful to him for instilling such values in my son at an early age. In India, we spoil our children with credit cards, loads of pocket money and all kinds of luxuries. We think we need to do all this to compensate for the lack of time with our children.

We justify it by saying that we want our children to have the best. I could not have chosen a better teacher than Hoddy.

Today, I can see how his influence has helped Rajiv to become a complete professional. He is hard-working, focused, and keeps a low profile. His training and education has helped him chart a whole new growth path for DLF. Hoddy can take credit for that.

The stint at Hillsdale helped him to get into MIT. He graduated in mechanical engineering before moving back to India. MIT helped Rajiv develop a fine perspective on business and management. MIT is a much sought after institute for its excellence in engineering, research and management education.

My last memory of George Hoddy is of my visit to Owosso to celebrate his hundredth birthday a few years ago. Till his end came in June 2010, at 107, he refused to let growing old change his lifestyle. He used to get up very early every morning, dress in a suit and tie, and then sit down for breakfast just the way he did all the years before leaving for office. He even used to drive but his daughter stopped it by hiring a chauffeur when he crossed hundred. I will truly miss my dearest mentor, philosopher and guide, George Warren Hoddy.

7

DOING BUSINESS THE HARD WAY

IT DID NOT take me very long to discover that in the India of the 1970s, political minefields dogged businessmen every step of the way. The state of Haryana, particularly, was a hotbed of politics and all factory-owners were vulnerable to pressures, especially during elections and rallies, when all industrialists were expected to make sizable donations to political parties. At that time I was looking after the Faridabad unit of American Universal. Since I was new to business, finding my feet was a bit of a baptism by fire. In that overheated atmosphere, the Congress party decided to hold a big political rally in Faridabad and I got involved as president of the Faridabad Industries Association.

Bansi Lal was the chief minister of Haryana at that time. He was a popular Congress leader. After the formation of Haryana in 1966, much of the state's industrial and agricultural development, especially the creation of modern infrastructure, took place because of him. He was elected seven times to the Haryana assembly, the first being in 1967. He parted ways with the Congress in 1996 to set up the Haryana Vikas Party.

He had asked Faridabad's deputy commissioner to raise money from industrialists. An official went around various companies in the area seeking contributions. When the official met the management of Escorts, the leading tractor company, he was told that the business rules of Ford Motors, the American partner, forbade any political funding. When this was conveyed to Bansi Lal, he was enraged. Some days later, the trade unions at Escorts went on strike.

The chairman of Escorts was Hari Nanda, a highly respected businessman who carried tremendous clout within the industry as well as the political leadership in Delhi, all the way up to the prime minister. He was worried as the lightning strike in all the Escorts plants, which was without any valid cause, had already lasted four days and the striking workers were refusing to come to the table to negotiate their demands. He tried to contact the chief minister but got no response. He then turned to me and asked if I could arrange a meeting.

I had developed a good equation with Bansi Lal in my capacity as head of the local industrial association but, despite that, he refused to give Nanda a hearing when I made the request during our meeting. I used all my persuasive skills and finally he agreed to give Nanda an appointment at 10 a.m. one day in his Chandigarh office.

That meeting turned out to be a humiliating one for Nanda, as I discovered when the Escorts chairman returned from Chandigarh and related his experience. He had reached the chief minister's office at the appointed time and was taken to his room on the fourth floor of the secretariat building. This was more like an auditorium with numerous rows of chairs. Nanda was asked to sit in the last row. When he asked why he was being seated so far back, the CM's secretary said he had specific instructions to seat him there.

Bansi Lal walked in half an hour later and completely ignored Nanda while conducting one meeting after another with his officials. On two occasions, the Escorts chairman got up and asked the chief minister if he could come forward and meet him. The answer was a curt 'No'. Bansi Lal did not even establish eye contact. At about 1.30 p.m., the chief minister left for lunch without bothering about Nanda. He returned at 4.30 p.m. and resumed his meetings till 5.30 p.m. When Nanda finally got up and said he had been waiting the whole day to have a word, Bansi Lal sternly replied, 'I know you are Hari Nanda of Escorts but why have you come alone? Where is your Jimmy Carter? I believe that you cannot do anything in your factory without the permission of your American partner. Unless you bring him along, I cannot meet you.'

He then walked out.

I got a desperate call from Nanda again asking me to intervene. I went back to meet Bansi Lal and told him that Hari Nanda was a senior and respected business leader with political connections that went right to the top. I sensed a change in attitude. In my presence, Bansi Lal directed the labour commissioner to resolve the Escorts strike. Nanda, however, was still worried and shaken by the episode. He tried to improve his relations with Bansi Lal through various political emissaries, but failed.

Years later, his son, Rajan Nanda, who had taken over the running of Escorts, did manage to establish a good working relationship with Bansi Lal when he took over as CM in 1985 and again in 1996, but it was a wake-up call for all of us with business interests in Haryana. Indeed, doing business in a politically sensitive state like Haryana required one to learn how to keep a cool head and avoid any unpleasantness. Those qualities were in peak demand during the mid-1970s when memories of the strike at Escorts came to haunt me at our own factory in Faridabad.

I had worked hard to build up a good rapport with the 3,000

workers at American Universal. Of all the lessons I learnt from Hoddy about management and running a company, perhaps the most important was to earn loyalty and respect from your employees. I had noticed how Hoddy got the best out of his employees. Time and again, he told me that if one had to get optimum work out of employees and also earn loyalty, one had to work very hard on building relationships with them. He would say, 'Get them to feel that they are part of the family, become a patriarch who genuinely cares. It helps in the long run.' It certainly did in my case when I was the target of powerful people and my factory was in deep trouble because of union problems. It was because of one man whom my family had helped many years earlier that we were saved from near disaster.

I had made Hoddy's advice the cornerstone of our management–worker relationship. Mahabir Hooda, my personnel manager, had been instructed to prepare a list of workers with their family details. I had him collect information on four crucial areas of each employee: son's education, daughter's marriage, wife's health and any legal disputes he may be involved with. He would also brief me if there were individual problems like a serious illness in the family or difficulty in getting school admissions, and similar problems. Every employee had a dossier with a full-size photograph.

Before taking a round of one part of the plant, I would study the details carefully, including the photograph. That way, when I talked to them, I did it at a very personal level, addressing them by their first names. They were surprised and taken aback that I knew so much about them and their family, but also appreciative of the personal touch. It gave them the reassurance that the company cared for them and they reciprocated by giving their best when it came to work.

Often I would send Mahabir to the house of a worker who was involved in a legal dispute so that we could help him out. It might seem a public relations exercise but it was much more than that. I would spend a lot of time counselling employees on personal issues and also helping them out in whichever way I could. Sometimes it would be a sudden medical emergency, school admissions or even helping with jobs for their family members. This built up a relationship of trust and my workers never forgot the things I did for them. It did wonders in terms of their loyalty and commitment. When there was a problem, I was able to easily diffuse it. This particular work ethic that Hoddy taught me helped me later too when I was attempting to build DLF into the giant it would become. In India, however, all the hard work and effort can be derailed by one word: politics.

Devi Lal had become chief minister of Haryana in June 1977. It was a period when there was a sudden outbreak of union activity and labour unrest in Faridabad. It was directly related to the post-Emergency period when unions and labour, which had been repressed for twenty-one months, tried to reassert their influence under the new mood of political freedom. In particular, the Communist Party of India (Marxist)- and the Centre of Indian Trade Unions (CITU)-led unions became very aggressive. Because of the relations I had built up, the labourers in my factory had no interest in strikes but were instigated by external communist-run unions. When the local union in our factory was hijacked by the larger, more powerful communist union, they had no option but to join the strikes that had affected Faridabad's industrial belt. My senior executives and I were caught totally unawares because we had built up such good relations with our workers. We were even more shocked when, instigated by the unions from outside, they turned violent, even beating up some of my managers.

It was my first real crisis as a business manager but I still remained optimistic. My father was well known to Charan Singh, who was the home minister in the Janata government at that time. I went over to see him along with my father. Charan Singh expressed surprise at the sudden muscle-flexing by labour unions leading to violence. He telephoned Devi Lal and asked him to take strong action to control the law and order situation. He then asked me to meet Devi Lal and explain the background to the labour unrest. I met the chief minister and gave him the details, whereupon he instructed Bhajan Lal, his labour minister, to act immediately. Bhajan Lal, whom I had already briefed, asked the deputy commissioner of Faridabad to impose Section 144 as the sudden violence by workers at American Universal had spread to adjoining industrial units.

Emboldened by the actions taken by the Haryana government, I decided to sack some four hundred workers who were involved in the violence at the factory. Before doing so, I called the local union leader and asked him what was going on. He admitted that the workers had no real issues and that the strike was actually being orchestrated by an aggressive communist labour leader. He gave me the name.

I decided to meet the leader, who used to operate from Vithalbhai Patel House in Delhi. I was told that it was the operational hub where communist leaders decided on their plans of action. I arrived there and was taken to meet him. He was a tall, imposing personality. Initially, he pretended not to know who I was but gave the game away by immediately launching into communist jargon and their standard propaganda line: all businessmen are crooks and only out to exploit labour. I had, however, an ace up my sleeve but whether it would work I had no idea. Before meeting him, I had researched his background and discovered that he was from Muzaffarnagar, the Jat hinterland of western Uttar Pradesh, which I knew well. I spoke to him in typical Jat dialect and informed him that workers in my factory had gone on strike without any valid reason and had resorted to senseless violence. He did not react.

I then played the ace in my hand. I told him that I was just a small businessman from Bulandshahr who was trying to set up a business and facing great difficulty. As soon I mentioned Bulandshahr, he started asking me about my background. I told him I was from a middle-class family and my father was a lawyer. That did the trick. As soon as I mentioned my father's name, the labour leader's demeanour changed. He was smart enough to throw questions at me to ascertain whether I was really telling him the truth. Once he was convinced, I sensed victory. I had presumed the Bulandshahr connection would be enough but as it turned out, it was stronger than that. It emerged that during the period my father was the public prosecutor, he had saved one of the labour leader's close family members from a murder charge. From then on, his attitude and tone became positive. I pushed my luck even more by telling him that we had excellent relations with our workers, which is why we had never experienced labour problems. Now that many of these workers had resorted to violence, I wanted to sack four hundred of them. I thought he would react adversely but instead, he remarked, 'Since you are Chaudhry Mukhtar Singh's son, and I owe him a lot, I will help you. The factory strike will end. You don't have to worry.'

I dared not believe the sudden change in attitude and fortunes but the very next day, when the workers called off the strike and returned to work, I went ahead and carried out the mass dismissals. There was not a squeak of protest. Our factory even got protection from the communist cadres.

My Jat origins and family were to come to my rescue on another occasion, this time in a rather bizarre incident. The partnership between DLF and ESB Inc. of the US had resulted in the creation of another enterprise, Willard India. The factory of this industrial venture was established in Sikandrabad in Uttar Pradesh, where Willard batteries were manufactured. I had to visit the factory frequently and looked forward to the journey as it was close to Khandera, the village where I was born. I always used the opportunity to go home and meet my family members and relatives.

On one of the trips, during the mid-1970s, I was on my way back to Delhi. It had been an exhausting day and I had dozed off in the back seat of my car. Suddenly, the car screeched to a halt. It was around 9 p.m. and quite dark. I realized we had been stopped by dacoits. The road was notorious for such incidents but I had never imagined it would happen to me. There were four gang members and they dragged me out of the car and checked the vehicle but found nothing of great value. I was not carrying a great deal of money either. Angry and frustrated, they blindfolded me and frog-marched me along a canal, obviously wanting to create fear and panic and perhaps hold me for ransom. My army training helped me to stay calm and confident.

'Why are you not carrying any money?' one of them demanded.

I told them I was not a rich man but from a village called Khandera. They obviously thought I was lying.

'Are we fools? Do you think you will be allowed to leave just like that?' the gang leader shouted.

He must have thought I was trying to pull a fast one and fired a volley of questions at me related to the topography of Khandera. I answered confidently, and then dropped my father's name as he was well known in the area. The gang leader still thought I was name-dropping.

'Really? You are Chaudhry Mukhtar Singh's son? Do you take us for imbeciles?' He laughed loudly and the others joined him.

He then asked me to describe my house, presuming I would be caught out in a lie. I described it in meticulous detail. He was taken aback and his tone softened. He walked up to me, hugged me warmly and said that my father had saved a family member from the death penalty. He added that he had visited my Khandera house numerous times for meetings with my father when the case was being heard.

'I have great respect for him,' he said.

The entire gang also became very apologetic and even offered me a glass of milk which they brought from a nearby house. It was their way of apologizing.

It was one more lesson on how good relationships can prove so decisive in one's life. As Universal Electric was a part of ESB, the latter had wanted to establish a battery-manufacturing facility in India. They had asked Hoddy for recommendations and he suggested that ESB get into a partnership with me. That is how Willard India Ltd was conceived in the early 1970s. It introduced me to the varied complications involved in doing business in India.

Getting a manufacturing licence from the Ministry of Industrial Development was the first hurdle, as batteries were on the banned list for foreign collaborations thanks to aggressive lobbying by Indian battery manufacturers. Getting an approval and a licence to establish the Willard facility was going to be a Herculean task since it meant negotiating a complicated system of obtaining approvals. It was a bureaucratic maze as the file had to move from one ministry to another and one department to another. There was also the lobby of local battery manufacturers who did all they could to prevent Willard from getting the nod of approval. It became a prestige issue. I was determined to push it through come what may, just to prove how archaic and regressive some of our industrial laws really were. I personally handled every facet of the approval process and after many sleepless nights and exhausting days spent in various ministries, I finally managed to get a waiver to set up Willard batteries.

It was my first real experience of negotiating the Great Indian Government Labyrinth. I had to meet several officials dozens of times to argue my case and persuade them to see reason. The first reaction was always one of suspicion: in the bureaucratic mindset, entrepreneurs and industrialists always have a hidden agenda. I needed to convince them it was actually going to benefit the country. As Willard employed advanced technology, it saved lead consumption. At that time, India was importing lead using foreign exchange. As Willard saved lead, it would save foreign exchange, which was extremely scarce at the time. I used this argument to convince political leaders and government officials to make an exception and grant the manufacturing licence. I finally got permission and the Willard factory came up in Sikandrabad, about 60 km from Delhi on the way to Bulandshahr. The technical operations were handled by ESB. As its first managing director, I handled the commercial aspects.

It was state-of-the-art technology but ironically, that proved to be a handicap in the Indian market. Since this technology involved making very thin grids for the batteries, they could not be recycled like the other brands in the market. The result was sales stayed sluggish. Also, the thin grids saved lead but could not withstand the load from the inefficient electrical systems in the automobiles of that era. Bad roads added to the problems. We discovered that a large number of our batteries were being returned by vendors as they were lying unsold. The company started running into losses. ESB had invested a lot of money to set up the factory in India and spent a lot more trying to adapt the product to local conditions. Normally, any failure in a business leads to finger-pointing and bad blood.

In the case of Willard, the ESB interests were represented by John Davenport, president, ESB International. He was a farsighted businessman. Due to my excellent personal relationship with him, he said that he would set the problems right at the cost of ESB. Such business practices were unheard of. The Industrial Finance Corporation of India, which was the lead banker, was surprised too. That is why I firmly believe that it is very important to invest in building relationships with business partners. In times of adversity, they stick by you. Eventually, Willard was received well in the market, but it took five long years. This led to banks and financial institutions restructuring their loans to enable the company to continue its operations.

It also meant a restructuring of my personal business goals. When I got into the battery business, I was optimistic about turning it into a profitable venture, but because of banks and financial institutions being involved, we got into litigation with one of the banks, Citibank, which filed a 'winding up' petition against the company in the Delhi High Court. I could have easily negotiated with Citibank to drop proceedings by repaying them an initial amount, but it had forced me into a period of deep thought about where my future lay.

The Citibank incident opened my eyes. The bank was trying to make DLF part with some of its assets to repay the loan. At that time, DLF did not have any worthwhile assets and it did not make sense for DLF to meet financial commitments on behalf of Willard India. DLF had no money then but when Citibank pushed me into a corner, I took an instinctive decision to try and revive it. DLF had established an excellent reputation in the market as a leading property developer and it would be tragic to allow that to wither away.

The Citibank episode had forced me to ask myself some hard questions: was I in the right business? Should I be investing my future in trying to grow the battery business or should I be trying to revive the family company in which I was a major shareholder? Did I have it in me to break away and revive a business that had stalled thanks to ill-considered government policies? I suddenly remembered Hoddy's advice about lobbying for change in the laws rather than evading them or trying to break them. He had also taught me about 'productivity in decision making', to marry the macro picture with micro reality. I did agonize over the decision since it meant another major turning point in my life – abandoning a running business and getting back into a business fraught with risks.

Most of my friends advised me to continue with the battery business and not dispose off Willard. Their argument was that once the loans were rescheduled and restructured, I would be fine. Looking back, I can say that if I had taken their advice, there would be no DLF as we know it today. There were other, more practical reasons for my decision. If we continued in the battery business, very heavy investments would have to be made to make Willard profitable. I came to the conclusion that greater long-term rewards lay in capitalizing on the DLF brand and convincing the government to bring in reforms in the real estate sector. Finally, I decided to sell my shares to exit the business. I sold it in 1977 for a song to B.P. Bajoria, a businessman from Kolkata.

My experience in industry had taught me a great deal, about business relationships, handling colleagues, workers and unions, the intricacies of corporate finance, and, most importantly, dealing with the bureaucracy and politicians. I learnt that bureaucrats and politicians have one thing in common. There are always stereotypes but also contrasts. For every five bureaucrats who are obstructive and negative, there will always be one or two who are open-minded and positive. It's exactly the same with politicians, even at the very highest levels. I discovered this from first-hand experience.

Being head of an industries association provides a ringside view of how governance works in India and how one prime minister can be such a contrast to the one before. I recall accompanying industrialist L.M. Thapar as part of a delegation of businessmen to meet Prime Minister H.D. Deve Gowda. We had requested the meeting to apprise him of the deteriorating state of the Indian economy with suggestions on what needed to be done. In the prime minister's office, Thapar started his presentation but we got the distinct impression that Deve Gowda was not listening. We had all heard of his habit of dozing off during discussions. Suddenly, he sat up and exclaimed, 'I am glad that the economy is doing well!'

Thapar immediately corrected him saying we had come to meet him to tell him that the economy was in dire straits. He promised to get various government departments to look into the suggestions we had offered. Nothing happened and the economic situation continued to deteriorate.

In direct contrast to this meeting was the one on 3 November 2008 when industry captains met Dr Manmohan Singh to discuss the repercussions of the global meltdown. The prime minister listened carefully to every word we said. Being an economist, he understood our concerns and suggestions. Barely a few days later, he announced a slew of measures to re-energize industry and provide the much-needed impetus.

I had earlier written to Dr Singh about the challenges the Indian economy faced, and he had immediately reacted by calling the high-powered meeting. He called in the finance minister, P. Chidambaram, the commerce minister, Kamal Nath, the deputy chairman of the Planning Commission, Montek Singh Ahluwalia, the governor of the Reserve Bank of India, D. Subbarao, and other top bureaucrats of economic ministries. The prime minister then invited each one of us to give our views and recommendations. He formed a committee on the spot and assured us that they would be available 24x7 if any problem was to be redressed. India was one of the few countries to survive the recession relatively unscathed. It was reassuring for the business community to have such sure-footed leaders at the helm who understood what growth of the economy means to the future of India and its people.

8

ACQUIRING LAND

WHEN THE IDEA first took hold of me that a world-class city could be built on the vast tracts of desolate land at the foot of the Aravalis in Haryana, nobody took me seriously. Reactions ranged from open ridicule to concern for my sanity. It is sheer fantasy, I was told, don't waste your time even thinking about such an impractical scheme.

Somehow, I just could not stop myself from driving down to the outskirts of Delhi and staring for long hours at the wide open spaces all around with nothing but miles and miles of rocky but austerely beautiful landscape. In my mind's eye I could see modern, tall buildings made of glass and steel, I could visualize wide, tree-lined avenues with smooth-moving traffic and people walking on them and children playing in lush green parks.

It was not as if I was not conscious of the overwhelming odds against turning my impossible dream into a reality. It was not as if I was ignorant of the complexity of the project I was contemplating. Such was the compelling nature of my obsession that I went to extraordinary extents to closely analyse the numerous steps involved before I could even get started.

First of all I had to ensure that the land I had my eye on was in conformity with the master plan of the area notified by the government of Haryana. Then I had to make sure that two or three thousand acres of contiguous land were available for purchase, because no city could be built unless every inch of land in the project area had been acquired and was under the ownership of the developer. I was also acutely aware that I needed to raise huge sums of money to pay for such a vast swathe of land. In those days there was no question of any bank entertaining a loan application from a real estate developer. Once the land was purchased, there were other colossal risks. For instance, there was no guarantee that I would be able to procure the licence to begin development work.

Even after overcoming all these hurdles, there would be a maze of legal and bureaucratic procedures to be gone through – applying for change of land usage, environmental approval, obtaining clearances under a never-ending plethora of laws: Right of Pre-emption Act, Agricultural Land Ceiling Act and so on.

It was easy to indulge in daydreams about creating a mega-city but the ground realities were formidable and even demoralizing. That was why even my well-wishers tried their level best to dissuade me from pursuing the project. When I recall those days today, I myself sometimes wonder what gave me the strength to persevere. Perhaps it was the power of my own vision and faith in the possibility that sometimes, fairy tales do come true. As it turned out, this actually happened in the rise of a gigantic dream city – Gurgaon.

Undoubtedly, it took many long years of hard work, many morale-sapping disappointments and traumatic setbacks and a great deal of faith and self-belief before the fantasy could become a reality. But, apart from the saga of numerous hardships, twists and turns of fate and indescribable joys of ultimate triumph and achievement that form such an integral part of these chronicles of my life, when I look back on those early years of my Gurgaon dream, I sometimes marvel at the relative ease with which I was able to acquire the 3,500 acres of raw land on which a large part of the city of Gurgaon stands today.

All the more so because, as every real estate developer in India knows, one of the most difficult tasks is to acquire large tracts of contiguous land for any development work. Look at the anachronism staring India in its face. Here is a young nation on the crossroads of history trying to grow rapidly but it is thwarted by scores of legal disputes on land acquisition that will take years to resolve. The disputes are mainly to do with farmers challenging forcible land acquisition or inadequate monetary compensation. In recent years, states across India have witnessed agitations by farmers whose land was forcibly taken away by government agencies. Their anger stems from the perception that they are not being given enough to compensate for parting with property which has been in their families for generations and for losing their traditional source of livelihood. As a nation on the move, India needs to find humane and pragmatic solutions to these problems in order to ensure that development plans do not get delayed and derailed.

Land acquisition can and should be managed successfully by adopting the right approaches and policies. My own experience of building DLF into the country's largest real estate company is founded on the basic premise that land acquisition is a transaction which should be a beneficial proposition for all concerned – the seller, the buyer, the community and the end user. It gives me an immense sense of satisfaction that DLF was able to acquire thousands of acres of land in Gurgaon without a single case of litigation against us or even a hint of violence or protest. I do believe that there are certain aspects of our approach that need to be reviewed critically and, perhaps, adopted by others to make land acquisition a less traumatic and contentious issue.

When I set out to revive DLF, I knew that my dream of developing a city in Gurgaon could only be achieved if a huge amount of contiguous land was acquired. But there was a problem. The labyrinth of outdated and sometimes illogical laws in India made decades ago can be quite mind-boggling. I discovered almost two dozen such laws in Haryana when I started to acquire land to build Gurgaon. Of them, the most bizarre was the Punjab Pre-emption Act of 1913. It essentially gave the right to any family member to lay claim on property that was duly sold by the person who legally owned the property. So, if anyone bought a piece of land from a farmer who legally owned the land, any distant relative of the seller could surface years later to challenge it. I was taken aback by the irrationality of this provision – how on earth would I ever be able to acquire thousands of acres from hundreds of farmers with such a law hovering like a threat over my whole project? I could have been engulfed in an unmanageable flood of litigations that would take years to resolve. No land development, leave alone a gigantic endeavour to build a city, would ever have been possible with such archaic laws in force.

I immediately got down to studying it very carefully and found that a similar law had been prevalent in Punjab and had been repealed on the grounds that it was out of tune with the development needs of the state. It struck me that if Punjab had scrapped such an irrational piece of legislation, why could not the neighbouring state of Haryana do the same?

I met bureaucrats and politicians to explain the logic of why Haryana could not afford to continue to have this law on its statute books. Even though everyone I spoke to accepted my contention in principle, they were hesitant to do anything about changing the law because no one wanted to be seen doing anything that would help private developers in politically sensitive Haryana. But I kept on trying to convince them that such a law would seriously retard the development of the state. It took time, but after scores of meetings, things finally started moving and in due course the Punjab Pre-emption Act of 1913 was repealed. This success came as a great boost to my morale and was an early sign that if logical arguments are used, governments do listen and with patience and perseverance, nothing is impossible.

Acquiring land and convincing the government to repeal archaic laws was one of my greatest challenges. I knew it was not going to be easy as farmers in Gurgaon had small holdings. Moreover, they were emotionally attached to their land even if it was unproductive. Persuading them to sell their land was a Herculean task. The acquisition of land was meticulously done over a period of time, taking every farmer or landowner into confidence. It was unprecedented and probably will be the only case of its kind for years to come. The millennium city of Gurgaon was built after acquiring land piece by piece. Most of the land we acquired from local farmers was desolate and barren. There were small patches of green where they grew cyclical crops, but they also faced a severe shortage of water. I based my land-acquisition strategy on those prevailing conditions.

When I set out to buy land in this area, I was firm that we would not take the farmers for a ride. They were simple folk and not many knew what the right compensation should be. We wanted to pay them adequately so that they would not feel cheated. I myself came from a rural background so I knew their realities. We never forced or arm-twisted a single farmer into selling his land. Farmers were initially reluctant to sell. Land has always been an emotional issue in India. It is not just the security of ownership it provides; it is an integral part of the lives of our farmers. We understood this and to allay their fears we spent weeks and months on building a relationship with farmers whose land we wanted to buy. We spent time in patiently explaining the logic of how they stood to gain if they sold their land. We also told them that we would also gain, of course, as we needed land to build a modern township that would be the state's pride and in several ways beneficial to the sellers as well.

We started land acquisition in Gurgaon in 1979 to build residential colonies. I remember sending Amritlal, our land purchase manager, on a motorcycle to do a survey of the area. He found land in Chakkarpur village in what is now Phase I of Gurgaon. He was excited about the prospects but I wanted to be sure if it would be worth it. I must have inspected it over a dozen times. We bought the first piece of land in Chakkarpur from Surajmal, a farmer, on 29 October 1980. It was a small plot of land – just 0.375 acre. With that purchase of less than an acre, we had taken our first baby step towards establishing India's largest real estate company, and, in the process, building the new, modern city of Gurgaon.

In those days, an average landholding in Gurgaon was no more than four to five acres; thus the acquisitions meant dealing with 700-odd families each with five to six members. I must have visited at least 500 families numerous times, personally interacting with each one of them. Gradually, I developed a great relationship with them. It was the only way to convince them to sell and for DLF to buy so many contiguous plots of land belonging to so many different families. They were decent people but nobody's fools. They would only listen to me if they believed I was sincere and related to them at a personal level. It was the human touch that was the key, not money or greed. Fortunately, my rural and army background was a great advantage. Every second family in Jat- and Ahir-dominated Haryana had a family member in the army, either serving or retired. They also admired the fact that after a stint in the army, I was trying to establish a business. I also had the advantage of being able to converse with them in their own language and at the same level.

Yet, it was to prove the biggest challenge of my career as a developer. The land was mostly owned by the Ahir community who are traditional agriculturists. They mostly cultivated wheat, mustard, bajra and gram, while some also grew vegetables. There was absolutely no culture or history in the community of selling their land and as such there was a strong emotional attachment to property bequeathed to them by their forefathers. They lived a simple life, ate simple food and lived in simple homes. They were not inclined to do business or even to increasing their wealth. Selling land just to have a better lifestyle was actually a disturbing concept for many of them. They were happy with what they had and did not want to move out of their comfort zones. The lure of big money as compensation did not tempt most of them.

Convincing them to sell their land was not easy. I had to do this on a personal level, not delegate it to any of my managers in DLF. I would plan my day, keeping in mind their daily routine. I used to go and meet them early in the morning just after sunrise or after sunset when the farmers would be at home. I sat with them, discussed various topics and had endless glasses of milk, tea or buttermilk. Spending a lot of time with them helped me understand their lives and needs much better. Over time I virtually became a part of each family and was soon involved in settling family disputes, arranging school admissions, helping with medical care and other issues in which they needed my advice and help. I attended scores of birthday parties, birth and marriage ceremonies, funerals and other functions even after they had sold the land. I saw them as family. It helped create a relationship of mutual trust and respect, even affection.

It also helped that my parents-in-law belonged to Haryana and were a leading family in the state. Rai Bahadur Lalchand, my wife's grandfather, was a prominent lawyer of Rohtak and a minister in pre-Second World War Punjab. My roots in Haryana, therefore, went deep. The name of Chaudhry Saheb also worked wonders for DLF as he had built a clean reputation.

He once shared his philosophy: 'When you do business with someone they also should prosper with you. If this is a part of your business philosophy and practice, partners will do anything for you.' I remembered this while dealing with the farmers. Having closely observed and studied how Chaudhry Saheb had used this method to acquire land in Delhi in the 1950s, I decided to attempt what to begin with seemed impossible – going to each farmer and persuading him to sell his land. I learnt to talk like them, dress like them, eat like them, in effect, I became one of them. I used to dress in a kurta-pyjama, wrap a shawl around my shoulders, and wear a beret on my head. I would squat on the floor of their huts and drink the refreshment they offered. I even shared a few puffs of smoke from their hookahs as it would have been impolite to refuse! My early days in Khandera village and later Bulandshahr helped me to adapt to the village culture in Haryana and understand their way of life. I was totally comfortable with them. I got my management team to follow my example in the way they dealt with farmers whose land they wanted to buy. In my father-in-law's experience, it helped to pay the farmer more than what he expected. 'They should not feel they are being cheated,' he had cautioned.

I did not do all this on my own. There were several executives at DLF who helped me pave the way for the company to acquire the contiguous plots of land we required to build the brand and meet our escalating ambitions. Among them, the prominent managers were Saroop Chand Ansal and Amritlal Jain, who contributed in a major way to the growth of the company and making it the giant it is today. These were the two persons who accompanied me on my trips, often at dawn or late at night. They liked the fact that I was a patient listener and carried no ego. I could meet anyone at any time they thought I should meet and talk with.

Looking back, I think that the ability to deal with people at all levels and in an informal way was the key factor in helping me to succeed in my objective. Amritlal supplied me with detailed information on what land was available, who owned it, why they were selling or not selling and any genuine problems they faced. I think they also respected the fact that I wanted to not just buy land but also genuinely help the farmers lead a better life. They also probably respected the fact that I repeatedly instructed them to never do anything that was unethical just because we were desperate to buy land. I told them that the price we would pay for unethical practices would be very high in the long run and if our hands were clean, it would convince others to deal with us for future acquisitions. It pays to play the game by those rules. There is no right way to do the wrong thing.

There were numerous times when they would disagree with me. I listened to their arguments and if they made sense, I would change my decision. Perhaps that is why they worked with such dedication and commitment. Amritlal had superb public relations skills while Saroop Chand made our life easy by handling all the complicated paperwork and legal issues. They worked on low salaries but were completely dedicated and never looked at the clock. I cannot forget their sincerity, dedication and contribution. Every morning, Amritlal would set out to meet villagers. He would begin by telling them the worth of their land and why it would be a good idea to sell it. If they agreed, he would then work with them to complete the complicated paperwork, fill various documents, execute agreements and register sale deeds. Villagers used to visit him at his home all the time to get such work done. I insisted that he be with them till all the formalities were over as they needed the guidance.

When I was felicitated by DLF employees in April 2010 on being awarded the Padma Bhushan, I made it a point to mention their contribution, called them on the stage and got the audience to give them a standing ovation. I wanted everyone to know that

DLF would not have been what it is today had it not been for their effort. Ultimately, it is employees like these, humble, dedicated, hard-working and intelligent, whose contribution helps build an organization.

It took me time to get farmers to see the logic of the argument I laid out for them. Most of them had unproductive land and only small sections were under cultivation and earning some little money for them. My pitch to them went like this: 'So far you have a total landholding of four to five acres which is unproductive. If you sell the present land to me I will arrange for ten times more land for you which would not only give better agricultural yield but also give you a sense of security.' In Gurgaon, there was a problem of water for irrigation and the land was also quite poor. As cultivation was minimal, yields were low. I convinced them that it made sense to sell the land at fairly good prices and then invest in fertile land somewhere else. We made them realize that if they sold one acre in Gurgaon, they could easily buy eight to ten acres of fertile land if they moved 20 to 30 km away, between Sohna and Alwar. It took many months, however, before they began to see the logic of my reasoning. The emotional connection was extremely strong.

There was another problem. Under the Hindu Undivided Family law, women have an equal right to ancestral property. When ancestral property is sold, they too need to sign the sale deed otherwise the title remains invalid. Many of the patriarchal families did not want money to be divided among the married daughters or sisters. The common argument was that the family had spent enough money on their marriage ceremonies and dowry. They also did not want us to pay the women. We therefore had to find ways to compensate the women using a lot of tact and subtlety. In many cases, I went over to the women, paid them their rightful share, and asked them to sign the documents. In some families, there was no problem about paying the women in front of other family members. But in most cases, they had to be paid secretly. Many were so clean-hearted that they did not accept the money but went ahead and signed the papers. It was such experiences that made us feel that we must do all we could to help them live a better life. Each case had to be handled differently. Before I proceeded with the acquisition of any piece of land, I used to ensure that Amritlal and his team prepared a detailed dossier on the family that would have details other than the quantity and quality of land. It would have information on the family, their personal traits and any problems they faced. If Amritlal found that a villager's wife was suffering from tuberculosis, I would get her admitted to a TB hospital and ask my officials to look after her needs in hospital. Till she was cured and back home, we would not discuss anything about the land we proposed to buy from her husband.

In a quite different case, Amritlal told me of a farmer who was not ready to sell his land and did not have any particular reason for not doing so. I decided to go and meet him. I was told he was a rough type with an ego. I first went to the adjoining house and spent some time with the family. Then, I swung by his thatched mud hut as if I was just passing by, saying 'Ram-Ram' in greeting. It was late in the evening and darkness had set in. A small kerosene lamp was the only source of light within his hut as there was no electricity. Villagers are very hospitable and take pride in welcoming even uninvited visitors. He welcomed me with the traditional, 'Namaste, Kaptan Saheb.' I sat on a charpoy and started a conversation. Before visiting him, I had identified one of his main concerns – he had a problem getting one of his children into school. I chose to focus on that rather than talk about the land. I assured him that it would be done and made sure it happened. It is only after helping him out that I talked to him about selling his land. He agreed. In retrospect, I can see that the genuine friendships we cultivated went a long way in helping us assemble the land we wanted in Gurgaon. Getting his child admission to a good school was not a big thing for me, but for the father, it was akin to securing the future of his child.

Some of the farmers were plain stubborn. One of them did not want to sell his land nor even hear anything about how he would benefit if he did. I went and met him again and again. Once, he offered me a huge tumbler of milk, which is a normal practice in any Haryana village to welcome a visitor. Milk was in plenty as they had plenty of cattle. I noticed a fly floating in the frothy milk in the metal tumbler. If I refused to drink the milk, he would have seen it as an insult. If I had told him that there was a fly floating in it, he would have felt slighted as it would show that he was a sloppy host who could not even offer a clean glass of milk. More than anything else, he was quite a brusque person and would have taken his wife to task. I kept slowly blowing the fly to the other side of the tumbler with every sip. I sipped very carefully. The villager noticed this and realized what was wrong. He appreciated it that I had not complained. His attitude towards me changed. It was only a matter of time before he agreed to sell the land. For the villagers, such minor things went a long way in establishing trust, confidence and respect.

The other strategy we adopted was to be absolutely straight with them so that there was no room for doubt or suspicion. We told them we wanted land for developing a city and were ready to make them partners if they so wished. DLF needed money for developing land and the partnership model was the best way forward. After handing over the money for their land, I would ask them if they needed all that money. Invariably, they said that they had never seen so much cash and did not need it for their kind of lifestyle. I then asked them to invest the money in DLF and become partners who would progress together with us. There were times when we bought land, handed over the money and then got them to give it back to us as investment in DLF on the very same day! It was a win-win situation for them and for us. We offered them an interest of 12 per cent.

In the 1980s, this was substantial money for most of them and higher than what banks were offering. It was an attractive proposition as they could withdraw the principal amount whenever they wanted. In case they wanted the money midway, we readily paid without any questions. After all, it was their money. We had a jeep that would go from house to house distributing the interest between the first and the sixth of every month. We never defaulted on payment even once.

They often needed money for marriages and other sundry needs. We allowed them to withdraw it in such emergencies and this helped DLF build tremendous credibility and acquire more land. When you make an effort to hold hands with your partners, they always back you. Mohar Singh, for instance, had around ten acres of barren land in Gurgaon. He was happy to get Rs. 5 million for it. All his life, he had not seen even Rs. 10,000 in cash. I told him that he would gain if he deposited the entire amount back with DLF to make it grow. He readily agreed. Touched by his trusting attitude, I asked him if we could help in some way. Mohar Singh said he would be glad if DLF employed his son as a watchman. Here was the ultimate irony: someone who had five million rupees was asking me to get his son a menial job. I desperately wanted that money to develop land and all it required was one small favour from me. I got his son employed by DLF. A job, however ordinary, made them feel useful and secure. We were dealing with villagers with such modest dreams.

DLF would not have grown into what it became without our partnership with these uncomplicated and honest farmers with such basic needs. We only had to persuade people like Mohar Singh who did not want to pursue farming to invest in DLF. The other villagers who wanted to buy land elsewhere were free to do so. The fact was that none of the villagers ever needed the kind of money they were getting for their land. At that time, the selling price ranged up to Rs. 500,000 an acre. Today, it is over Rs. 40 million an acre. There is no parallel in India to what DLF did in terms of helping farmers whose land it had bought. We saw it as a part of our commitment. After all, for these villagers, it was akin to their livelihood being taken away. DLF is what it is today only because of the farmers who decided to sell their land to us. We often forget those who help us after we make it big. The contribution of these farmers who supported us financially by reinvesting the money we gave them to develop the land is today part of India's corporate history.

What we achieved at DLF is a miracle in business terms. DLF had no money when it started. More interestingly, ordinary farmers ended up financing DLF to take it to being a leader in its field. It was history in the making but it did not happen incidentally. Even today, I salute those farmers for having trusted and believed in me enough to sell me their land and in return, I am glad I did everything I could to safeguard their interests. They were our lifeline. I recall Amritlal's words at one function. 'Because of the work culture that DLF had, we now have a reputation in Haryana and can easily acquire the land we want. We understood villagers as few real estate developers did. If DLF wants money today, villagers will line up with cheques! They trusted us. We were very transparent with the farmers. We became what we are today as there was meticulous planning and a follow-up on every single thing pertaining to the interest of the farmer.'

One of the real challenges for me at a human level was to ensure productive use of the money farmers got from selling land. Otherwise, they would indulge in reckless spending that often came with sudden riches. I saw that happen with some families with tragic results. They were so carried away by the rush of wealth that they spent it on amassing pointless consumer goods they could easily have done without. Despite our counselling, many bought expensive cars or SUVs as these became a new status symbol of progress. Some blew it up on a newly acquired lavish lifestyle. They carelessly spent on clothes, expensive restaurants and hotels, alcohol, shopping and travel. Soon, the money dried up. The result was that many farmers were sucked into a life of debt and poverty. This is certainly not what I wanted to happen to those who had helped DLF by selling their land.

This is precisely why we counselled them on why it was important to invest their money wisely so that it would grow. For instance, we got many of them to use the money they got from the sale of their Gurgaon farms to buy larger tracts of land in nearby areas of Haryana and Rajasthan where land was more fertile and productive because water was available in plenty. Many of the farmers had got their daughters married to Jat or Ahir families in these areas. So, they also felt good about being closer to their daughters' families. More than anything else, they could get back to farming, which would be psychologically good for them as they would feel rooted to the soil again. I made it a win-win situation for them.

DLF did not abandon them after we got their land. In fact, we financially assisted many of them with tubewells, pumps and agricultural equipment. Numerous families benefited by this turnaround in their lives and they saw their living standard rise; they had money to ensure quality education for their children besides earning more than ever before from their newly acquired productive land. I also helped many young men get government jobs. Fortunately, I had a lot of friends within the government who would not say no to a recommendation. None of the farmers ever forgot what we did for them.

When I look back, it is clear that my strategy of land acquisition was successful as I gave a lot of attention to rehabilitation of farmers who sold their lands to us. As events proved in the years to come, it became apparent that it was a decision of critical importance. Just paying money to farmers was not enough; they needed to be counselled on how to use the money and helped with rehabilitation as well. I saw this as an essential part of our business. I believed we had a moral responsibility to settle those whom we had displaced. I also believe that without this attitude, development will never happen in India. This is why DLF is, perhaps, the only organization that does not have a single court case against it by a farmer whose land we acquired. In all the villages where we bought land, Amritlal is still in touch with them though he has retired from DLF. Almost three decades have passed since we acquired their land, but we still value each of them. Many bought land a few kilometres away from the city of Gurgaon and are millionaires today. Others got into business activities, managing shops or operating buses or taxis. It feels great to see how they have prospered along with DLF.

Amritlal often talks of the high trust level farmers had with us. These days, we are so very careful about property documents and wonder if we have been cheated. In those days, farmers would not even demand copies of agreements and sale deeds. In fact, many of them would deposit their sale deeds and documents with Amritlal saying that they would ask for them if needed! Do we have a lesson to learn here? DLF worked out of a small two-room office on Mehrauli Road in Gurgaon but we managed to acquire thousands of acres. In a business like real estate what matters is trust and not just having plush, glass-fronted air-conditioned offices. If the government wants to acquire land, it just has to pass an order, pay compensation at the price it chooses to fix and take over the land. But for a private developer, it is far more complicated. We had to negotiate with each farmer. By the time a deal was finalized, the price of the adjoining land would have risen and some farmers would come back to negotiate. Even after agreeing to sell their land, some would refuse to sell at the last moment. Some would agree and sell their land, but later turn bitter if they had heard that some other farmer had got a better price. Upset, they would not agree to the transfer of the title to the land. For us as developers, unfettered possession was crucial as without it, no development work could be started. But we kept our communication lines open with the farmer. Ultimately, the difficulties would be sorted out by straightforward communication.

There are lessons to be drawn from the DLF experience. Land acquisition in India will always be a problematic issue, so it should be handled with sensitivity. If the farmer stands to gain, he will willingly be a part of change and progress. He has to be made a partner in progress, just the way we did at DLF. We are proud of our role in land acquisition. It has given India a new model of urban growth where land can be acquired without rancour and farmers can be made partners in urban development. Ironically, even today both the government and private developers try to browbeat the farmer into taking their land at the lowest price possible. Clearly, no lessons have been learnt from the success of the DLF model. We had gone the other way, taking the farmer with us, ensuring his rehabilitation and that he invested his money in such a way that he gained financially. Even the government has run into serious problems where it acquired land for creating infrastructure or building special economic zones. DLF, I can say with all humility, has a model that can be followed elsewhere in the country.

Just paying compensation to farmers is not enough. There has to be awareness within industrial houses that they have to go several steps ahead in ensuring rehabilitation. Our economic development is being seriously affected because of the failure of proper land acquisition. We need to acquire huge tracts of land if

India has to take the next big leap, but it has to be done properly and ethically. To understand the essence of how to do that, we have to see the fallacy of land acquisition today. All regulatory mechanisms in India are conceived and managed by urbanites. So they look at something like land acquisition in the typical way that urbanites would. They look at their own interests and not those of the farmer from whom the land and with it his livelihood are being taken away. To cross-subsidize land for the urbanites, those acquiring the land float a mechanism that will acquire it at low prices. The end result is that the farmer actually pays for the urbanite to get land at a low price. As long as cross-subsidization happens, the farmer will never get the right price. Nowadays, farmers are not ready to be browbeaten. That is why we are seeing numerous agitations all over the country demanding a better price for land. Our policies should be such that we take care of the interests of the farmer and avoid giving cause for any agitation.

Haryana is one Indian state which is trying to set things right by ensuring that regulations are changed to protect the interests of the farmers. Other states must follow with legislative measures to ensure that there should not be cross-subsidization to benefit an urbanite to the farmer's detriment. I once had an occasion to meet Charan Singh when he was home minister in Morarji Desai's cabinet. He was always dismissed by the media as a rustic leader, but what he told me made immense sense: 'I see a big fallacy in the way we make our budgets as enough allocation is not done for agriculture. This is because there is immense pressure for industrialization. If the purchasing power of Indians has to increase, allocation for agriculture has to be increased.' For so many decades, India did not do this and it is only now after more than six decades of independence that we have started to rectify this anomaly through introduction of a new Bill in parliament. However, one hopes in its final enactment, it is balanced enough and does not adversely affect the growth of urban infrastructure in India.

As I was deeply involved in tackling the hurdles of building Gurgaon, it became obvious to me that the only way to make things move was to personally network with everybody from a patwari (low-ranking revenue official who handles land records) to the chief minister. Networking had also to be done at the Centre with all the concerned ministries as it was then a closed economy. One had to sit down with politicians and bureaucrats and explain the need for a new way of looking at urban development. One also had to get proactive in creating awareness about the need of changing archaic town planning and land-related laws. At that time, the idea of the private sector creating a township was unknown. It was also unacceptable to most government officials. At times, it seemed like a lonely battle, and I had to single-handedly do everything including helping to prepare replies to call attention notices in parliament on subjects relating to urban development. I also had to deal with all kinds of people – farmers, low-level revenue officials, politicians, bureaucrats. I had to coordinate at the higher levels too – the chief minister, the prime minister and even international management gurus like Jack Welch. I had no choice but to learn micro-management. The more one deals with multiple issues, the more one learns. But, I enjoyed it all. At the end of the day what really mattered was what one achieved.

In India, networking helps. Once, I was at the Hemsley Palace Hotel in New York getting ready at around 7 a.m. to attend an international advisory board meeting of GE. I was to present the India story at the meeting which was being attended by the former US secretary of state, Henry Kissinger, who was a special invitee. I was just getting ready to leave my hotel room when my phone rang. It was Amritlal, then a senior manager of DLF, complaining how a low-ranking revenue official in Gurgaon was openly flouting government regulations by acting as a broker of other land dealers and inciting the farmers not to sell land to DLF unless his demands were accepted. Since Amritlal had been told to ensure ethical practices in such dealings, he wanted me to talk to someone. Wasting no time, I called the chief minister and requested him to look into the matter. I was later told that the revenue officer was transferred within twenty-four hours. Today, it seems strange if one has to call the chief minister of a state to sort out such small issues. In those days, it was part of my day's work.

9

A BATTLE FOR SURVIVAL

A COCKTAIL PARTY for a jet-setting couple, a powerful political leader inviting himself for dinner, a tactless remark made by a tipsy guest, an angry walkout, a senseless misunderstanding – these were the ingredients for the worst nightmare of my business career. Overnight, from being a rising star in the corporate world and the favoured protégé of the chief minister of Haryana, I became the target of a relentless campaign to destroy my company and image as a businessman of the future.

The genesis of that unfortunate episode lay in my role as president of the Faridabad Industries Association, a role, ironically enough, foisted on me by that same chief minister. At that time, in the early 1970s, I was just beginning to make a mark as a young and upcoming entrepreneur in charge of the American Universal factory in Haryana. Faridabad was an emerging industrial hub in north India with some reputed companies like Dunlop, Goodyear, Escorts, Bata, Thomson Press and Kelvinator based there. Being hungry for success, I had worked very hard to make myself known in business circles, which is probably why I got noticed by

Bansi Lal, a powerful political leader who was then serving the first of his three separate terms as chief minister of Haryana. He had the reputation of being a tough Jat politician with strong likes and dislikes.

The first time I got an inkling that I had caught the chief minister's attention was when I received a call from the office of the deputy commissioner of Gurgaon asking me to meet him. He was quite candid and came straight to the point – the chief minister wanted me to contest for president of the Faridabad Industries Association. This surprised me, because I was still a junior compared to the other business stalwarts in Faridabad, who had been there much longer. But the deputy commissioner was insistent and said all I had to do was file my nomination papers and I would win, because the chief minister would mobilize enough support for me. I wondered why a chief minister would want a newcomer like me to contest when there were so many well-known and respected industrialists to choose from.

I had met Bansi Lal just once or twice at informal gatherings, since my father-in-law, an influential man himself, knew him well. On one occasion, I had invited him to visit our American Universal factory in Faridabad. It was just a casual invitation extended out of politeness. I hardly expected him to take up the offer, but he surprised us by turning up and taking a keen interest in the factory and the way we operated. While leaving, he remarked that I had a good future as an entrepreneur in Haryana. That was our first serious encounter.

The election to the industries association took place soon after and, true to his word, I was elected unopposed, much to the chagrin of several senior businessmen. I did not let their frowns upset me, and instead focused on what role I could play. There were certain issues connected with state taxation, industrial disputes and labour unrest which had caused friction between the state government and the industrialists. I saw myself as a bridge to build a better relationship between the government and business so that an environment could be created for industry to grow in the state. Initially, I had been reluctant to contest the election as I was just starting out as an entrepreneur. Years later, I saw it as a milestone in my business career. It was a great learning experience and stood me in good stead when I was elected president of the PHD Chamber of Commerce and Industry (PHDCCI) and subsequently as president of the Associated Chamber of Commerce and Industry of India (ASSOCHAM). These exposures were invaluable as they helped me press the government on reforms and for regulatory changes necessary for the country's economic growth.

Haryana was widely regarded as a progressive state and my appointment as president of the local industries association was a feather in my cap. It involved frequent interactions with the chief minister. I found him quite receptive and reasonable when it came to ironing out problems faced by the business community. Naturally, my popularity grew, especially since I steered clear of the kind of factional politics which plague some business bodies. The Faridabad association represented several important companies and our success in working with the Haryana government to promote industry in the region even earned the praise of the PHDCCI, which was the umbrella business chamber covering the four states of Uttar Pradesh, Punjab, Haryana and Delhi.

I had established a good personal rapport with Bansi Lal but was careful not to discuss politics with him. Whenever I met him, formally or informally, our conversations were confined to industrial growth and other issues concerning Haryana state's economy. Before long, I became known in local business circles as being very close to the chief minister and as a result I was invariably nominated to most committees that had some connection to Haryana. I could sense that Bansi Lal himself was pleased with my rising profile and he soon became even more informal and friendly, even to the extent of dropping in at my home in Delhi's Panchsheel Park for dinner or just a cup of tea, sometimes without telling me in advance.

Unfortunately, it was this very informality that was the undoing of our relationship. From being a well-wisher and benevolent patron, Bansi Lal all of a sudden turned into a bitter foe who, for the next two decades, directed his power to try to bring me down.

Even today I do not know for certain what triggered the change in his attitude towards me and why I so suddenly fell out of favour with him and became the target of his anger. I also cannot say how I was able to survive the onslaught and to somehow withstand his intense animosity and overcome all the upheavals that it brought in its wake. All I know is that some inner strength within me refused to allow him to crush my spirit and to dent my determination to succeed in realizing my Gurgaon dream, come what may.

The turning point in my equation with Bansi Lal came on a fateful evening in December 1975. He was then the defence minister of India, having risen from being an imposing regional political satrap to the status of an even more influential and feared figure in national politics. He had emerged as one of the most vocal supporters of the controversial Emergency regime under Mrs Indira Gandhi and was regarded as being close to her son Sanjay Gandhi. One evening, as I was preparing to host a private dinner party at my home for some celebrity guests from abroad, the phone rang. It was the secretary to the defence minister, informing me that Bansi Lal would like to drop in at my residence for dinner. There was nothing unusual about that since he had often done so in the past. But this time, I was caught in a quandary. The dinner I was hosting was in honour of Charles Lachman, co-founder and a substantial shareholder in Revlon, the global cosmetics corporation. He was accompanied by the glamorous and strikingly beautiful Countess Jaquine of

Rochambeau. Both were famous personalities and were the toast of fashion magazines like *Vogue*. They were true jet-setters from New York. I wondered whether Bansi Lal would be comfortable in such company.

In keeping with the background and interests of my guests, I had spent hours carefully finalizing the list of around fifty celebrities from Indian high society who I thought would mix well with them. The prospect of Bansi Lal's unexpected arrival had upset my meticulous planning. In those days, I lived in a relatively small house and I was in a dilemma as to how I was going to accommodate two divergently different groups. Cancelling or re-scheduling the party was out of the question since many of the Indian guests were coming from outside Delhi and Lachman himself was a global figure with a crowded schedule. Since I did not want the defence minister to feel uncomfortable in the company of the champagne-and-caviar set, I decided to quickly call up some prominent Jat leaders like Balram Jakhar, Ram Niwas Mirdha, Natwar Singh and my uncle, Surendra Pal Singh, and request them to join us for dinner, hoping that Bansi Lal would feel more at home in their company.

I hastily changed the seating arrangements so that the political leaders could be together and not necessarily have to mix with the others. I also partitioned the dining room into two separate areas so that both groups had their own space. While making such elaborate last-minute preparations, I did not in my wildest nightmares imagine that the dinner party would impact my life in such traumatic and stressful ways for the next two decades and almost destroy my dreams as an entrepreneur. Indeed, things went well in the beginning and the party had warmed up considerably by late evening. As far as I could judge, everyone was happy.

But I had not bargained for what followed. One of my guests was a senior army officer posted in the defence ministry at that time. He was also quite influential through his family connections. We were good friends and I considered him a fine gentleman. His only weakness was that he liked his drink and was prone to consuming one too many, especially if there were friends around. When Bansi Lal entered with his entourage, I escorted him to the section of the room where the other Jat leaders I had called were seated.

Upon seeing the minister, the army officer sauntered over, champagne glass in hand. I was not near them at that moment and I was told later that he greeted Bansi Lal in a familiar way by putting his left arm around him saying: 'Mr Bansi Lal, you are doing a pretty good job. If you like, I will put in a good word about you to Sanjay Gandhi.'

This was perhaps the most tactless and condescending thing for an army officer to say to his defence minister. He went red in the face and stormed out of the party without uttering a word and without waiting for dinner.

I was busy looking after the other guests and was completely unaware of what had happened. It was only when I looked for him while dinner was being served that I was told he had left in a huff.

The next morning, I rang up his secretary in all innocence and enquired if the minister was all right as he had left without having dinner. I was taken aback when the secretary told me that Bansi Lal was furious because one of my guests had deliberately insulted him under the influence of liquor. He added that the minister was angry with me for having dared to serve liquor in his presence. I tried to explain the situation and asked to meet Bansi Lal to apologize and set the record straight. He flatly refused to meet me.

I found it difficult to believe that an incident for which I was in no way personally responsible could so affect our relationship, that too with somebody who was a powerful political figure and defence minister at that time. But as I soon discovered, from that day onwards, I became persona non grata for Bansi Lal. Overnight, I had gone from hero to villain in his eyes.

I was stunned. How could our warm relationship have turned so cold because of a remark made by somebody else? There were no answers. Bansi Lal was that kind of man – if he liked someone he would go out of his way to shower affection and goodwill, but if he had decided to cut somebody out of his good books, nothing on earth could persuade him to change his mind.

Again and again, I tried to meet him and apologize. I tried to approach him through mutual acquaintances, politicians and family friends. But it was all to no avail. He had shut the doors on me forever. The feedback I received was that Bansi Lal had sworn he would never forgive me or forget the insult.

I had always respected him for being a strong administrator and admired him for his many bold and visionary policy decisions that helped Haryana develop faster than any other state. But my special relationship with him had ended. It was the start of a long and gruelling battle for survival for me and my company.

One unfortunate fallout of his sudden animosity towards me was the damage it did DLF. Both DLF and I were pilloried with numerous false charges which we had to counter. Soon after DLF's first licence was issued on 20 April 1981 to develop urban land measuring around 40 acres, stiff opposition was launched by Bansi Lal who was not a minister or chief minister at that time but still had considerable clout in the state. He protested to Bhajan Lal, the then chief minister, over the licence. Undeterred, we went ahead and applied for more licences to develop the land. Usually, these licences would have been issued sporadically as the ownership of land had to be established and the investigative processes of the local government had to be completed. By 1982, we had started developing the elite residential area of Qutab Enclave in Gurgaon now called DLF City. By the end of February

1983, without any fuss or publicity, we had secured licences to develop a total of 556 acres.

Evidently, the progress that DLF was making was not to Bansi Lal's liking and he got some serving bureaucrats loyal to him to issue a notification by the state government to acquire land around the areas that DLF was developing. The idea was to prevent us from acquiring contiguous land. DLF's strategy was to acquire land piece by piece, because we needed thousands of acres of contiguous land to create a township. Bansi Lal was out to thwart this process. One morning I was taken aback to read newspaper headlines saying that the Haryana government had issued a notification for the acquisition of 187 acres of land abutting the licensed area of DLF. This was on 25 March 1983, just a few weeks after we had acquired licences for 556 acres of the land we wanted to develop.

Ostensibly, the purpose of the acquisition by the Haryana Housing Board was to construct houses for medium- and low-income groups. The measure was obviously targeted at DLF for the area covered under the notification would make it impossible for us to extend our reach beyond the land we had already acquired. Moreover, the action was taken by the Housing Board without clearance from the Directorate of Town and Country Planning Department. I decided to find out more about the notification and its origins. I met the housing minister. I found him completely clueless about the notification. He did remember that he had signed a notification for acquisition of land for the Haryana Housing Board but said he had done it without looking at its implications for the private sector, which was beginning to play a bigger role in developing Gurgaon with the state government's approval and encouragement. When I explained the entire background to him, including the fact that the Gurgaon township project had the blessings of Rajiv Gandhi, he asked me to submit a representation requesting him to reconsider the issue and cancel the notification.

We submitted a detailed representation through the director, Town and Country Planning. While sending his recommendations, the director emphasized the need for de-notification as the area formed part of the expansion plans of DLF. After several weeks of follow-up, our representation was finally accepted and the land de-notified and released for private sector acquisition again. I had done all this with the least amount of publicity as I did not want our counter-strategy leaked. I feared that if Bansi Lal got wind of the steps I was taking, he would do all he could to stop their progress. Armed with the de-notification orders, I happened to meet Bhajan Lal and told him what had happened. He was quite surprised as the original notification went against the policy that his government had formulated. He did not want something like this to happen again and demanded a thorough enquiry. He also wanted to send a message to the officers who had done this arbitrarily that they could not violate the rules. He appointed the chief secretary, L.C. Gupta, to head the enquiry.

After three months, Gupta submitted his report supporting the decision of the government to issue a de-notification order. More importantly, it laid down clear guidelines for the future so that such arbitrary steps were nipped in the bud. It prescribed that any department wishing to acquire land would have to route their requests through the director, Town and Country Planning and only after getting a no objection certificate would they be entitled to acquire land.

However, that was when fate decided to play its hand again. In July 1985, Bansi Lal became chief minister of Haryana for the second time. One of his first acts was to suspend an upright bureaucrat, G. Mahadevan, director, Town and Country Planning, as he suspected that Mahadevan had passed orders that had been beneficial to DLF in the early 1980s. This scared off other bureaucrats and town planners. Subsequently, no bureaucrat was prepared to have anything to do with decisions regarding real estate involving private sector developers. Bansi Lal then asked his Town and Country Planning minister, Seth Kishan Das, to cancel all licences given to DLF. He also tried to reopen the de-notification issue, but as the L.C. Gupta Committee of Enquiry had gone into it very thoroughly, he could do nothing about it.

The Haryana government machinery must have been kept busy trying to frame charges against DLF. The Haryana Vigilance Department conducted raids on DLF both in Gurgaon and Delhi on 11 September 1986. They carried away a truckload of documents. Several inspections were carried out by revenue officials to determine whether DLF had encroached on any adjoining government lands. When the areas involved are so vast, sometimes mistakes occur while demarcating land, particularly land that is under the ownership of local government bodies. I had ensured that while demarcating and taking possession of land which was adjacent to government property, we would deliberately occupy less land than we were entitled to. I did not want to give anybody an opportunity to accuse DLF of encroachment.

Thanks to that policy, none of the 'inspections' could establish that even an inch of government land was encroached upon by DLF. However, the orchestrated raids were highlighted by the media and adversely affected the image of the company. The biggest blow came when all our licences were cancelled on 5 November 1986. Newspapers featured prominent Haryana government advertisements warning people not to make any further payments to DLF. Naturally, thousands of our clients all over the country panicked.

This was the same Bansi Lal who had encouraged me at every stage. He had predicted that I had great promise as a businessman and would do well. Overnight, because of one foolish act by a tipsy guest at my residence, the tables had turned and I was now facing the might of state machinery against me and my company. Bansi Lal issued instructions that although there was a separate minister dealing with town and country planning, no government approval would be given without securing the chief minister's prior consent. Dealing with him became almost impossible.

Many senior bureaucrats, as for instance, R.S. Mann, the town and country planning commissioner in Haryana, sympathized with me but were compelled to follow the orders of the chief minister. He was an upright IAS officer but did not have the courage to defy the all-powerful Bansi Lal. Actually, no one could defy him. Even his ministerial colleagues dreaded him, let alone bureaucrats. During these tumultuous years, I made several attempts to reach out to Bansi Lal to try and mend fences. But, he not only refused to meet me but also brushed aside pleas made on my behalf by senior political leaders like Balram Jakhar, Natwar Singh and Ram Niwas Mirdha.

In desperation, I finally turned to Uncle Surendra, who was a minister in Indira Gandhi's cabinet and had a good relationship with Bansi Lal. When I told him about the events concerning DLF, he volunteered to take me with him to meet the chief minister. Accordingly, I accompanied him to Bansi Lal's Akbar Road residence in New Delhi. He greeted my uncle warmly, but as soon as I entered the house, the chill was obvious. He did not even ask me to sit and instead showered me with expletives in typical Haryanvi dialect. I kept my cool and said that I had come to apologize.

'You are a friend of my enemy, Bhajan Lal. Your days are numbered. I will put you in jail,' he shouted.

Despite the attacks on DLF, it was still a shock to see him behave in such manner, that too in my uncle's presence. As I have mentioned elsewhere in these memoirs, my uncle had been a great influence in my life. He was the one who helped me take the momentous decision to leave England to return to India. He had also been a minister in the Union government numerous times in both Nehru's and Indira Gandhi's cabinets. He was influential in political circles and had considerable clout. As he was the Congress observer in Haryana, he tried his best to reason with Bansi Lal that he should let me be instead of making me and my company the target of baseless charges. Bansi Lal ignored even his request.

On my part, I continued to treat Bansi Lal with the utmost regard. Whenever he came to Delhi on official work and stayed at Haryana Bhavan, I always made it a point to leave my business card with his secretary saying that I had only come to pay my respects. I knew full well that he would not grant me an audience. Nevertheless, I continued to drop in and leave my card. I wanted to drive home the point that despite all that he was doing, I personally bore no ill will against him. His secretarial staff was very courteous and his secretary even told me that he felt very embarrassed as Bansi Lal never reacted when he was told I had dropped in to see him. I ignored all the snubs. One principle that has defined my life is that humility pays in the long run while egoism gets us nowhere.

Meanwhile, the company was suffering. During Bansi Lal's rule, all DLF activities pertaining to urban development had come to a grinding halt. We were under serious threat. The Haryana government had issued press releases warning investors to be careful as the licences of DLF had been cancelled. Naturally, our clients had no way of knowing that there was a personal feud involved. Thousands of them lined up demanding their deposits back. I instructed my staff that every single one should be refunded in full.

To make matters worse, the media was being used to report negatively about DLF and the entry of the private sector into urban land development. In fact, the media mirrored the views of Bansi Lal, and his bureaucrats planted stories which were slanted against private sector developers. This prompted an *India Today* correspondent to ask me in an interview what I felt about the turn of events.

'No laws have been flouted, no rules have been twisted. If they cancel these licences, the national capital region plan is a dead duck,' I replied.

Lightheartedly, I had added that the action of the chief minister in cancelling DLF's licences was akin to a rampaging bull in a china shop. My statement was quoted in the 31 August 1986 issue of *India Today*. Bansi Lal got even more furious. I was told later that he had ordered his officials to demonstrate just what kind of a bull he was!

Once again, the vagaries of fate intervened, as was to happen right through my life and career. Rajiv Gandhi, after staying away from politics, had suddenly been elevated to take over as prime minister in December 1984 after a landslide victory in the general elections following Indira Gandhi's assassination. After assuming office, one of the first things he did was to start meeting ordinary citizens in the lawns of his residence every morning where he would address their grievances on the spot. There were no appointments given and everyone had to stand in a queue.

Although I had a personal equation with Rajiv, I decided to underline the urgency of my problem with Bansi Lal by standing in the queue one morning. Rajiv spotted me and, surprised, asked why I was in the queue. I was quite frank and told him that I had not slept the whole night as I was very troubled and needed to talk to him. Rajiv asked me to meet Sarla Grewal, his principal secretary, to brief her on what the problem was. That same day, I met Grewal and told her how the Haryana government had stopped DLF from functioning. Sarla fixed an appointment for me to meet Rajiv the very next day as she realized the seriousness of the situation. I knew from my earlier interaction with Rajiv that he had taken a keen interest in the development of Gurgaon.

When I met him and related my problems, he was surprised to hear about Bansi Lal's war against me and DLF and the reason for it. I also told him how badly and unfairly it had harmed DLF. He could not believe that the incident involving a tipsy army officer had become such a bone of contention; he even laughed at how ridiculous it was. After a patient hearing, he said he would deal with the matter and that I would hear from his office.

I later came to know that immediately after the meeting, Rajiv asked Grewal to ensure that the orders of the Haryana government were reversed and that the urbanization of Gurgaon continued without any hindrance. I felt that at long last, my troubles were coming to an end. My hopes were soon belied. Grewal spoke to Bansi Lal but to no avail. He was known to be stubborn. In fact, the commissioner for town and urban planning expressed his inability to ease the pressure on DLF. When Rajiv went to Haryana to inaugurate a facility, he met Bansi Lal and told him that since I was trying to build a world-class city in Gurgaon I should be encouraged and not hindered. But, Bansi Lal remained inflexible and continued to target DLF. Some days later, I got a call from Gopi Arora, special secretary to Rajiv Gandhi, asking me to meet him urgently. Gopi was a high-profile bureaucrat who wielded considerable power in the Prime Minister's Office. He didn't beat around the bush.

He simply said, 'I have a message for you from the prime minister. First, you must immediately legally protect yourself and your company as Bansi Lal is bent on arresting you.'

He then reassured me that the issue would be sorted out soon. I sought his advice as to what I should do to protect myself.

'Go into hiding for some time,' was his response.

It suddenly hit me how serious the situation was. I stopped going to office as I feared it could mean trouble. I was proved right as officials from the Haryana Vigilance Department arrived there to conduct more raids. If I were present, there would be the likelihood of my being arrested. I decided to approach Uncle Surendra again, as he had always been a pillar of strength for me. He was also familiar with the campaign against me. He suggested

I move to his estate in Unchagaon, in Bulandshahr district, as no one would think of looking for me there. It is about 110 km from Delhi and close to the banks of the Ganga. It is full of mango groves scattered among the agricultural fields.

I followed his advice but also got prominent lawyer H.K. Sibal to file a writ in the high court asking for a stay on the cancellation of licences, which in due course was granted by the high court. But the threat of my arrest still loomed when, on 19 June 1987, I got word that Bansi Lal had stepped down as chief minister and elections to the state assembly would be held soon. For the first time in many years, I breathed easy and felt safe enough to return to Delhi and my office at DLF.

A month later, on 17 July 1987, the polls saw Devi Lal riding to power with a thumping majority. Now that he was no longer the chief minister, I again tried to mend fences with Bansi Lal, but got the cold shoulder as before. I found that his son, Surender Singh, and daughter-in-law, Kiran Chaudhary, who were in politics themselves, were sympathetic towards me, but were not inclined to interfere in a matter involving Bansi Lal's personal likes and dislikes. I continued trying to open a line of communication with Bansi Lal but without any success.

That situation continued for many years. I went back to rebuilding DLF and expanding its presence in Gurgaon. It was not easy starting work at DLF again. The company had lost several years in the battle with Bansi Lal. DLF's reputation had been damaged. It had been forbidden to take any instalments from customers after its licences were cancelled. It also could not conduct any transactions. Cancellation of licences reduced the cash flow, which had almost dried up. But providence has its own ways of compensating. Fearing that their land would no longer attract a premium, owners were ready to sell it cheap. Instead of drowning in depression, I saw this as a great opportunity. As banks would not loan me money, I arranged short-term finance at exorbitant rates of interest from non-banking agencies to acquire more and more land. Many thought I was crazy to be assembling land at such a fast pace at a time when all our licences stood cancelled. I was borrowing at an interest rate of 24 per cent to pay for the land. When the time for repayment came, I borrowed more.

I took this decision as land was cheap and I was convinced that it was the right time to buy. It was a calculated risk. At that time, land in Gurgaon was available for as low as Rs. 40,000 an acre, but DLF had no money to buy. Today, the same land would cost several millions of rupees for an acre. Looking back, I think the whole experience with Bansi Lal had made me stronger. Maybe, if he had not cancelled the licences, I would not have fought back like I did to survive, succeed and shine. I kept telling myself never to give up. I knew I had to continue building relationships and have the tenacity to fight a hostile political system. My dogged determination finally helped.

The cancelled licences were eventually restored on 31 January 1989 by Devi Lal, who had become the chief minister of Haryana. In 1986, we were selling land at Rs. 600 a square yard. But when the licence got restored, the rate had gone up to Rs. 2,000 a square yard. Fortunately, we had bought a lot of land in those three years at a stable price. I kept buying small pieces of land while the assault by Bansi Lal was on. The media was also hounding me and the banks were not giving finance. Nothing seemed to be going right, but I saw this as an opportunity while most felt that DLF's days were numbered. My family members, like my father-in-law, felt that I should be cautious as there was a long legal battle ahead. It all depended on how successful I would be in persuading policy makers to change their mindsets.

Then, just as DLF was regaining customer confidence and the demand for our properties was peaking, fate stepped in once again. Bansi Lal became chief minister for the third time, under the banner of the Haryana Vikas Party, in May 1996. I again tried to mend fences with him, but he remained as aloof as ever. As it was common knowledge that he was against DLF and me personally, some of his bureaucrats started feeding him negative stories about DLF. I was told he would not even try to verify these allegations and accepted them at face value. The cold war between him and DLF resumed. As time passed, everyone in the Haryana government became aware that Bansi Lal was against the entry of the private sector in the business of urban land development in the state. Accordingly, everything was pitted against me – the bureaucracy, the political setup, financial institutions and the media which kept echoing unsubstantiated allegations.

A very exhaustive procedure has been laid down for finalization of a development plan of a notified urban area in the country. This procedure involves inviting public objections against the plan which the government intends to finalize. Such objections and comments are thereafter heard properly to ensure that the final published plan is in conformity with the aspirations and needs of the people affected by its implementation. In Gurgaon the same procedure has been followed by the government while finalizing its development plans. Any amendment to the final published development plan has to follow the same procedure of publication and thereafter invite public objections and comments. Although a chief minister is the head of the government, he is not empowered to make any changes in the finalized development plan without following this prescribed procedure. While normally such a procedure was being rigidly followed in Haryana, some exceptions were made to it during Bansi Lal's tenure. He would often issue direct instructions to make changes in the published development plans and if such changes were not implemented, the concerned officers were threatened with transfer to punishment postings.

Most bureaucrats knew about Bansi Lal's feud with me and that as a result any project involving DLF would therefore be affected, directly or indirectly. One of these happened to be a road. In any area notified by the government for residential development, sector roads would normally be constructed in keeping with the projected growth of habitation. One of the major roads that was planned in the Gurgaon development plan was called Bypass Road No. 9. It was meant to divert traffic coming from Delhi, Faridabad and Jaipur so that the upcoming city of Gurgaon was not affected by traffic blockages. Government officials had issued a notification for acquisition of land to construct the road in March 1998 and procedures were in place to start construction.

However, some of Bansi Lal's loyalists in the local administration told him that the road was being constructed to benefit DLF. As I gathered, their sycophantic zeal prompted them to inform him that the road was passing through areas where DLF had developed large residential sectors. Bhaskar Chatterji, commissioner, town planning, was ordered to stop all work on Road No. 9 and de-notify the land which had been acquired for the purpose. The de-notification order was issued in November 1998. This was against all established rules, which laid down, inter alia, that even a chief minister could not change a development plan without following the prescribed procedure.

This is probably the only instance in India when a chief minister actually stopped construction of a road that was designed to decongest inter-state traffic at the cost of thousands of residents of Gurgaon and adjoining areas, all because of his campaign against me. None of his officials dared to inform him that what he was doing was illegal and also illogical. The result was that residents of Gurgaon suffered endless traffic snarls and resultant pollution. It also affected economic activity and led to countless man hours of work being lost. Bansi Lal did not appear to be bothered even though the evidence of his actions was there for all to see. This continued till he lost the assembly elections once again.

By then, protests by the numerous resident welfare associations against the traffic mess had got so serious that the incoming chief minister, Om Prakash Chautala, re-notified the land again in August 2003 so that this road could be constructed. But the fact is that a major road affecting thousands of commuters and residents was delayed for years just because of one man's whim!

In another similar case, someone had told Bansi Lal that most of the commercial areas in Gurgaon were being created by DLF. He brought in a new policy whereby anyone with two acres of land could apply to get a licence to develop commercial areas. Suddenly, there were scores of new developers who were given permission to make swanky malls on the Gurgaon–Mehrauli Road without any regard to traffic and other infrastructural constraints. In the original plan, such commercial activities were spread out to ensure that traffic and infrastructure facilities do not get overloaded in one area. Unfortunately, Bansi Lal's ad hoc decision making destroyed DLF's – and Rajiv Gandhi's too – vision of setting up a world-class city.

At the height of the campaign against me, with DLF backed into a corner and suffering huge losses, I took inspiration from unexpected sources. Many friends asked me how I was still managing to keep my cool in the face of such adversity and I could trace it back to a meeting with a former army chief. I had gone to the Delhi Gymkhana Club to play tennis during November 1962.

The crisis created by the India–China war was at its peak and I was amazed to see Gen. J.N. Chaudhuri looking very relaxed though he had just taken over as the army chief, on 19 November. The war ended on 20 November. How could he be at the club when the war had just ended? A number of media persons had surrounded him. Since Lt. Gen. Wadalia and General Chaudhuri were close friends I had got to know the chief well. Curious, I walked up to his car when he was answering a volley of questions by the media.

I could not help saying to him, 'Sir, I am very surprised to see you here as you have just taken over as the chief and the country is trying to cope with the aftereffects of the war.'

He smiled and said, 'KP come and see me when you swing by Army Headquarters to see your former boss Lt. Gen. Wadalia and I will tell you why I am here.'

Although I had retired from the army, I still used to visit Army Headquarters occasionally to brief Lt. Gen. Wadalia about the developments in the stud farm. The next day, as I was at the headquarters, I used the opportunity to meet General Chaudhuri. He remembered what I had asked him and said something that I adopted with great effect for the rest of my life.

He said, 'I deliberately went to the club while the war was at its peak knowing that the media will blow up the event. In fact, I wanted it to be highlighted as I want to send a message to everyone that the Indian Army is a very superior force manned by officers who do not panic and are confident of victory. I may be worried, but my face should not show that to the outside world. The best commanders are those who remain calm, cool and confident during adversity.'

It was an important lesson which I recalled and practised often during my battle with Bansi Lal. I was under tremendous pressure, even depressed at times, but outwardly, I was calm and the employees at DLF were motivated by that attitude. Even after we were raided and our licences to develop land were cancelled, our employees stuck with me as I had sent out a signal that there was no reason to panic. Thank you, General Chaudhuri.

Another person who inspired me during those trying times was H.D. Shourie. I used to meet him whenever I was particularly low. He was a respected retired bureaucrat and the father of senior journalist and BJP leader Arun Shourie. He was also a great friend of my father-in-law. HD was a spirited fighter and was running Common Cause, an organization dedicated to fight for consumer rights and common people's grievances. I poured my heart out to him about the political campaign against me. It was then that he recited an Urdu couplet that has always given me courage.

Kunde mukhalif se na ghabaraye eh akab / Yeh to aata hai tujhe uncha uthane ke liye. (O Eagle, do not get scared by the gusty storm coming from the opposite side / It is coming only to uplift you.)

Whenever I feel depressed, as was often the case during my troubles with Bansi Lal, this couplet has always inspired me to face any adverse situation with grit and hope.

Ultimately, all of Bansi Lal's actions against me invariably had an impact on the residents of Gurgaon, as was the case involving the DLF golf course. It had come up during his last tenure as chief minister during 1996-99, when his campaign against DLF was still continuing. As there was nothing that could be held against us in terms of our real estate operations, his administration targeted the golf course that was becoming the talk of the town. It was a first-rate facility but Bansi Lal's attitude almost destroyed it. His officials decided that the road leading to the golf course entrance was to be dug up as we had made it wider than what was planned.

We were appalled when earthmovers came in to destroy the road we had built. We had deliberately widened the road as it was built on our land and not on public property. A wider road also added to the ambience of the golf course. This is probably the only case in India where the state government tried to crack down on a developer who was building a wider road on his own property and at his own cost! The earthmovers dug the road so that it could not be used at all, inconveniencing hundreds of members and their guests. Bansi Lal had also directed his officials to issue a notification on 12 April 1999 for compulsory acquisition of 215 acres of land in Gurgaon for another golf course, this one to be built by the Haryana Urban Development Authority (HUDA). He may have thought that a rival golf course would compete with DLF. His officers did not have the courage to tell him how prohibitively expensive it would be and that public funds were just not available.

As if this were not enough, his officials filed an FIR on 26 April 1999 against the managing director of DLF on grounds that were patently false. We quickly moved to secure anticipatory bail. As this was clearly a mala fide order, the court accepted our petition. Thanks to the courts, we also resumed construction of the road leading to the golf course. I often remember this incident when I drive into the golf course and it only strengthens my belief that in the end, it is truth that wins. Towards the end of his tenure, Bansi Lal, who had been hailed as a visionary by Gurgaon's residents, turned into a reactionary. As soon as he was out of power, the acquisition of the land he had notified to build a golf course lapsed, as no government that followed would ever earmark huge public funds for such a project when there were other pressing infrastructural requirements.

Bansi Lal felt that enough had been done for Gurgaon and often said that he had other cities to develop. He had diverted his attention from Gurgaon mainly because it was being developed by DLF and also because it was being done at the behest of Rajiv Gandhi, who had given his blessings to the project. While Bansi Lal was very close to Sanjay Gandhi, his relationship with Rajiv was quite formal. As time went by, there was a marked change in the relationship. Eventually, he drifted away from the Gandhi family and formed the Haryana Vikas Party. Had he kept the interests of the state above personal biases, we would have seen a different Gurgaon today. It would have been the best city in

India and an important investment destination in Haryana. Bansi Lal's Haryana Vikas Party government fell on 23 July 1999 as the Congress withdrew its support. Om Prakash Chautala came in as chief minister. That signified the end of Bansi Lal's chequered career. He became a loner.

Various chief ministers had come and gone, from Bansi Lal, to Bhajan Lal, Devi Lal and his son Om Prakash Chautala. They all had their strengths and weaknesses. Devi Lal had his own peculiar way of dealing with issues. He was helpful, but could not prevail upon his bureaucracy as much as Bansi Lal or even Chautala. Both had a rough, peremptory style so no one opposed them. Devi Lal was mostly guided by his ministers and the bureaucracy. Being a mass political leader, he had a knack of surrounding himself with people from all walks of life and was easily accessible. It was also one of his weaknesses since all sorts of individuals had his ear.

One such person was H.L. Sanghi, a former small-time real estate player in Delhi. He convinced Devi Lal that if the Haryana Urban Development Authority were to take over urban land development completely from the private sector, Haryana would make so much money from this sector that it could become a zero-tax state. Devi Lal fell for the idea even though it was quite unrealistic and met with stiff opposition from the bureaucracy and even his political colleagues. Sanghi became an extra-constitutional authority around the chief minister and was also made the ex-officio head of HUDA. Almost a year was lost before Devi Lal realized that the ill-conceived plan had only led to chaos and delay of the infrastructure development of Gurgaon. Sanghi was removed but he had done enough damage. His idea of how the public sector would exclusively dominate urban development in Haryana was illogical, unworkable and antiquated but it showed how individuals could affect the future of an entire city. The idea was impractical as experience since Independence had shown that exclusive authority to the public sector to bring about urban development had never worked. Developing Gurgaon would have been too much for HUDA to do alone.

When Devi Lal came to power, I put my case before him regarding the cancellation of DLF's licences. I had struck up a good working relationship with him and we had a series of meetings to discuss revoking the cancellation of our licences. I must have met him at least fifty times on this issue. After every meeting, nothing would happen. Finally, he advised Virendra Singh, the town planning minister, to restore the licences. It taught me the importance of perseverance. DLF was back in business. It is a historical fact that Devi Lal and Bansi Lal were arch rivals. Bansi Lal's campaign against me was well known. Naturally, Devi Lal had a soft corner for me as he understood what I had been made to go through.

Jats in Haryana have a great sense of humour and a very distinctive style of narrating a joke too. On more than one occasion, I found that Devi Lal's barber, in the course of his conversation, would suddenly mention the kind of rumours afloat in the market about what Bansi Lal was saying about Devi Lal. This would immediately infuriate Devi Lal, who would shower the choicest Haryanvi abuses directed at his political rival. One day, I asked the barber why he dropped Bansi Lal's name so often. In a matter-of-fact way, without even the hint of a smile, he said, 'It is very difficult to give Devi Lalji a proper haircut, because he has so little hair. But when I mention Bansi Lal's name, all the hair on his head stand up, making it easier for me to do my job'!

I had my ways of trying to make things easier for myself. Because of the general lack of awareness among policy makers about the importance of the real estate industry and the intricacies of town planning and urban development, I found it necessary to meet informally with politicians in power and bring them around to my way of thinking. The best time to catch them in a receptive mood, I discovered, was early in the morning, as early as 6 o'clock sometimes, when their minds were fresh and not yet cluttered with the problems and stresses of the day.

My interactions also gave me insights into their personalities. I found Om Prakash Chautala politically shrewd and savvy, capable of taking bold decisions quickly. There was a general impression that he was against industrialization of the state, but this was a myth, because it was Chautala who was actually instrumental in giving a big push to IT-related projects like DLF Cyber City in Gurgaon. If he was convinced that a policy initiative could help faster development of the state or that jobs would be created for young people in rural areas, he had the courage to disregard the cautions of his bureaucrats and take a positive decision.

I believe that in India, strong and decisive leaders, in politics, of course, but also in other spheres, are needed for all-round progress to take place. Only someone with guts and vision can take unpalatable decisions and put the interests of the state or the country above everything else.

Building relationships with the political leadership helps ease the way, even though the effort can sometimes boomerang. Many ministers often fall prey to misinformation by bureaucrats and unscrupulous people, but a frank, face-to-face discussion invariably helps clear the air. History will remember Bansi Lal, who pushed an aggressive agenda of reform and development in Haryana during the early years of his tenure as chief minister. He had the great ability of getting his bureaucrats to perform. He could rightly take credit for having made Haryana one of the fastest growing states in the country at that point of time. Unfortunately, his detractors often said that he had a 'ziddi' streak in him, suggesting that he had a stubborn style of governance.

I have often wondered if a cursory remark by an army officer at a party could make a political leader like Bansi Lal suddenly turn against me. There were probably other reasons. To begin with, Chaudhry Saheb's brother-in-law, Sardar Hari Singh, from Dabra, who was an important figure in Haryana politics, chose to join the opposition and it might have slighted Bansi Lal. This also might have triggered his antipathy against Chaudhry Saheb, as he too soon fell out of favour with him. Secondly, and more importantly, Bansi Lal was against the involvement of the private sector in urban land development as he felt this should only be done by the public sector. I seriously disagreed with him. Although the Punjab Scheduled Roads and Controlled Areas Restriction of Unregulated Development Act, 1963 and the Haryana Development and Regulation of Urban Areas Act, 1975 existed for allowing the private sector to develop urban land, Bansi Lal did not allow this to happen. However, I pioneered the movement to allow the private sector to enter the domain of urban land development, which was until then with the public sector. The first licence to develop urban land in Haryana was granted to DLF by Bhajan Lal, who was well known to be an arch rival of Bansi Lal. All these factors must have perhaps combined to turn Bansi Lal against me over a period of time.

In the end, he was reduced to a sad and lonely man, abandoned by his followers and political colleagues, while I had moved on in life. I had tried to build bridges with Bansi Lal after he was out of power and out of the Congress party that had given him so much. Even then it did not work. He was also badly affected by the sudden and tragic death of his son Surender in a helicopter crash in 2005. I went twice to Bhiwani, in Haryana, about 120 km from Delhi, to be with the family after the tragedy. For the first time, I saw a broken man. He was such a powerful force in

Indian politics but the death of his son left him shattered. The wall between us was still there. He did not even look at me when I went to offer my condolences. 'Thank you' was all he said. It was more like a formality.

I travelled to Bhiwani once again a month after his son's death. This time I found him a completely broken man, sitting alone with an air of being lost and lonely. I gently told him that I had come to share his sorrow. For the first time in many years, I saw a mellow Bansi Lal. I told him that I continued to respect him despite the misunderstanding. It is only then that he said in a faltering voice and with deep emotion: 'Because of me you have suffered a lot. I always tried to hurt you and your company. But now I realize I was wrong, I was misled. You are a good man.'

After all the trials and tribulations I had gone through, after all the rancour that I had endured, I accepted these words as an expression of remorse from a man who, despite everything, I had always admired for his administrative skills. I was glad that my sustained efforts to reach out to him had finally brought about some kind of peace between us, howsoever belated.

While I struggled to build Gurgaon, I realized that unless one developed a good working relationship with the incumbent chief minister, it was virtually impossible to get things done. Some bureaucrats and politicians were wary of real estate players, perhaps rightly so. Many builders had dubious track records; others were fly-by-night operators indulging in all kinds of shady deals and malpractices, and unauthorized building activity. At that time, only a few professional developers had a good reputation. Among them were Ansals and Unitech. Since the first licence was issued to DLF, vigorous lobbying was carried out by me, Sushil Ansal of Ansal Builders and Ramesh Chandra of Unitech calling for reforms in the existing antiquated town planning and state laws. The three of us made numerous visits together to Chandigarh to convince town planning officials, bureaucrats and the politicians to bring in reforms. It was hard work, but often yielded results. When you have collective strength, even if you are competitors, you can achieve your objectives.

I might have suffered for many years in Haryana but at least I could ensure that urban development stayed in the hands of the private sector. If Bansi Lal had had his way, it would have gone to the public sector and Gurgaon would not have grown the way it did. DLF ensured that Gurgaon was a pacesetter in urban development and many more examples like ours will hopefully be seen in the years to come in different states of the country.

10

DLF

EVOLUTION AND REBIRTH

IT WAS JANUARY 1975. I picked up my pen to sign a share transfer form. I was about to sell all my shares in DLF. On the desk before me was a cheque in my favour for Rs. 26 lakh, or 2.6 million, being the approximate book value of the shares. It was the amount I would get for severing my links with DLF forever.

Sitting in front of me at my Willard office in the Hindustan Times building in New Delhi was Y.S. Tayal, DLF's chief financial advisor, who had been sent by Chaudhry Saheb with the share transfer form. Had I signed it, my DLF story would have ended there and then. My life would have been entirely different and, perhaps, this memoir would never have been written.

But at that moment, there were no misgivings in my mind. The decision to sell my shares had been taken for me by my father-in-law. One does not even think of questioning the family patriarch, one simply does what one is told to do. That was the culture in our families.

Just as I got ready to sign away my stake in DLF, Tayal, who was a mild-mannered person, cleared his throat and spoke. He said: 'Once your signature is on that paper, you will lose DLF forever. So before you sign, please think about it carefully.' However, he cautioned that since DLF had not undertaken any worthwhile real estate projects in almost a decade, its financial health was extremely poor now.

I was caught in a dilemma. But before I could react, he continued: 'I will be retiring from DLF in a few weeks, so I can speak my mind freely. I feel it is my moral duty to apprise you of the implications involved. Once all of you sign all the share transfer forms and accept the cheques, it would mean that your family will get permanently disassociated with DLF forever. Please think about it.'

It was a wake-up call for me. In a flash, I realized the truth of what he was saying and the implications of giving away my DLF shareholding.

Tayal had been sent to inform me that Chaudhry Saheb's younger brother Devinder Singh had made a proposal that we should either sell our shares to him or agree to merge DLF with his company, Industrial Cables. On the assumption that we would have no objection to sell, a set of DLF share transfer forms and cheques had been prepared for me, Indira and Prem. On the basis of the book value of the shares, Prem was to get around Rs. 2 million and Indira and I were to get around Rs. 2.6 million each as per the book value of our respective shares. Tayal had come to me first and was planning to then approach Indira and Prem to get their signatures.

My father-in-law had almost retired from DLF in 1972. It pained him that neither his agricultural operations nor the real estate ventures of DLF were making any progress. He had almost closed DLF down after private sector developers were forced out of the business of urban land development because of government regulations.

He also had doubts about whether Shamsher, who was preoccupied with his own ventures, had the time, inclination or temperament to handle the tedious, time-consuming and often tricky tasks of navigating the plethora of government departments. He also would have to network with officials at the highest and lowest levels and navigate the maze of micro-level glitches that invariably crop up in real estate development.

At that time, the only visible asset DLF possessed was an old two-storey building on Parliament Street in the heart of New Delhi. Known as Narendra Place, it had been bought for a paltry sum. But, it could be made commercially viable only by demolishing the existing structure and constructing a modern, highrise office building in its place.

The plans were at a standstill because of one major hurdle, which appeared insurmountable. The property was located right next to one of Delhi's most famous protected monuments, the historic Jantar Mantar, the unique observatory built in the early 1700s by Maharaja Sawai Jai Singh II of Jaipur. Without the permission of the Archaeological Survey of India (ASI), no development work could begin in the monument's neighbourhood. And such permission was not forthcoming because the ASI experts said that erecting any tall building in the vicinity would cast a shadow on the ancient sundial and other instruments that make the Jantar Mantar such a scientific marvel.

There were also many other regulatory stumbling blocks. The DDA's sanction was needed to delink the property from its Comprehensive Re-development Plan of the Janpath Lane area to enable us to construct a building on an individual plot development basis. The Central government's consent was required to convert the land usage from residential to commercial. Approval also had to be secured under the Urban Land Ceiling Act (ULCA). Finally, the thirty existing tenants of Narendra Place, who had been living there for five decades, would have to be persuaded to vacate the premises. Not surprisingly, the project showed no hope of getting off the ground.

It was in late 1974 that my father-in-law's brother, Devinder Singh, expressed a desire to take over DLF. He had already started real estate operations in Punjab and around Delhi and was keen to exploit the DLF brand to expand his business. Since Industrial Cables was doing well, he tried to convince Chaudhry Saheb that he had enough cash flow to turn the company around. But since he held less than 12 per cent of the shares of DLF, he needed to buy out the other shareholders and take full control. Chaudhry Saheb had used his earnings from the Qutab Stud Farm to acquire shares adding up to about 28 per cent. But since my wife Indira, sister-in-law Prem and I held over 55 per cent of the shares of DLF, Devinder would have to buy shares from us in order to get a controlling interest.

I could understand why Chaudhry Saheb considered Devinder's proposal. It was not just because he was his younger brother. He had evidently looked at all the angles, especially about Shamsher, Prem's husband, and me. Even though both of us had a cavalry background, he knew that we were quite different when it came to dealing with people. I had the benefit of having been brought up in rural India and a small town like Bulandshahr, so I could easily mix with rural folk. I was very comfortable sitting on the floor in a thatched hut in a village, cracking jokes about Jats and drinking their sugary tea. I could speak and behave just like them.

With his Doon School background, Shamsher was more at ease interacting with the higher bureaucracy – when it came to dealing with junior officials and clerks, he lacked the ability to come down to their level. Nor had his background prepared him for dealing with humble farmers. His father, Sardar Nawab Singh, had been a member of the Indian Civil Service and Shamsher's upbringing was more suited to an urban lifestyle and sophisticated business ventures rather than the real estate business where one was constantly dealing with villagers and lower-level district officials.

That is probably why Chaudhry Saheb must have felt that real estate was not the right business for Shamsher. About me, too, he must have had his doubts, and rightly so. I knew nothing about real estate. My networking skills were untested at that time. My experience was limited to the manufacturing business I was running.

In contrast, Devinder was familiar with the intricacies of the real estate business and also had the knack of dealing with people from an urban or rural background alike. Since Shamsher was no longer interested in DLF in any case, and I was busy with Willard and American Universal, the logical conclusion that Chaudhry Saheb had come to was that Devinder would be able to take care of DLF's operations better than either of us.

Yet, even though I knew that there was much truth in my father-in-law's assessment of the situation and his solution seemed the most pragmatic one, Tayal's words sparked off a disturbing thought – did I really want to sever all ties with DLF? Was it in our interest to sell our shares or accept a merger of DLF with Industrial Cables? Should the DLF brand be allowed to die, which I knew was the last thing that Chaudhry Saheb really wanted? Was I really incapable of reviving DLF and making it profitable? What would it take to make this happen?

There was another angle I had to factor in. At that time, I was quite excited to head Willard. It had just started in India, but it was a solid company with an international reputation for using the latest technology. The thought of making it a commercial success in India was tempting and would be a huge ego boost.

My mind was in a whirl. I needed time to think. I asked Tayal to leave the share transfer papers with me for a few days and told him I would inform him the moment I had taken a decision.

I realized that I badly needed dispassionate advice. As luck would have it, S.S. Bagai, DLF's tax advisor from Mumbai, happened to be visiting Delhi that day. Bagai was a hard-nosed professional who was always forthright in his views and I thought he would make a good sounding board. I asked him to drop in at my office.

Bagai was already aware that Chaudhry Saheb had deputed Tayal to my office to get the stake sale proposal implemented.

'I am aware of Chaudhry Saheb's views, but since you have asked for my personal advice, I want to be very frank and truthful. In my experience, I have seen many industrial houses go from the peaks of success to the depths of failure,' he said. 'It would be unwise of you to put all your eggs in one basket by concentrating only on Willard and American Universal.' He was quite firm about it. It was not in my interest, he said, to sell the DLF shares. Nor should I agree to a merger as it would mean getting into a minority position in the new company.

'Instead,' he continued, 'you should be investing your time and effort in reviving DLF.'

Bagai's parting advice was that I could use my earnings from the Qutab Stud Farm and income from my property in Bulandshahr to revive DLF and ensure that the control of the company stayed with my wife, my sister-in-law and me.

The more I thought about it, the more sense it made. I spoke to Prem and Indira. I told them what Bagai had advised. Their reactions were identical – we should neither sell, nor give DLF away.

None of us could have foreseen just how prophetic those words would turn out to be; that there would come a time in the distant future when DLF would become the biggest and the most respected real estate company in the country. Nor could we have imagined how different our future would have been had we taken any other decision. Life is made up of turning points such as these, when we take a crucial decision without knowing at that time how crucial it is going to be for our very existence in the future. It is only after you reach your destination that you can look back and say you took the right road.

With the full support of the two sisters and my mind firmly made up, I called Tayal a few days later and told him that we did not want to sell our shares. He then arranged a meeting with Chaudhry Saheb, Devinder and me to discuss the matter at the old DLF office at F-40, Connaught Place. Chaudhry Saheb began by saying that DLF had declined in the past few years. He wanted someone to revive the business and ensure that it did not die. I fully empathized with him as DLF had seen much better days under his leadership. Devinder then outlined his plan of how acquiring the DLF brand would help him expand his real estate business. He said he was ready to either pay an enhanced price for the shares or merge DLF with Industrial Cables Ltd.

I politely but firmly said that I had discussed the matter with Indira and Prem and none of us wanted to sell our shares and break all links with the company that Chaudhry Saheb had created. I would work hard to revive it, I said.

I could tell that my father-in-law was very pleased by the determined tone of my voice. He, however, reminded me that my manufacturing business at Willard and American Universal needed all my attention and financial resources to succeed. Apart from that, he pointed out, being a developer involves much more than just hard work. I would have to deal with all levels of bureaucracy, regulatory authority and political leaders both at the state and Central government levels, to sensitize them about the needs of the real estate sector and persuade them to change existing policies. Besides, the impending Urban Land Ceiling Act had a disastrous effect on private land developers. Banks were forbidden by the Reserve Bank of India to give loans for real estate ventures.

Then, with his eyes moist, he told me, 'I have no finances to help. All I can offer you are my blessings.'

'That is all I want from you. I never wanted your money. I am going to find it myself,' I replied.

Having obtained his blessings, I politely declined Devinder's offer to buy our shares or merge DLF with Industrial Cables Ltd.

'Despite my continued involvement in Willard and American Universal, I am determined to revive DLF regardless of what it might take,' I told him.

It was a make-or-break decision but as things turned out it was the right one. Despite this, my relationship with Devinder continued to be as close as ever. He respected my stand as much as I understood why he was keen on getting control of the DLF brand. Much later, Devinder was the happiest person when I had managed to revive DLF and taken it forward from near oblivion to success.

I have never forgotten that it was Tayal's hint and Bagai's advice that ended up making DLF what it is today. If they had not advised the way they did, I would have perhaps stayed in charge of Willard which was destined to fail, largely because of unforeseen technical circumstances.

Invariably, employees fear being shouted at if they speak up and so sycophancy develops. But, Hoddy had taught me to encourage employees to speak up so that one could get fresh ideas. What is important is to have patience, a cool temperament and the right body language to enable employees to speak without fear. Bagai spoke frankly only because I encouraged him to do so and listened intently to what he said. Both these qualities are important if a leader wants fresh ideas. One also has to be open to ideas so that these can be evaluated unemotionally. Having professionals with you who can offer clear-headed advice without bias or succumbing to sycophancy is one of the most invaluable assets any responsible and aspiring business can have. The boss is not always right. It was an important lesson in decision making.

If I had ignored what Bagai had said or not taken Tayal's hint,

DLF would not have been what it is today. I was also glad that both Indira and Prem had backed me all the way. I look back with gratitude for their role in saving DLF from receding into history. It was truly a lesson well learnt.

Having made up my mind to refocus on DLF, I examined the situation objectively. The dice was loaded against me. DLF had not done anything worthwhile in real estate for nearly twenty years!

There were reasons for this. In the past, my father-in-law had faced very serious problems, some of which had little to do with business. In fact, there was a time in the 1950s when even the prime minister, Pandit Jawaharlal Nehru, had almost stopped DLF in its tracks because of political rivalry between two powerful politicians. The chief minister of Delhi at that time was Chaudhry Brahm Prakash, prominent Congress leader, who was a close friend of my father-in-law, who was getting drawn into politics. Inevitably, jealous rivals started floating false stories that DLF, then an emerging real estate company in Delhi, was actually a covert financial entity of Brahm Prakash. DLF had submitted plans for approval for the development of a residential area to be called Greater Kailash I. Nehru was shown the miniaturized blueprints and told that the clusters on the map were actually slums that a real estate company was clandestinely creating.

Nehru was very conscious of ecological and aesthetic requirements. Since Delhi was still growing into a capital city worthy of India, he wanted the upcoming habitations to meet certain standards. He accepted the falsehood as the truth and was naturally appalled that the state government was encouraging the growth of slums. So DLF became the target of his wrath. He summoned the health secretary, one Mr Pillai, and ordered him to stop DLF's work and make inquiries about the project before it exploded into a scandal. For some inexplicable reason, urban housing in Delhi was originally under the purview of the Union health ministry. There was no urban development ministry at that time.

Pillai was a straightforward bureaucrat with a no-nonsense attitude. He called Chaudhry Saheb and showed him the miniaturized plan and asked for an explanation. Chaudhry Saheb had brought along a detailed map that was to actual scale. It showed the completed township in Greater Kailash I in intricate detail. Naturally, there was no question of any slums. Pillai went back to Nehru and explained that the miniaturized blueprint had been misread. Realizing he had been misinformed and shown a wrong plan, Nehru told Pillai, not without a hint of embarrassment and a wry smile, to 'allow DLF to do what it was doing'. Subsequently, Nehru was gracious enough to visit the GK I area where he expressed appreciation of Chaudhry Saheb's developmental work in Delhi. Those were the years shortly after Independence when Partition and its effects were still very much in evidence.

In the bloodshed that followed Partition, millions of Hindu refugees fled from Pakistan to India, with most of them arriving in Delhi. The population of Delhi, which was just 0.91 million in 1941, ballooned to 1.79 million over the next ten years. The majority were refugees from Pakistan. More than half a million refugees had sought shelter in the capital and thousands of tents had been put up as temporary housing. In 1948, plans were drawn up for new townships on the urban fringes of Delhi by the newly created Improvement Trust for the Ministry of Relief. In 1949, a Central Coordination Committee for the Development of Greater Delhi was established as a part of the Central Public Works Department. Through improvisation, adjustment and resettlement, the refugees were moved into thirty-six rehabilitation colonies.

Ideas and opportunities have created empires all over the world. Here was one opportunity that, decades later, would give birth to an empire. DLF was at that time a real estate company in name only. It had no finances or backers. The sole visionary was Chaudhry Raghvendra Singh. After studying law at Lahore's Government College, he had joined the Provincial Civil Service. It was in those days a coveted job and he rose to become the secretary of the Punjab State Transport Authority. But Chaudhry Saheb was an entrepreneur at heart, and his pioneering spirit had influenced him to quit the service and start a real estate company called Delhi Land and Finance Pvt. Ltd.

As a government employee, despite the high official status, he did not earn much and his savings were hardly enough to start a business. He had not inherited any wealth either. What he did have in abundance was vision and an enterprising spirit. He had the foresight to visualize the increased demand for housing soon after Partition with Delhi being flooded with refugees from Pakistan. DLF was incorporated a little earlier, in 1946, with a capital of 5,000 shares of Rs. 100 each. While the majority shares were held initially by a Jain family, others were held by friends of Chaudhry Saheb and his family. He himself owned only fifty shares. In subsequent years, he took over two other ventures, Raisina Cold Storage Pvt. Ltd that dealt with manufacturing of ice, and DLF Housing and Construction Pvt. Ltd that dealt with real estate and construction activities.

In 1969, these three ventures merged to become DLF United Limited. Before the merger, it had a very small capital base. The shareholding of DLF United was held primarily by my wife, Indira, her sister, Prem Mohini, I and Chaudhry Saheb and the rest was held by hundreds of other shareholders. All his life, Chaudhry Saheb had been a selfless person who had inherited almost nothing in terms of wealth when he started his business. All he had was a small patch of agricultural land in Balhot village in Rohtak district of Haryana. What he had earned, though, was tremendous goodwill. The operations of DLF were supported mainly by friends and relatives. He emerged as a self-made man. He struggled to build whatever he did. Even his meagre personal holding in DLF was bought out of his earnings from the Qutab Stud Farm. Yet, he had the vision to see opportunity when it came knocking.

Under Chaudhry Saheb DLF was the most prominent private builder in Delhi at that time. It had built up a good reputation with the quality of its construction and materials and fair and transparent dealings with its customers. There was huge opportunity but very little finance to buy land for development. Chaudhry Saheb hit upon a unique idea to raise money, an innovation that was unheard of in those days and which I would later adopt to rebuild the company after it went through a long and challenging period.

His idea was truly revolutionary. He invited farmers from whom he was buying land to partner him in the real estate business. It was an ingenious scheme but needed daring and foresight to pull it off. As he had no money to pay the farmers from whom he wanted to acquire land, he requested them to give their land to him on credit. In return, he promised he would work hard to build a profitable real estate business and pay them as soon as he made money. The farmers were sceptical at first but soon brought round by his straight talk and confidence. He had the ability and the personality to invite trust.

The day DLF started giving returns he wasted no time in paying back the farmers. But in doing so, he added another audacious angle. He asked them to reinvest 90 per cent of the money they got from the sale of their land in DLF. 'I will make your money grow and also make sure you grow with DLF,' he promised them. He kept his word.

They already had a favourable view of DLF, thanks to his promise of prompt repayment. Between the first and the sixth of every month, he would pay them the interest on the money they

Father Chaudhry Mukhtar Singh introduced me to the world of sports. He was a very well-known and respected lawyer in western Uttar Pradesh during 1948-80.

Mother Rampyari Devi left behind fond memories of childhood.

Sister Vikramdevi Singh was very close to me.

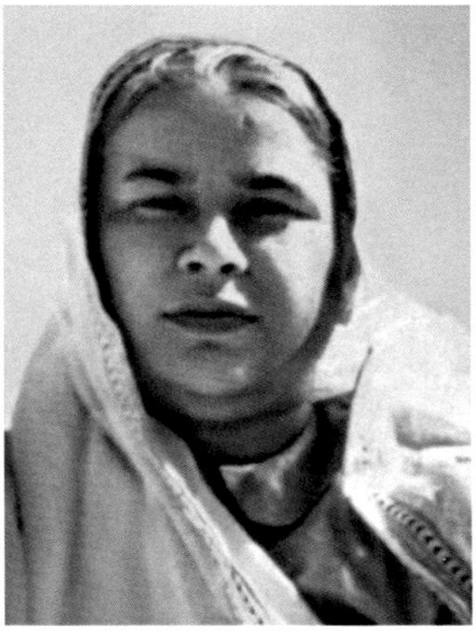

Aunt Mohar Kaur, whose brother Hon. Capt. Raghubir Singh was ADC to Viceroy of India, Lord Wavell.

Family photograph, 1941. Sitting left to right are father Chaudhry Mukhtar Singh, mother Rampyari Devi, aunt Nawabji and aunt Mohar Kaur. At the back I am standing on the left, Vikramdevi at the centre and uncle Giriraj Singh on the right.

Uncle Hon. Capt. Raghubir Singh, ADC to Viceroy Lord Wavell during 1943-46. He taught me horse riding.

With Julie's grandfather Fred Wells and grandmother Patricia Wells in 1949.

Julie introduced me to the world of English aristocracy.

Happy times. With Julie in 1949.

With Julie at the Polo ground in England where we often played.

At a polo game in England in 1949. I am at the extreme left with Julie's uncle Richard at the extreme right.

Maj. Gen. M.S. Wadalia inspecting the Sangro Company of the Indian Military Academy where I was Senior Under Officer in 1951. I am to the right of Gen. Wadalia.

Great Bonding:
A typical gathering of the Gentlemen Cadets undergoing training at the Indian Military Academy with the Chief Instructor Col Ranbir Bakshi. I am standing fifth from left.

Instructors at the Indian Military Academy: Battalion Commander Col Baljit Singh, who persuaded me not to leave the IMA, is seen standing third from right.

Maj. Gen. M.S. Wadalia inspecting the Sangro Company of the Indian Military Academy where I was Senior Under Officer in 1951. I am to the right of Gen. Wadalia.

My stint in the army during 1951-60 was one of the richest experiences of my life.

My stint in the army during 1951-60 was one of the richest experiences of my life.

Uncle Surendra Pal Singh during his visit to England in 1949. He was a great influence and anchor in my life.

Surendra Pal Singh as an officer of the Indian Army in the early 1940s.

Surendra Pal Singh emerged as a powerful political leader of western Uttar Pradesh and was a minister in Pandit Jawaharlal Nehru's and Indira Gandhi's cabinets.

Sister-in-law Prem was very close to Indira and me.

Chaudhry Raghvendra Singh as a young officer of the Indian Army.

Father-in-law Chaudhry Raghvendra Singh with mother-in-law Savitri Devi.

Grandfather of Indira, Rai Bahadur Chaudhry Lal Chand, a distinguished personality of his time, having been a minister of Bharatpur State and pre-Partition Punjab. He was awarded the title of Rai Bahadur by the British government.

Magical tie. With Indira soon after our wedding in March 1954.

Bundle of Joy. Indira and I with Renuka who is holding one-day-old Rajiv in her arms on 9 May1959.

Son Rajiv and daughter Renuka in their early years.

Savitri Devi with Prem and Indira. Renuka and Rajiv are beside their grandmother.

Indira with Renuka and Rajiv.

Rajiv and Renuka in their early years.

A picnic trip outside Delhi. Indira, Rajiv and I.

Carrying balloons at Renuka's birthday party. Rajiv is trying to pull me back while Renuka pushes me to move ahead.

Loving Bond: (from left to right) Granddaughters Savitri and Anushka, I, granddaughter Tara, Indira, grandsons Jai and Rahul. Standing behind are son-in-law Timmy Sarna, daughters Pia and Renuka, daughter-in-law Kavita, son Rajiv and son-in-law Rana Talwar.

Happy family with grandchildren.

Indira with grandchildren. From (L to R): Anushka, Rahul and Savitri.

Renuka with her husband Rana and son Rahul.

At Disneyland, Orlando, USA, with Rajiv, Kavita and Indira. In the foreground (L to R): Rahul, Savitri and Anushka.

Renuka and Rana.

Granddaughter Savitri.

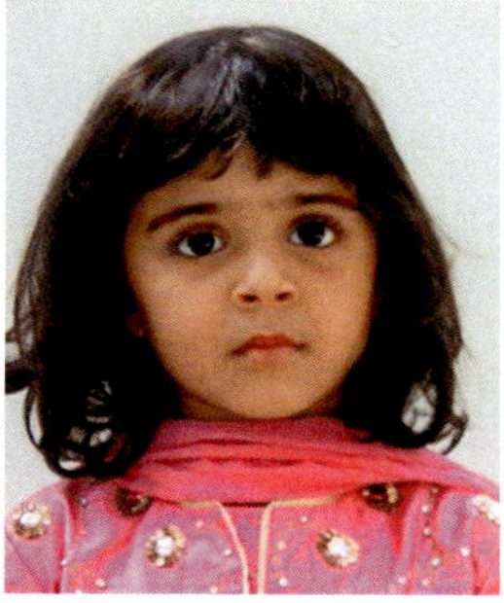

Granddaughter Tara.

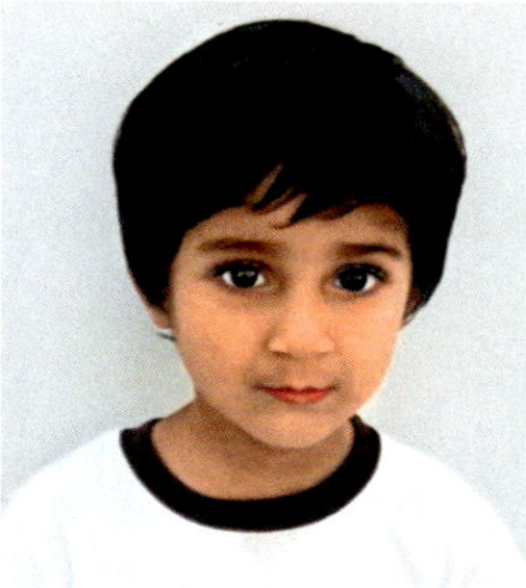

Grandson Jai.

Grandson Rahul.

With daughter Pia.

Granddaughter Anushka.

Rajiv and Kavita flanked by daughters Savitri (right) and Anushka (left).

Indira with cousin Brig. K.N. Singh, Prem and Punam Narender Singh.

Indira with Blackie, her pet Alsatian.

Indira in Mussoorie in 1998.

Indira in 1999, a year before her helicopter accident.

Rajiv with Kavita on their wedding day on 8 February 1984.

Renuka with Rana Talwar on their wedding day on 26 December 1995.

Pia and Timmy Sarna on their wedding day on 2 November 2003.

Daughter-in-law Kavita with Gilda Gourley, Pamela Harper, Suzanne Cohn and Hemi Bawa at Pia's wedding.

Dr Peter Harper and Robin Farkas wearing turbans with Pamela Harper (extreme left) and Carol Farkas (second from right) at Pia's wedding.

Norman and Suzanne Cohn at Pia's wedding.

With Dr Peter Harper on my right and Dr David Helfet on my left at Pia's wedding.

At a polo match with Lt. Gen. Wadalia in 1960. I am at the extreme left and Lt. Gen. Wadalia third from left.

Prem and Renuka with a group of yearlings and broodmares at Qutab Stud Farm.

Lt. Gen. Wadalia with a young foal and a broodmare at Qutab Stud Farm.

A portrait of Indira by M.F. Husain in 1970.

M.F. Husain at DLF Corporate Office working on a painting titled *The Enchanting Damsel of Delhi*, depicting the evolution of the historic city into a modern metropolis.

A painting that M.F. Husain made specially for me.

DELHI
The enchanting damsel
Across the conclave ceiling above, floats the enchanting damsel of Delhi. The contours of her sensuous body speak four different languages — Devnagari, Urdu, English and Gurmukhi. For centuries, the two dominant communities in the city, reflected by her two faces, one a burning sun, the other moonlit serene, have co-existed in perfect harmony.
She has played host to hordes of visitors over the years. Indra rode on a thousand elephants to meet her. Emperor Ashoka held his three-headed lion high on a pillar pinned to her chest. A Khurja earthen pitcher embraces his beloved Persian Surahhi on the banks of the river Yamuna.
In fact, the Yamuna has been a mute witness to the many lovers of Delhi who came and lived with her, many of whom betrayed her. The Moghals came and left their horses behind. The British tiger suddenly appeared on her back. Overseas traders put the famed Kohinoor diamond in the crown, which ultimately found its way to foreign shores.
And finally came the white bowl that symbolises the power that tamed the tiger and made it surrender to a non-violent challenge — Gandhi's struggle for freedom.
In the words of the great Urdu poet of Delhi, Meer :
"DILLI JO SHEHER 'THA ALAME-INTEKHAB"
دلی جو شہر تھا عالم انتخاب"

Golfing friends get together at the Delhi Golf Club. (L to R): K.C. Mehra, J.M. Khanna, K.K. Mehra, I and Indira.

Memorable golfing times at Belfry near Birmingham, UK. (L to R): K.K. Mehra, Madhvi Bery, Indira Dhody, Indira, Kiran Khurana and Prem Mehra.

Dil Se friendly Golf Tournament at Lahore between India and Pakistan. I am sitting in the middle with dark glasses. The Indian team members wearing dark blue shirts are seated while the Pakistan team stands behind.

Golfing trip in Austria. (L to R): Peter Thukral, Mohan Chadha, Manjit Chadha, I, Indira, Kusum Bedi, Mona Thukral, Jeet Bedi.

Friends at the Gary Players Ranch in South Africa. (L to R): Moni Varma, Shobha Varma, Gary Player, Indira, I and Aruna de Souza.

Relaxing after golf with Dr David Helfet in Delhi.

Golf at 'Old Head' Course in Ireland. (L to R): Hira Sehgal, Vijay Bhardwaj, Peter Thukral and I.

Maharaja Golf Tournament in Italy. (L to R): Paolo Fresco, Gino, I and Lucio.

Friends in a horse-driven buggy riding around St. Mortiz. (L to R): Jeet Bedi, Hira Sehgal, Mohan Chadha, Manjit Chadha, Indira, Barbara Sehgal, Kusum Bedi and I.

Golfing trip to Ireland. (L to R): Hira Sehgal, Jeet Bedi, Arjun Sahay, Vijay Thapar, Sudhir Vasani, I and Peter Thukral.

At a golf tournament at DLF Golf and Country Club. From (L to R): Jeev Milkha Singh, I, Pradeep Mehra and Rajesh Dhingra.

Playing golf with Vijay Singh, the No. 1 golfer in the world in 2004, at DLF Golf and Country Club.

Day out with pigeons. Marlene Fresco with Indira and me in Milan.

Paolo Fresco with wife Marlene in Agra.

At Tiger Tops in Nepal. (L to R): Marlene Fresco, I, Indira, Corry, Paolo, Gino.

Some scenic views of DLF Golf and Country Club. (Contd.)

DLF's Gateway Tower has become an iconic landmark office complex in Gurgaon.

DLF's Corporate Park was instrumental in making Gurgaon one of the top Business Processing hubs in India. GE started its BPO operations from here.

Pinnacle, a classy residential condominium in Gurgaon, has set new standards for community living.

DLF's Plaza Tower was one of the early highrise office complexes in Gurgaon.

The DLF Cyber City in Gurgaon, spread over 17 million square feet, is one of the largest commercial complexes in the world providing workspace to lakhs of professionals. It has emerged as a major Business Process Outsourcing hub in India.

Residents of Aralias, luxury residential apartments, enjoy a scenic view of the DLF Golf and Country Club.

Promenade, one of the shopping malls created by DLF in New Delhi, brought in a new elevated shopping experience.

DLF's Emporio in New Delhi is India's first state-of-the-art luxury mall that houses numerous top international brands

Our family estate Lynndale: Spread over 110 acres in Mussoorie, at the foothills of the Himalayas, is a peaceful, pine-covered area full of natural beauty. (Contd.)

With Indira, Robin Farkas and Carol Farkas.

Standing (L to R): Tishi Khanna, Carol Farkas, Robin Farkas and James Gourley. Seated from left: I, Lily Khanna, Suzie Rose, Indira, Elie Rose and Gilda Gourley.

In Mussoorie. Standing in the back row (L to R): Gajindar Khurana, Kiran Khurana, Maj. Gen. Bery, Lily Khanna, Renu Puri, Madhvi Bery, Bugly Bambawale, Chander Talwar, Lalie Khanna and Tishi Khanna. Seated (L to R): Indira, I and Sati Puri.

DLF's Board of Directors. Sitting (L to R): Ms Pia Singh, Mr Rajiv Singh, I, Mr T.C. Goyal, Mr M.M. Sabharwal. Standing (L to R): Mr Ravinder Narain, Mr G.S. Talwar, Mr K. Swarup, Dr D.V. Kapur, Mr K.N. Memani, Mr B. Bhushan, Brig. (Retd.) N.P. Singh.

With Amrit Lal Jain on my left and Swarup Chand Ansal on my right. Amrit Lal Jain played a crucial role in acquiring large tracts of contiguous land in Gurgaon while Swarup Chand Ansal ensured that such transactions did not involve any legal hassles.

During the prize presentation ceremony of the DLF IPL Final in South Africa on 24 May 2009.

Striking the gong at the listing ceremony of DLF IPO at the Bombay Stock Exchange (BSE) on 5 July 2007.

Powerful influence With George Hoddy during his visit to the American Universal factory site in India. Hoddy was a mentor and guide to me.

With Marlene Fresco at a formal dinner party in New Delhi.

George Hoddy with wife Louis in Owosso, Michigan, USA.

Jaquine, Countess de Rochambeau, during her first visit to Delhi in December 1975.

At a dinner party in London (L to R): Ashi Burman, I, Kumkum Talwar, Indira and Nicky Talwar.

Ken Langone and his wife Elaine in Tuscany, Italy.

Trip to Lake Tahoe in USA (L to R): I, Mani Thapar, Tiny Thapar, Lakshmi Walia, Marilyn Spiegel and her husband Tom.

(L to R): Paolo Fresco, Anthony Lo Frisco, Lucio Lussu, Adrienne, Eleanor Lo Frisco, Marlene Fresco, Indira, Gino Fiore, Corry and I.

With Indira, Leonard Lauder and his son William.

A group of friends during a pheasant shoot with Lord Devonshire, James and Gilda Gourley in England. In front row standing: Indira is third from the left, Gilda Gourley fifth and I am sixth.

With Evelyn Lauder in New York.

Receiving a Doctorate from His Excellency Shri B.L. Joshi, Governor of Uttarakhand and Vice Chancellor of Dr Pant Agricultural University.

Family photo taken at the time of award by HSH Prince Albert II of Monaco. From left: I, Savitri, Pia, Timmy, HSH Prince Albert II of Monaco, Rajiv and Kavita with Indira sitting down.

Receiving the award of 'Officer of the Order of Saint Charles' from HSH Prince Albert II of Monaco. Daughter Pia and granddaughter Savitri are in the background.

The Padma Bhushan.

The 'Officer of the Order of Saint Charles'.

Receiving the Padma Bhushan from the President of India, Her Excellency Smt. Pratibha Devisingh Patil, on 31 March 2010.

had invested in DLF. He became their banker and business partner rolled into one. It was a unique model and it succeeded as there was not a single default in payment. Every month, on the allotted time and date, the DLF jeep would drive into the village with envelopes containing cash and documents to be signed. The villagers had become so trusting that most signed the documents without even asking what was written in them.

With this model of transparent transactions, DLF's reputation steadily grew. What consolidated it even further was that if any of the farmers wanted their money back, it was given without question. Many of them needed money for emergencies or weddings, and it was never refused. That was how DLF's financing worked. It was perhaps the only business model of its kind in the world. Chaudhry Saheb used it to develop DLF's first residential colonies across 5,800 acres in Delhi during the period shortly after Independence. By the mid 1960s, DLF had developed twenty-four colonies in Delhi, Ghaziabad, Gurgaon, Faridabad and Patiala. In Delhi, colonies like Hauz Khas, Greater Kailash I and II, Kailash Colony, Dilshad Garden, South Extension and Model Town had made DLF synonymous with quality and integrity. They are familiar names to any Delhi-ite. The company had created housing in areas where no habitation existed before. It was an extraordinary story of what out-of-the-box thinking can achieve. I don't know too many entrepreneurs in India who have built a flourishing business without any capital.

As in all Indian success stories, politics played a part. Chaudhry Saheb's close connection with Brahm Prakash almost led to his downfall. Brahm Prakash had been active in the freedom movement and was jailed several times during the Quit India movement. Back in 1945 when the British still ruled India, he had the vision to realize that cooperative societies could alleviate the hardships of poor villagers. He started organizing village and agriculture cooperatives. His organizational skills and commitment put him on the fast track and he rose to become chief minister of Delhi in 1952, a position he would hold for the next three years. As chief minister, he convinced Chaudhry Saheb to enter politics, giving him a ticket to contest the Delhi assembly elections from Delhi Cantonment as a Congress candidate. Chaudhry Saheb won and thereafter in the 1960s he was nominated as an alderman of the Delhi municipal corporation. In the 1967 parliamentary elections, Brahm Prakash again got him a Congress nomination to contest for the Lok Sabha parliamentary elections from south Delhi. This time, he lost. Politics would prove to be a bitter experience.

Jealousy and rivalry, both personal and political, would lead to the impression being created that the closeness between Chaudhry Saheb and Brahm Prakash had a more sinister motive and that DLF was actually owned and run by the chief minister with Chaudhry Saheb as a dummy proprietor. This, of course, was an outright falsehood, but opponents of Brahm Prakash within the Congress found it a clever ploy to undermine him. An attack on DLF was an attack on the chief minister. Although he had ceased to be chief minister after 1955, his popularity among the masses in Delhi remained high and he was a formidable political force. He was also in Nehru's good books but later fell out of favour. A silent but sustained campaign had been launched by his opponents to embarrass Brahm Prakash but the direct fallout was on DLF, which was the proxy target. His political career went downhill and with it, so did Chaudhry Saheb's. Later, he would realize that getting into politics had been one of his greatest mistakes. It was a lesson he learnt at a great cost.

Politics, however, can be an alluring temptress. Despite my father-in-law's negative experience, I too was almost seduced by the idea of standing for election. It was in the 1980s when I was doing well in business. I was assembling land to build Gurgaon and had become a familiar figure in the villages there. I used to spend a lot of time with the villagers, trying to convince them to sell their land, and became quite close to them. I knew the families well and had gone the extra mile to help them when they needed it. Seeing my popularity with them, major political parties started sending me feelers asking me to contest the 1986 parliamentary elections. I was flattered by the attention. In those days, it had become a fad for businessmen to contest elections. Hari Nanda of Escorts, for example, was one of them. I seriously contemplated taking up the offer. When I talked this over with Chaudhry Saheb, he narrated the lessons he had learnt by getting involved in active politics. He advised me that for a business like real estate, it was essential to maintain good relationships with all political parties and not be seen to be aligned with one party. Any active role on my part on behalf of one party, he said, would be suicidal.

I am glad I set my ego aside and had the sense to take his advice. Earlier, when he was an active player in politics, fate intervened in the form of the DDA. It signalled the end of DLF's rapid growth which, in fact, came to a sudden halt when the DDA Act of 1957 came into force. It gave the state-owned company the sole right to acquire land for property development. This meant that DLF could only develop the land it had acquired before the Act came into force. With DLF's growth path blocked, Chaudhry Saheb decided to diversify into manufacturing. It took me into an entirely new business trajectory, as head of two companies, American Universal and Willard India Limited, both joint ventures with US-based partners.

It was a whole new experience, one with new challenges and opportunities, but it was tragic to see what was happening to the capital's development with DDA coming into the picture. The agency started building residential flats and shops in Delhi at a frenetic pace, with little regard for aesthetics, construction standards, or quality of material. Sadly, what characterized its buildings were pathetically poor design, shoddy construction, and indifferent finish. Structures raised by the DDA were without any character and almost looked like clones of Soviet housing projects.

But for the middle classes in Delhi, the dream of owning a house was so all-encompassing that they were prepared to overlook the tacky interiors, poor construction material, uneven flooring, and congested neighbourhoods. The housing shortage was so desperate that these house owners were actually happy when they got an allotment in any DDA colony. They, of course, had no choice.

Today, construction flaws in these apartment blocks are visible in colonies like Mayur Vihar, Vasant Kunj, Sarita Vihar, and elsewhere. Due to poor construction, many of them are crumbling and in a state of disrepair. Those who invested their life savings in these flats had to pay a heavy price. One can often see cracked floors, peeling plaster, broken staircases, and seepage weakening the walls and structure of these flats. It was a depressing scenario, but I was certain about one thing: sooner or later, there would be a demand for quality housing. That was why the idea of returning to the real estate business stayed uppermost in my mind for the next decade or so. It did not take great intelligence to figure out that the housing needs of our rapidly growing cities could never be met by government agencies alone. Private developers would have to be allowed in some time in the future.

The ULCA, enacted in 1976, put a cap on the size of land ownership in urban India to prevent the possibility of real estate being concentrated in the hands of a few. Similar restrictions existed in neighbouring Noida in Uttar Pradesh. That left only Gurgaon in Haryana. Around that time, most of the urban land development in Gurgaon was done by the public development agency called Haryana Urban Development Authority. Licences to develop urban lands were not given to any private sector agency.

With DLF's expansion plans in cold storage, I got fully involved in the manufacturing business. In 1964, Chaudhry Saheb floated American Universal as a joint venture with Universal Electric Co. of USA and put me in charge of the project. The second venture was Industrial Cables Limited (ICL), where initially Chaudhry Saheb was the major equity holder. Its management was supervised by Devinder Singh, his younger brother. Later, Chaudhry Saheb transferred his entire equity holding to Devinder and disengaged himself from ICL by resigning as chairman of the company. ICL remained a profitable venture for several years.

As DLF was not pursuing any worthwhile real estate business at that time except the ongoing projects, it diversified into agricultural operations in north India by taking over the contract management of Sibia farm near Jind in Haryana. In south India, it had acquired large tracts in Karnataka and Andhra Pradesh for seed farming and grape cultivation. The business activity of DLF was thus divided into two separate entities. One related to agricultural operations and the other to its real estate business. While Chaudhry Saheb exercised overall control of all the DLF businesses, he continued to look after all the agriculture operations exclusively. He left the real estate operations predominantly to Shamsher Singh.

In retrospect, getting into agricultural operations was one of the most imprudent diversifications that DLF ever made. It had no experience in the area and because of this strategic error, DLF started suffering losses. It also diverted attention and focus from the real estate business. At that time, several other developers were aggressively engaged in the construction of commercial buildings on land acquired from DDA through auctions. As DLF did not participate in these auctions, it missed out on the golden opportunity that was staring it in the face. Instead, the energies of the company were being frittered away in pursuing its agricultural operations. As Shamsher did not see much promise in DLF due to its losses, he started his own business ventures that were unconnected to the core business of DLF. This led to the continuous decline of the real estate business.

Against this depressing background, the decision to revive DLF was one of the most crucial decisions I ever took. I gradually realized that my future was not in manufacturing batteries but in real estate. Having faced problems with the battery unit, I was determined not only to revive DLF, but also to succeed. Willard India may not have been a success, but it had taught me many lessons in running a business. When I disinvested Willard, I was only left with DLF, which had no worthwhile business and finances but had a good reputation and brand recognition. It wasn't an easy transition. There were virtually no similarities between the manufacturing business and the real estate business. They were like chalk and cheese. Acquiring land was a very different ball game requiring one to deal with a senior bureaucrat and a villager on the same day; both needed different styles of communication. Micro-managing all this required enormous effort and a good deal of research, and I was doing it all myself.

Those were tough times. Every day brought new challenges, new disappointments. But, somehow I kept trying, refusing to let my optimism flag. I kept looking for silver linings and deep within, I knew I could make it. Then, out of the blue, DLF received a windfall. In the late 1970s, the Supreme Court awarded DLF a monetary compensation of Rs. 1.38 crore (Rs. 13.8 million) as the government had acquired a lot of its land in Greater Kailash II in the early 1960s. However, since most of it would go in paying tax, we needed to figure out a way to get access to additional finance to grow the real estate business. Our financial advisers came up with the option to merge American Universal with DLF for more efficient tax planning. When I examined this proposal in depth I observed that since a substantial percentage of equity shares of American Universal were held by Universal

Electric, our family shares in the merged entity would drop to below 50 per cent after the merger, and we would effectively lose control of the company. Notwithstanding these complications I decided to take the risk of going ahead with the merger. Having taken this decision I remained focused on achieving my twin objectives, namely, merger and thereafter acquisition of Universal Electric shares. However, I encountered an unforeseen problem. The control of Universal Electric had by then shifted to Electric Storage Battery Inc. (ESB) in Philadelphia, which was against the merger. I flew to the United States to ask George Hoddy to help me to prevail on ESB to give their consent. The positive aspect was that overall control of all international activities of ESB, including Universal Electric, had passed to John Davenport.

The challenge, however, remained since I had to convince the top management of ESB to not only agree to our merger proposal but also to selling their entire equity shareholdings in our Indian venture. At my request, Davenport called a meeting of top officials of ESB and Universal Electric. As was to be expected, there was strong opposition by ESB to the proposal for Universal Electric to sell their shares in India. For me, a merger without subsequent sale of shares by Universal would have been meaningless. In the merged entity, Universal Electric would have remained a dominant shareholder.

I shuttled between Philadelphia and Owosso to mobilize support for the merger. Hoddy proved to be the catalyst. It was he who finally convinced Bill Lawson, who was president of Universal Electric, to back my proposal. When the final meeting was chaired by Davenport, Lawson and Hoddy supported the move while the legal and business heads of ESB opposed it.

Over the years both Indira and I had developed a close personal relationship with Davenport and his charming wife Suzaine. Suzaine and John were a happily married couple. He was a widely travelled person and had acquired considerable contacts all over the world. They were both easy to get along with. Indira also had the uncanny knack of getting along with my friends abroad. Her closeness to Suzaine helped me in forging a long-lasting friendship with Davenport. Prior to the meeting mentioned earlier, Indira and I had visited Davenport at his residence. Over a drink that evening, I asked for his help in getting me a positive decision in the forthcoming meeting. I explained my predicament and told him that by deciding to revive DLF recently, I had taken the biggest gamble of my life. I needed his support to get ESB to agree to the merger of DLF with American Universal and thereafter to sell all the equity holdings of Universal Electric to me in India. I also explained to him the complicated government regulations involved in granting permission to foreign companies to offload their shares to Indian entities.

I continued to shuttle between Owosso and Philadelphia several times over ten days till Davenport was finally able to obtain concurrence from other senior executives of ESB. I had been pestering Davenport for his help to resolve the problem. One day he remarked, 'KP – what you are asking is a very tall order, but for you I will do it.'

True to his word, he overruled the legal department of ESB and went by the advice of Lawson and Hoddy to approve my proposal.

After the courts in India had approved the merger, we put in an application to the Government of India to permit Universal Electric to disinvest their shares in India. In those days, there was a stipulation that if a foreign organization wished to dispose off its shareholding in India, it had to first offer the shares to public financial institutions and government-owned insurance companies. Only if they refused to purchase the shares would permission be given to an Indian entity to buy the shares. At that point my family shareholding of DLF Universal Limited was 59.47 per cent. Without our acquisition of ESB's equity this would have dropped to well below 40 per cent after the merger.

It was vital to my plan to revive DLF that I should retain absolute control by a majority holding through acquisition of Universal Electric's shareholdings. Since I was not sure of obtaining government permission, we launched a rights issue which was not subscribed by Universal Electric but fully subscribed by me. This was basically a contingency plan to ensure that if the government did not give permission, I would still have a slender majority in the company by owning 50 per cent of the shares. In contemporary parlance, it is called 'Plan B', and it is, in my view, an essential strategy to deal with the uncertainties of doing business in India.

To ensure I was on the right track, I decided to seek the advice of the under secretary in the office of the Controller of Capital Issues in the Ministry of Finance. Venkatraman was a low-profile but highly knowledgeable bureaucrat who was an expert on the complicated rules and intricacies of the Indian financial markets. He was an encyclopaedia on such matters. He was also an expert on dosas, which brought home the fact that sometimes the way to a man's mind is through his stomach! One day, on a visit to his office, I saw him devouring dosas from the office canteen. 'I understand you are a great connoisseur of dosas?' I remarked.

'Nothing can match the crisp dosas that my wife makes,' he replied and then asked, 'Why don't you drop in at my flat in Kaka Nagar over the weekend for breakfast?' I gladly accepted.

He was a godfearing man and would smear his forehead with holy ash every morning after puja. We hit it off. I started relishing the taste of dosas and we discussed a range of subjects. What struck me was how he made complex laws so easy to understand. A few weeks later I told him about my dilemma regarding acquiring the shares of Universal Electric. He studied the issue and found that when we established American Universal there was a collaboration agreement between DLF, the Indian promoters, and Universal Electric. The agreement had a clause that if either party wished to disinvest partially or fully, its holding would be offered to the other party first and only then to outside investors. Venkatraman pointed out that as the clause was approved by the Government of India, a case could be made out to allow disinvestment to the shareholders of DLF instead of public financial institutions. The only hitch was that it required a special approval from the Controller of Capital Issues.

Normally, a top corporate lawyer would have been hired to handle such a complicated case but I chose to handle it myself. Venkatraman had shown me the way to proceed and I was confident I could use his advice to get the official decision in my favour. He had also suggested that I meet Nitesh Sengupta, the Controller of Capital Issues. Sengupta was an intelligent bureaucrat with a positive attitude, always willing to listen to an argument with an open mind. When I met Sengupta I showed him the clause of the collaboration agreement that required Universal Electric to offer its shares to its original Indian co-promoter, DLF. His view was that though it may be legally correct, it would not be possible for the government to give approval to ESB to sell its shares directly to DLF. Instead, the government could consider permitting ESB to offer its shares to all shareholders of DLF Universal since it was already a public limited company.

Armed with this information, I again flew to Philadelphia along with the draft of the application that Universal Electric needed to submit to the Controller of Capital Issues in India seeking permission to disinvest its equity shares in DLF Universal. Since it had to be cleared by the legal head of ESB who had earlier opposed it, I did not want to take a chance and decided to be there in person to ensure the application was worded exactly as advised by Venkatraman, and conformed to existing government regulations. As I had expected, ESB's legal head objected to the issue of having to sell their entire equity holding to me.

Once again, Davenport came to my rescue and invited us both

for dinner, where he convinced his legal adviser that since ESB had already decided to sell the shares, it might as well be done gracefully the way I wished. I waited till the document was ready and signed and brought it back with me. The application was filed and thanks to my dosa breakfasts with Venkatraman, I finally got official approval for DLF shareholders to buy all the shares of Universal Electric.

I had some savings but not enough to buy the shares, so I decided to sell my property in Bulandshahr. The acquisition of Universal Electric shares was crucial to my future plans. Once government permission was granted, we were able to acquire a substantial portion of the shares. It raised our holding in DLF Universal from 59.47 per cent to 71.65 per cent. Since additional capital was needed to finance the growth of DLF, we mobilized this through successive rights issues in 1984 and 1989, raising my family's holding to 86.18 per cent. This gave me a great sense of satisfaction and was a huge confidence booster. I had battled very hard and succeeded in getting absolute control of DLF. Had I not, our family would have been reduced to a minority and the DLF story would have had a very different ending. That experience was to prove invaluable in the coming years as I got down to dealing with the challenge of turning DLF into an organization on par with the best in the world.

That dream would be incomplete without a corporate headquarters that symbolized what DLF stood for in the real estate space. It had to be dominant, architecturally eye-catching, and the first of its kind. Just a few days after I had taken the decision to revive the DLF, Chaudhry Saheb called me over to his office. Reaching there, I found R.K. Jain, DLF's company secretary and head of the legal department, with Prithpal Singh, the then chief engineer of DLF, and R.K. Dhawan, a former assistant engineer who had started his real estate business after quitting DLF. Chaudhry Saheb realized that getting government approvals for Narendra Place was going to be very cumbersome and as Dhawan had good networking skills, he might be a better choice than anyone else in DLF. He had therefore approved the signing of a collaboration agreement between DLF and Dhawan based on equal partnership with Dhawan giving a token advance of Rs. 2.5 million as his consideration of entering into this agreement. R.K. Jain had drawn up an agreement making Dhawan a partner with DLF to develop Narendra Place. Chaudhry Saheb remarked that although the agreement had already been vetted by Jain, I might wish to see it before he signed it. As it was a bulky agreement and would take time to read, I told both Dhawan and Prithpal to see me the next day. After they left, I requested Chaudhry Saheb to withhold his decision and let me deal with both of them.

'We should not go ahead with giving Narendra Place to Dhawan. We should do it ourselves,' I said.

Chaudhry Saheb was a bit sceptical of my newfound enthusiasm.

'Getting all the permissions to develop Narendra Place is a complicated and long-drawn affair,' he cautioned. 'I don't believe you can do it as you don't have the experience.'

I reacted by saying, 'I know I'll be able to do it. Please, leave this to me to handle in my own way.'

Finally, he agreed. I told Dhawan the next day that I was not interested in his proposal. I could see the surprise on his and Prithpal's face when I told them, 'The scenario has completely changed. I am now a buyer. If you have any proposals where I can buy something worthwhile or collaborate, I might be interested.'

It was my way of sending a message to the market that the position in DLF had changed. From being passive players we were now aggressive acquirers. To start with, I tried to see what we could do to kick-start the DLF business. The only worthwhile asset we had was Narendra Place. It was a semi-circular structure constructed in 1928 by renowned builder Sobha Singh, the father of writer Khushwant Singh. It needed to be demolished and rebuilt to create value but it was occupied by tenants who had lived there for over fifty years. Even if we managed to get them to leave after paying compensation, we would still need myriad regulatory approvals. I spent the next two weeks understanding these. Then I analysed every step required and decided to oversee the procedures. I deliberately avoided delegating the job of interacting with officials of government departments to get the permissions as I realized that it was best to do the networking myself.

The immediate challenge was to get the plot delinked by DDA from its comprehensive area development plan to an individual plot development basis. It called for the highest level of networking with the DDA and the state and Central governments. We spent a couple of years trying to make these officials see reason, arguing that if they did not allow construction on an individual plot ownership basis, the area would not get redeveloped. It would be almost impossible for all owners in the Janpath Lane area to agree to a common plan of development. Fortunately, S.C. Gupta, commissioner of planning at DDA, was willing to listen. Our architects made numerous presentations before they finally secured DDA's permission to delink the Narendra Place plot from the comprehensive redevelopment plan of the adjoining area. This entitled DLF to construct a building on this plot in accordance with the prevailing building and town planning regulations.

At that time, basements were allowed to be constructed only within the building limits of a property and not extend beyond it. Basements were reserved for car parking and housing of service equipment like generators and not for commercial or residential use. We anticipated that with economic growth, there would be a dramatic increase in the number of cars. We wanted permission to create multi basements up to the setback lines of our property. Our reasoning was straightforward, but it took several months to convince DDA officials. Eventually, it was worth all the trouble we went through. After we got permission, it became a norm for all commercial buildings in Delhi. The end result was that thousands of vehicles can now be parked underground.

The toughest hurdle was to get permission of the Archaeological Survey of India (ASI). Since it was next to Jantar Mantar, we were told that we could only construct up to a maximum height of three floors as going higher than that would obstruct the sun's rays from falling on the monument that told the exact time of day. This sounded like a valid argument and I thought our dream of building a ten-storey corporate office was dead in the water. Yet, I still looked for a way out. As micro-management was embedded in my DNA, I asked the architect of our project, S. Bose, to show me how the sun moved every day of the year. We were amazed to find that the sundial would not be affected at all as the rays falling on it were not coming from the side where our building was to be constructed but from a totally different direction. Logically it should not matter even if we built a skyscraper.

Initially, even our architects were sceptical, but after a detailed survey they realized that we had a possible way out of the stalemate. We made a detailed presentation to top ASI officials about the movement of the sun all through the year. They were equally amazed at what we had found, but wanted to do an independent study to make sure that we were not trying to fool them into giving permission. After their own exhaustive survey, the ASI granted a no objection certificate to the New Delhi Municipal Council to sanction our building plans for up to ten floors. What was once considered impossible became possible by just following a passing thought to its logical conclusion. However, that was not the end of the matter. We still had to get permission under ULCA, permission from the Central government for changing land use, and, most importantly, persuade the tenants to leave.

I was well prepared with enough background and research and I felt I had the necessary skills to convince officials of my intentions and how it would benefit the city. I must have made hundreds of visits to meet various officials over nearly nine years to get this done. A lot of people ask me how I managed DLF and also kept going for all those years chasing different levels of bureaucracy to negotiate the intricate aspects of regulatory approval. My answer is simple: I respected and understood the apprehensions of officials who worked under the complicated and cumbersome norms set by the government.

In the bureaucratic work culture, nobody questions the wisdom of rules and regulations, however illogical they may be. It is for entrepreneurs like us to get them to see reason so they start to question some of the archaic rules that they operate under. There will always be some officials who see the need for legislation to be changed or tweaked to meet the needs of changing times. I knew it was only logic that would succeed at the end of the day. All it required was good research, patience and stamina to keep chipping away at the steel frame, as the bureaucracy was called. It was not that I did not trust other colleagues to do the networking. It is just that it was a very complex job and one needed to multitask all the time, dealing with sensitive people at different levels of authority. I felt it was for me to handle the task, and the responsibility for success or failure had to be mine.

Once we had secured all the necessary regulatory approvals, we were ready to start construction, except that we now faced the challenge of convincing nearly fifty tenants who had acquired rights of continued occupation under the rent control Act. It took a combination of persuasion and substantial monetary compensation to the tenants to make them leave the building. All of them eventually accepted the generous financial terms we offered and moved out, all except one feisty lady.

Ruksana Sultana was something of a media celebrity, an

influential political leader who had been close to Sanjay Gandhi during the Emergency. She was a glamorous, vivacious woman with film connections: she was the daughter of Zarina, the elder sister of Begum Para, the Bollywood siren of the 1950s. Ruksana lived in a ground-floor flat, was financially well off, and refused to move. DLF was forced to file a petition in the court to have her evicted. The court passed a decree asking her to vacate. Her political influence had waned but she was as stubborn as the proverbial mule. A bailiff from the court along with the police arrived to evict her but she locked herself in and refused to open the door. It was a stalemate. The police were wary because of her background and the fact that she was a divorced woman living alone (her daughter would later marry actor Saif Ali Khan).

My office was on the second floor of the building, and I could look down from one of the rear windows into her courtyard. One of her windows was slightly open and I could see a number of rough-looking men armed with spears. I was told that they were her supporters from the Jama Masjid area. If the police tried to break in, it could become a communal issue. It was a volatile situation. In an impulse decision, I decided it was not worth confronting Ruksana like this, and I should deal with her using patience, perseverance and tact. In today's parlance, you might call it 'Gandhigiri'. I ran downstairs and requested the bailiff and the police to leave. They showed me the court order and said they could easily force her out of the house, but I told them it was not required. They left wondering why I was taking her side when I was the one trying to get her out.

Jain, who had fought the case in the court and then got the bailiff to oust her, was livid. He told me that I was doing the wrong thing and that she would have to leave on that very day. He was a senior employee, and one I respected, but I had to overrule him and said that Ruksana should be left alone.

She was no stranger. She was well known in Delhi's social circles and I had met her on a number of occasions at parties and gotten to know her fairly well. I had always found her warm and friendly. Thanks to the media hype around her political affiliations, she was much misunderstood. Later that day, I knocked on her door.

'I know why you are here. I have absolutely no intention of leaving,' she said gruffly as soon as she opened the door.

I smiled and replied, 'I am not even asking you to leave. Shamsher has praised your coffee-making skills and I thought that I could sample those today.'

She was not taken in by all this but she was a cultivated woman who would never refuse a coffee to a visitor she knew. We had met just the previous night at a dinner party. We sat in her living room and chit-chatted for a while, enjoying the coffee and the small talk. Before taking leave, I said to her, 'Your coffee is excellent, you will have to send me a cup every day to my office or you will have me knocking at your door.'

Of course, she did not send coffee to my office, which gave me a chance to go down to her flat and talk with her almost daily. Numerous cups of coffee were downed as we chatted about various subjects, never once bringing up the eviction issue. As time went by, she started enjoying our coffee chats.

In fact, we actually became good friends. Weeks and months passed. I wanted to win her over to my side and not have her thrown out. It was a friendly gesture on my part and it worked. One day, I bumped into her at a dinner-and-dance party when she inquired, 'Am I becoming an obstacle to your construction plans?'

'We have got the necessary approvals but you can continue to stay there as long as you want,' I told her. 'Or, alternatively, we can help you find another apartment.'

'I would like to leave and not be a problem for you any more,' she replied.

I would have even agreed to pay her more compensation than the other tenants, but she refused. She moved out without any anger or bitterness. We continued to remain good friends even after she had vacated the flat. It was yet another lesson in life, that the spirit of friendship, communication and tact can work better than legal threats and force. It's an approach that has helped me numerous times in growing our business.

We kept in touch even though she used to spend a lot of time in Goa. Suddenly, one day the news came of how the outgoing and effervescent Ruksana was no more. It came as a great shock as she was so full of life and spread that energy wherever she went. She was too young to die, but a sudden illness robbed us of a good and genuine friend who always brought cheer in every gathering she attended.

After Ruksana left Narendra Place, we started work on our corporate office called the DLF Centre. As the company was growing and I had ambitious plans, I wanted a building that would stand out for its design and grandeur. I was too busy securing approvals and so my son, Rajiv Singh, took on the task of managing the project with Rajiv Malhotra as his project engineer and India's leading architect Hafeez Contractor in charge of the design.

It was my son's idea to make the building eye-catching and also set new standards of maintenance that subsequently became the gold standard for corporate offices in the country. DLF Centre became the second building in India after the American Centre in Kolkata to have granite slabs on its exterior. The granite was sourced from Sadahalli near Bangalore. Trains full of granite slabs accompanied by artisans came all the way from Karnataka. Rajiv wanted it to be special so he set high standards with its design, construction and aesthetics.

International clients, who had negotiated for office space, were equally particular. British Airways, for instance, sent four specialists from Heathrow in London to inspect the building's firefighting equipment and returned fully satisfied. Other corporate offices followed our design. The DLF Centre was a gamechanger in corporate office design and maintenance. It changed the skyline of Parliament Street and also changed the fortunes of DLF. After we moved into it in October 1992 the company has gone from strength to strength.

In quieter moments, I often think of the mental and physical struggle I went through for almost nine years just to get regulatory approvals. I wonder how I kept going and never ever thought of giving up despite all the people who told me it would never happen. Today, the DLF Centre stands majestically next to Jantar Mantar, the modern and the ancient, both symbols of a proud and innovative India. Having an architecturally impressive headquarters and well-planned interiors that are maintained to the highest standards acts as a motivation tool for our employees. The DLF Centre is something everyone who works at DLF is proud of.

I was once asked what the secret of my success was. I have followed a simple strategy: quickly assess what is doable and what is not. If a regulation can be changed by advocacy, it is doable. If the law has to be broken to achieve something, it is not doable. To understand this, we need to equip ourselves with enough knowledge of the subject and therefore determine what can and cannot be done.

Determination, courage, prudent risk-taking and perseverance have always remained my key traits. DLF had to go through so many challenges and hurdles before we could make it what it is today. We had to deal with a biased Central minister and later chief minister of Haryana who was determined to crush DLF. He managed to keep us in check for almost twenty years, from the 1970s to the 1990s. But for this, DLF would have grown much faster and much earlier. There were numerous false allegations, court cases and punitive actions which his government indulged in to checkmate DLF. It was a lonely and exhausting battle but we fought every step of the way, never allowing personal vendetta to affect our pride and ethical standards.

I also had to deal with laws such as the ULCA which affected practically every state in the country. It was steeped in socialist thinking and stipulated that if a person was holding land in excess of certain prescribed limits, it would be taken over by the government. In the case of Delhi, this limit was arbitrarily fixed at about 500 square metres. DLF was the most affected since most of our properties were sold to buyers who had made payment on instalment basis spread over many years. Accordingly, the title deeds of such properties stayed with DLF and were handed over to the buyers only after all the instalments were paid.

In 1976, when this Act came into force, there were thousands of plots sold in different colonies in Delhi where ownership remained with DLF till the full instalments were paid by the customers. It was a Catch-22 situation. The government, using the Act, could club holdings of all unbuilt properties together to ascertain individual permissible ownership limit. This meant that DLF customers who had made substantial part payments for their properties earlier could be deprived of ultimately owning them. The implications were frightening not only for DLF but also the property owners. Both stood to lose. Many of those who had invested in DLF plots and were paying instalments panicked.

It required out-of-the-box thinking. I made an announcement that all clients who wanted refunds were free to get them from DLF. In fact, I asked T.C. Goel, DLF's deputy general manager, finance (now, DLF's MD), to quickly arrange for short-term loans so that refunds could be made. I did not want a single client to feel that we had shortchanged him. Goel and B. Bhushan, vice president, taxation, formed a good team and worked hard through the crisis and succeeded.

Although the Act was full of loopholes, it had checkmated DLF. There was a general perception amongst the public that this Act was aimed at hindering the growth of DLF. I have always seen that when life closes one window, it opens another somewhere else. While there was a general gloom in DLF, Jain, our company secretary, who was a seasoned colleague of Chaudhry Saheb, gave us a ray of hope. He rushed into my office one day and showed me a clause in Section 20 of the Act that empowered state governments to give exemptions under certain conditions. After studying it, I was convinced that the next step was to work towards getting the Central government to issue guidelines to various state governments authorizing them to grant exemptions in certain cases of hardship.

I am proud to say that hardly any of DLF's clients asked for refunds as they trusted us fully to safeguard their interests. Instead they joined us to plead with the Central government to issue guidelines for exemption under Section 20. It was apparent that unless exemption was given to such cases where instalment payments had been made, a grave injustice would be done to the public. It could also trigger agitations around the country. It was therefore logical for the government to grant such exemptions as this was in the public interest. It called for intense networking with the Ministry of Housing and the Ministry of Law. I spent months interacting with government officials at various levels to convince them why such exemptions should be granted. I also got various chambers of commerce to represent the interests of plot holders.

Finally, I succeeded in getting the guidelines issued by the Central government. It was this one single action that enabled thousands of property owners of DLF colonies in Delhi to become millionaires overnight. This brought tremendous credibility to DLF which continues even now. Many of them went on to invest in new DLF properties and became goodwill ambassadors of the company.

Real estate in India is in a constant process of discovery. Norms of revenue measurement that are in vogue even today were prescribed during British times! Once, when I was casually looking at one of our legal documents, I noticed that it did not distinctly specify the exact size of the plot and instead used the word 'admeasuring' before the word 'size' in reference to the plot. I found the same terminology in numerous other documents. For example, if the property was 500 square metres, in the sales agreement, it would say, 'admeasuring 500 square metres'. I wondered what it meant and so asked Saheb Singh Patwari, one of our revenue officials, about it. He had joined DLF after retiring from the Delhi government. I took him on as he was an expert on revenue matters. He said that while it was easy to measure a flat piece of land, it was almost impossible to accurately measure undulant land. So, the word 'admeasuring' was used to indicate the approximate size. This methodology had carried on since British days. I kept thinking about it. Land measurements cannot be so vague or approximate.

Around the same time, I happened to visit Greater Kailash II with Saheb Singh. This area was mostly uneven and sloping. I asked him to show me what 'admeasuring' meant in the context of that particular area. He explained that conventional methods would not work to measure such land. That got me thinking about the implications of the word 'admeasuring'. I wondered how one could reconcile the figure of total land purchased by

DLF with the land handed over to property buyers and the common spaces given to the Municipal Corporation of Delhi (MCD). Eventually these figures must reconcile with each other. But Saheb Singh felt that it might not be possible in case a colony was built on uneven terrain.

The issue kept haunting me and I decided to plunge deeper into it. I constituted a special task force under Saheb Singh along with a town planning architect to go into the matter in depth. They worked extensively and finally determined that DLF had purchased much more land in Greater Kailash II than what had been handed over to plot holders and the MCD. The reconciliation of this excess land was necessary in view of the growing market value of properties in the colony.

I went and met the chief town planner of MCD, who was a very knowledgeable person. Listening to Saheb Singh's reasoning, he quickly understood the anomaly and implications but said that it would be impossible to re-assess the issue as DLF had already handed this colony over to the MCD several years earlier. I then met the municipal commissioner and the chairman of the MCD's standing committee, Deep Chand Bandhu of the Congress party, as well as the leader of the opposition, Shanti Desai of the BJP, to apprise them of the peculiar situation arising out of the word 'admeasuring'. I wanted to apprise them about this discrepancy since it related to the sensitive issue of urban land. I also did not want DLF to be accused of trying to gain extra land or compensation that was not legally due to it.

Subsequently, several government agencies carried out a series of investigations. Eventually, they all came to the conclusion that there was some additional area in Greater Kailash II that belonged to DLF. To compensate for what DLF had lost, readjustment of the existing layout plans of Greater Kailash II was necessary. After a series of negotiations, spread over several months, MCD finally approved a revised layout plan of Greater Kailash II which resulted in the availability of an additional 3.6 acres to DLF for development of a group housing residential project. We accepted the decision even though our estimates said that we were entitled to get around 25 acres.

Around the same time, prolonged litigation was going on between the MCD and DLF regarding the ownership of community sites in Delhi colonies developed by DLF. All along DLF had maintained that these sites belonged to it. The MCD argued that these sites should belong to them, since they had been developed as part of the common areas. I noticed that the majority of these sites had been encroached upon. Nobody was benefiting from the prolonged litigation and growing encroachment of remaining sites. I said this to the commissioner and the chairman of the standing committee and added that it would be in the public interest to arrive at an out-of-court settlement. Finally, after long negotiations at various levels of the MCD, an amicable settlement between the MCD and DLF was reached. Many were surprised that opposing political parties in the standing committee of the MCD had reached a unanimous decision. Ultimately, logic was the winner. This was a milestone in DLF's history.

My curiosity to figure out what 'admeasuring' meant led to the company finally getting back some precious land. DLF is now developing the plot into a highrise residential area. DLF will earn more revenue from the sale of the built-up area of this small piece of land of 3.6 acres than it had earned since its inception till the date of this amicable settlement with MCD in 1989. Just one word in a legal document had tickled my curiosity and look where it led. I often use this example to tell our employees not to be afraid to question issues they do not understand or feel are unfair.

Today, it seems almost surreal to picture the trials and tribulations that DLF went through to arrive where it is. In 1975, it was on the verge of closing down. For twenty years, we were stopped in our tracks by a stubborn political leader. Then there was the long and arduous advocacy for change in archaic laws and town planning norms to get multiple approvals, discovering a loophole in the Urban Land Ceiling Act that averted a complex and commercially crippling situation, unravelling what 'admeasuring' meant and finally being able to develop Gurgaon into a modern city. It took years of my life and gave me more grey hair than I bargained for, but it was a journey worth taking. Mahatma Gandhi has said, 'Men often become what they believe themselves to be. If I believe I cannot do something, it makes me incapable of doing it. When I believe I can, I acquire the ability to do it even if I didn't have it in the beginning.' It is an inspiring thought that has helped me understand the power of dreams.

11

DLF

GROWTH AND TRANSITION

DURING THE SUMMER of 1980, I spent a great deal of time thinking about ways to revive DLF's real estate business, weighing various options, trying to create new opportunities. Uppermost in my mind was the need to launch a new land development project. I was not interested in small-scale, run-of-the-mill, bread-and-butter schemes. I was fired with the ambition of doing something on a scale that would give the DLF brand the image boost it needed to make an emphatic comeback.

I would have preferred to start land development activities in Delhi but that was ruled out, thanks to the rigid provisions of the Urban Land Ceiling Act. I had to look elsewhere. I had my eyes on a desolate stretch of land in Gurgaon district. The location seemed good, just a few miles across the border from Delhi, not too far from the airport and right on the main highway to the city of Jaipur. The land itself was a vast expanse of numerous small agricultural holdings, with large stretches of sparse vegetation and tiny villages dotting the otherwise inhospitable and uninhabited countryside.

I could sense the opportunities. But I had to make sure the land was available for purchase, I had to consider the commercial viability of the venture and I also had to find out more about local land laws and regulations. I made frequent visits to the site to familiarize myself with the lay of the land, striking up conversations with the few local inhabitants who approached me out of curiosity braving the heat of the day.

As far as I knew, Haryana was one of the few states in the country that had not enacted the draconian ULCA. This would later help the state grow faster than many others, but at that time nobody was interested in a place like Gurgaon, a featureless little town in the middle of nowhere. Paradoxically, that was precisely the reason I was keen on buying land in the area and taking up the challenge of developing it into a township that would become the centre of activity.

One site in particular had caught my eye. It was an area of around 40 acres situated some 50 metres away from the Gurgaon–Faridabad highway near Chakkarpur and Sikanderpur Ghosi villages. It was mostly wilderness with a terrain criss-crossed by small gulches where one could still find wild blue bulls roaming. To reach that spot, I had to pass the majestic Qutab Minar along the way. I would glance at the towering monument, wondering if it would bring me inspiration. It did, and of the most unexpected kind.

On one of these visits, on a particularly scorching day, I had parked my car near a village well and sat down to evaluate the potential. It was difficult to imagine anyone ever wanting to invest in a house or flats in the midst of a wilderness so far away from the heart of Delhi. In the 1980s, driving from Delhi to Gurgaon was nothing like it is today. It was quite an ordeal, without roads, without human habitation for miles around. Yet,

I was beginning to see the logic of starting a DLF project there. The way I saw it, once the city of Delhi started to expand to accommodate the growth in population, the Gurgaon area would provide the space for the spread of urbanization. To help myself think more clearly, I sought a small shaded area under some trees. It also offered an opportunity to chat with the villagers visiting the well where a camel was being used to draw up the water. I was sitting on a charpoy, the ubiquitous string cot used by the rural folk in the area, when an incident occurred that changed the course of my endeavours. In fact, it was this one incident that was to transform Gurgaon from a rural wilderness into an international city.

I was chatting with a villager when a speeding jeep screeched to a halt nearby. The driver of the vehicle emerged and asked if he could get a can of water as his engine was overheating. It was around noon and the midday sun was unbearable. I went across to ask the person to join me in the shade while the water was being fetched to cool the engine. It was only when I came close that I realized it was none other than Rajiv Gandhi.

Rajiv used to love driving out of Delhi and often used to visit his farmhouse on the outskirts of Mehrauli. He also liked to use the route across Gadaipur to a village called Mandi on the road towards Gurgaon. He was on one such trip when his vehicle had started to give problems. Rajiv had just quit his career as a pilot with Indian Airlines. He was taking his first hesitant steps into politics and was trying to get a broader picture of the country and its problems. He had collected some friends like Arun Singh, his cousin Arun Nehru and other bright young people to act like a think tank to brainstorm on various issues and offer suggestions to Prime Minister Indira Gandhi.

His entry into politics had been sudden and tragic, following the death of his younger brother, Sanjay Gandhi, in a plane crash. Rajiv had become a huge emotional support for his grief-stricken mother as she had been very dependent on Sanjay, her anointed political heir.

'What are you doing in such a desolate place and that too at the height of summer?' Rajiv asked me after I had introduced myself.

'I am in the real estate business and am inspired by the idea of creating a modern city on the outskirts of Delhi,' I replied.

He became interested and pressed me on the issue.

'What is holding it up and why don't you do it?' he asked.

I decided to be frank and upfront and told him all about the existing land laws and how the odds were stacked against private developers. I informed him that DLF had started acquiring land but there was little it could do unless regulations were amended to provide private developers a level playing field. I confessed that I was desperate and had my back against the wall trying to do something that seemed like an impossible dream. At that time, DLF had no money or business worth talking about. Banks were forbidden to give loans to purchase land. There was no such thing as housing loans. The only capital that DLF had was my optimism and determination to revive the company and make it a real estate giant. Rajiv sensed that.

Intrigued, he asked me for details on land legislation, statutes and town planning regulations which, I had told him, impeded urban growth and development and were out of sync with the needs and rising aspirations of modern India. As he grasped the overall picture, I could see his interest growing. We sat there for an hour and half, in the middle of nowhere, engaged in detailed discussions about the idea of creating an integrated, world-class township in Gurgaon.

That day I realized that this young politician could be an agent of change. He had an inquisitive mind, and an ability to grasp a complex subject very quickly and get to the core of the issue. He also came across as sincere and agreed that there was a need for fresh thinking on the subject. He expressed a desire to understand the issue in greater detail and suggested I meet him and Arun Singh at his New Delhi office on Motilal Nehru Marg where I could make a presentation, after which we could discuss what could be done.

I was elated at this chance encounter and the opportunity it offered me personally. I was just entering my fifties and while real estate was a high-risk business for private operators, age and existing laws were no barrier to dreaming big. I had experienced technical setbacks in my earlier business ventures but I was determined to make it as an entrepreneur. Since DLF was a family company in my control, with an established market reputation, I was convinced that my future lay in expansion into Gurgaon. In my dreams, night or day, I was already picturing a city with well-planned residential colonies and commercial and shopping areas. If one has to dream, dream big, I would constantly tell myself. My father-in-law had built colonies in an existing city; I would complement his efforts by building a city! A chance meeting with the future prime minister of India now offered me the opportunity to make that dream come true. I prepared myself carefully for the crucial meeting.

It had been a challenging and intense time in my life. The ULCA had been introduced, Willard India had to be kept afloat despite technological hitches and losses, there was no money, financial institutions were adding to the pressure and the burden of DLF was also weighing on me. Since I had taken an irreversible decision of reviving DLF, it became more than clear to me that the time had come to disengage myself from the manufacturing activities of Willard India and American Universal and instead concentrate on real estate.

On most mornings, I would go across to my father-in-law's house adjoining mine on Aurangzeb Road in the heart of New Delhi for a morning cup of tea and a chat about DLF. Chaudhry

Saheb, as everyone called him, kept saying that though DLF had lost heavily due to the ULCA, the private sector's role in the real estate business could not be ignored and it would be back with a bang. Such words of wisdom instilled a sense of added confidence and optimism in me. I also remembered George Hoddy's advice to me many years ago about lobbying to change laws rather than having to circumvent or break them. Now, with the meeting with Rajiv scheduled, I had a chance to do exactly that.

I arrived at Rajiv's office with a detailed presentation on how the urban landscape could be transformed if archaic laws were changed and the private sector made a partner in township development. I also tried to portray what it would mean for India in the long run. I started by outlining that the requirement of urban housing was falling way short of demand. I also explained how the private sector could play an important role in developing houses for the vulnerable sections in a planned manner. I then detailed the complexities of getting government approvals for any private housing project. Rajiv and Arun Singh listened attentively, interjecting with their own questions, and I sensed that this was a god-sent opportunity.

The biggest hurdle to private sector involvement in urban development were politicians, bureaucrats and policy makers who would have to be convinced about why it should be allowed. It required intense lobbying to drive home the logic and get the laws and regulatory norms changed. I knew I was the only one who could bring this about as the real estate sector at that time did not have anyone else who could or would put things in the right perspective. On the political front, Rajiv and Arun Singh had the clout and approach to bring about that change as well.

At the end of the meeting, they advised me to meet Bhajan Lal, the chief minister of Haryana, and lay out my plans for Gurgaon before him. Accordingly, I drove down to Chandigarh to meet Bhajan Lal. He had called in Khurshid Ahmed, the minister for finance and town planning in his government, to attend the meeting. Bhajan Lal was an astute politician and since I was meeting him on Rajiv's suggestion, he was eager to hear what I had come to see him about. I outlined my plan to develop a colony in Gurgaon.

Unlike other states, two laws existed in Haryana to regulate the development of urban areas. One law was called the Haryana Development and Regulation of Urban Areas Act, 1975, and the other one was the Punjab Controlled Areas Act of 1963. But according to a policy formulated by the Bansi Lal government in 1976, no licences were given to private agencies to develop such areas despite the existence of laws, thereby putting the matter in the exclusive domain of the Haryana Urban Development Authority (HUDA).

Khurshid Ahmed categorically stated that the government could not be seen violating a policy it had formulated. The meeting was a failure. I had no choice but to go back to Rajiv and Arun Singh. Several meetings followed as we discussed the issue in depth. I kept emphasizing that we needed to change existing policies and regulations that were not just outdated but a barrier to rapid urban development. During my interactions with them, it was apparent that both were fully convinced about the failure of the public sector to cope with the rising demand for housing. Both had a clear vision of how Gurgaon should become a model city through substantially private sector development. They, however, wanted clear stipulations that while licences were granted to developers they would ensure that the interests of weaker sections of society were taken care of. I fully endorsed that view.

Arun Singh, being from the private sector himself, would eventually play the biggest role in ushering in long-awaited and long overdue change in legislations concerning urban development in Haryana. He was the one who called Ahmed and asked him to develop policy guidelines which would ensure that, while granting approvals for private sector development in Haryana, adequate regulatory safeguards were provided so that a certain percentage of houses or plots for the weaker sections of society would also be made available at government-prescribed prices. These regulations were intended to open up and encourage urban land development. The guidelines ultimately helped DLF along with other private sector developers like Ansals and Unitech to get licences for development of land in notified urban areas of Gurgaon.

The guidelines stipulated that all developed areas should have large open spaces in the form of green areas. The costs of providing onsite and offsite infrastructure would have to be financed by the private sector. Whereas the private sector would develop the entire onsite infrastructure at its cost, they were also tasked with mobilizing financial resources from property owners. This would be in the form of external development charges which were to be paid to HUDA to finance the cost of laying offsite infrastructure to the Gurgaon township areas. Finally, Ahmed developed the new terms and conditions by which the state government could reverse its earlier policy and allow the private sector into development of colonies and urban settlements in Haryana.

Khurshid Ahmed was a far-sighted politician and once he was convinced of the advantages of what I had proposed, he went ahead, with Bhajan Lal's backing. As Rajiv Gandhi and Arun Singh were also behind the plan, Bhajan Lal too got enthused by the idea. At first, he had expressed reservations on allowing private sector land developers, but after numerous meetings, he saw the possibilities of what a modern city would mean to the image and future of Haryana. Eventually, he took the bold step of issuing the first licence to DLF in April 1981 to develop 39.34 acres. I celebrated, assuming my worries were over. It would prove painfully premature.

Soon after the licence was issued, former chief minister Bansi

Lal, who was a bitter opponent of Bhajan Lal, raised a hue and cry saying it was a retrograde step. He organized a group of fellow MPs to meet Prime Minister Indira Gandhi to plead that no such licence should be granted in Haryana as it would hamper the growth of the public sector. Bansi Lal also organized several call attention motions and agitations in parliament to ensure that the private sector was not allowed to enter the field of urban land development in Haryana. All this resulted in the creation of a committee headed by the cabinet secretary that included the chief secretaries of states like Uttar Pradesh, Rajasthan and Haryana to examine issues of urban development all around Delhi. Earlier the view had been expressed by a section of the bureaucracy that allowing the private sector into urban development would lead to urban chaos and spoil the character of the National Capital Region (NCR).

Bureaucrats also did not want the private sector to get into the area of urban land development since they wanted to retain exclusive control over this economic activity. They had managed to rope in the media which came out with stories insinuating that the government was succumbing to pressure from DLF and other private developers. I was already fighting with my back against the wall and over and above that I had to fight all kinds of rumours that were being floated. For example, as soon as DLF started its operations after the issue of the first licence in April 1981 to develop land, I was told that Arun Nehru, who was an intelligent and bold functionary of Rajiv Gandhi's core group, was upset as he had heard that DLF had heavily bribed Bhajan Lal to get licences for developing around 40 acres in Gurgaon. I felt really slighted. We had got the licences after fulfilling every requirement of the applicable town planning regulations. The deal had been totally above board. It had taken us several months of hard work.

I wanted to clear the air and requested Amarinder Singh, the erstwhile maharaja of Patiala, who was also a good friend of Arun Nehru, to arrange a meeting with the Congress leader. I just wanted to lay the facts before him as I saw him as a bright emerging leader with vision. I would even have benefited from his experience. However, the meeting turned out quite differently. As soon as I entered his office, far from gaining from his advice, I was told that he knew that DLF had paid Rs. 160 million to Bhajan Lal to get the approval. I was taken aback by the allegation but I kept my cool and explained that it was impossible. DLF works to high ethical standards and does not bribe, I told him. Besides, we had got a licence to develop only around 40 acres, of which only 50 per cent was saleable. The total saleable area thus worked out to roughly 1,10,000 square yards and as developed plots of land in Gurgaon, at that time, were abundantly available in the market for around Rs. 80 per square yard, we would only get around ten million rupees if we sold the entire 40 acres. How then, would we ever be able to pay a bribe of Rs. 160 million, I asked. But worse was to follow. I could even be arrested under the Maintenance of Internal Security Act (MISA), he warned. Despite my explanations, he was not ready to listen. MISA was a draconian law, the mere mention of which was enough to send a chill through the spine. So I politely exited.

I never had an opportunity to ever meet him again, but knew well that he would later figure out that he had been misled and that DLF was being caught in the crossfire between Bansi Lal and Bhajan Lal. I had to invest a lot of time and effort in talking to numerous political leaders at that point just to ensure that Bansi Lal's false allegations against DLF were set right. It was a lonely battle and when leaders as good as Arun Nehru are fed with wrong information, the battle becomes even lonelier.

Against this background, Mrs Gandhi was hesitant to support any deviation from the established urban land development policy. Thankfully, Rajiv and Arun Singh stood firm and backed Bhajan

Lal's stand. As Rajiv had been enthused by my idea of how a new city could be built around Gurgaon, Bhajan Lal got the encouragement to go ahead with his original decision to permit DLF to develop around 40 acres in Gurgaon. If Rajiv and Arun Singh had not stood by their convictions, urban development would have been delayed by at least another decade or so in India.

It was fortunate that Khurshid Ahmed had also come around to believing the move would change the face of Gurgaon and the image of Haryana. It was a major turning point in the history of urban development in India. It triggered new thinking on the role of private sector developers and set the stage for public–private partnership in the real estate sector. As I mentioned, Haryana was also not covered by the ULCA. Elsewhere in India, the Act had severely retarded the growth of urban areas and had encouraged illegal and unplanned construction with the tacit support of corrupt bureaucrats and town planners.

The Act was an anachronism. It had ended up freezing large areas of urban land and led to protracted legal disputes. Another negative impact of the Act was that it prevented private developers from buying contiguous land for future development. The Act provided de facto monopoly on urban land development to government developers such as housing boards or development authorities. The idea of the Act had emanated from Nehru during his honeymoon with socialism and the public sector. It was flawed from the start as, inevitably, some politicians and bureaucrats got involved with corrupt real estate developers. What followed was an explosion of illegal, unplanned construction and the development of unauthorized colonies. This one unfortunate decision made a mockery of the proper and planned development of land for housing in urban India.

However, with Rajiv Gandhi's intervention, the private developers now had a chance to make up for decades of lost time and unchecked urban chaos.

Despite this, hurdles remained. Chaudhry Saheb, with all his wisdom and years of experience in the field, often told me that in the years ahead, the real challenge would be to change the mindset of political leaders and bureaucrats at both the Central and state level as they had set ideas on urban change and development. They had to be made to visualize a different growth model from the ones they had been used to. More than anything else, both political leaders and bureaucrats would not easily part with areas of power and influence.

The weight was heavy on my shoulders. For not only was I the only recognized spokesman for private sector developers at that time, I also had the background of heading industrial federations. After a successful stint heading the Faridabad Industries Association, I had risen to the national level as president of the PHD Chamber of Commerce and Industry and later president of the Associated Chambers of Commerce and Industry of India. It was a prestigious position as the chambers exerted a fairly powerful influence in the interface between government and industry. It was thanks to bodies like these and the support of dozens of eminent people that the creation of the NCR became a reality. The NCR was to include the neighbouring areas of Delhi like Gurgaon, Faridabad, Ghaziabad and Noida so that development could be done in a systematic fashion, apart from relieving the pressure on housing in the capital. This was a momentous decision and it virtually saved Delhi from collapsing. The haphazard development and unprecedented growth of population, especially during the post-Independence years, had put severe pressure on Delhi's infrastructure.

With change finally taking place, I was optimistic but also in a very difficult position. As the Reserve Bank of India had banned financial institutions from giving loans to real estate companies, funding was a severe problem. I detested being in debt for land purchase and developmental activities, but was forced to borrow money on a short-term basis at exorbitant interest rates from non-finance lending agencies to fund my efforts at aggressively assembling land in Gurgaon. These loans were invariably for six months. When the time came to repay, I would borrow again to pay the loan. It was a dangerous way to live. But if I did not do it, there was a danger of the business collapsing. I was borrowing from Peter to pay Paul. Even in the most difficult circumstances, I found there was always a ray of hope.

I managed to keep my head above water only because the Haryana government at that time was allowing builders to collect an external development charge (EDC) from those who bought our plots. The EDC was to be handed over to the government so that it could use this money to develop offsite infrastructure in Gurgaon like roads, footpaths, drainage, water supply, parking and so on. Fortunately, the government allowed us to pay the charges collected by us after a few months. Using this liquid cash, we paid for our short-term debts. I could roll that money over but only if the market would keep on growing. Since the markets were stable and prices were going up, I was able to manage my finances without getting overextended. This was also the time our licences were cancelled by Bansi Lal and we were unable to collect any money from customers. As I said earlier, in every cloud there is a silver lining. There were no buyers for land in Gurgaon at that time apart from DLF, but vast areas of agricultural land were available. I used this opportunity to aggressively borrow short-term funds to buy any available contiguous land. In hindsight, it was a prudent move.

Even after Rajiv Gandhi became prime minister, he kept track of what was taking place in Gurgaon, since it had lessons for the rest of the country. He had become PM in October 1984 but lost the elections in 1989. By 1991, he was firmly on the comeback trail and was widely expected to win the mid-term elections that year and return as prime minister. Sometime in early April 1991, one of my security guards woke me up around midnight saying that a call had come from the Congress president's residence. At first, I thought it was a prank, but to make sure, I called back. It was, in fact, Rajiv Gandhi. He wanted me to come over to his residence immediately. This was shortly before the Congress was to release its election manifesto. Jumping out of bed, I drove down to meet him in the wee hours of the morning wondering at the reason for the call. Rajiv did not look the least bit tired though he had been working through the night. He was munching on a bar of chocolate. He said that he had written two paragraphs on urban development in the Congress manifesto which was to go to press soon. He wanted me to read it and see if it was in the interest of urban growth and was correct and balanced.

I read it carefully. What the Congress manifesto said was that most of our towns and cities faced severe pressure due to rapid and unplanned urbanization, migration and breakdown of municipal services, forcing a majority of India's urban poor to live in unhygienic conditions. The Congress, it said, was committed to implementing a National Urban Policy for the planned and holistic development of urban agglomerations and large and medium towns. Specific programmes to resolve problems of drinking water, sanitation, sewage and garbage disposal and recycling of waste in urban areas would be launched to ensure a healthy and pollution-free environment. It ended by stating that satellite towns would be created to reduce pressure on large cities. Had he lived and come back to power and implemented what was written in the paragraphs I had read, it would have changed urban India.

Not wanting to disturb Rajiv, who was busy finalizing the manifesto, I left saying what he had written was fine. The manifesto was cleared by the Congress Working Committee on 6 April 1991. As a real estate developer, I was encouraged by what Rajiv had done, but little did I or anyone else know that tragedy lay around the corner. I would never see him again. A few days later, on 21 May, at a late-night election meeting in Sriperumbudur in Tamil Nadu, Rajiv was assassinated by a suicide bomber of the Liberation Tigers of Tamil Eelam. It was a day I will never forget. The country lost a visionary leader and I lost someone who was instrumental in helping me realize a dream and also made me what I am today. Gurgaon would never have happened had it not been for Rajiv.

Today I look at Gurgaon and picture the bare landscape that existed when Rajiv and I had that first impromptu discussion on urban development. It is now a bustling modern city with glass-fronted office buildings, large glitzy malls and tastefully built skyscrapers towering over the landscape. There are over 500 companies, including virtually all the top multinationals, employing thousands of young professionals. There are, in addition, thousands of housing units with lakhs of residents.

The IT boom of the 1990s needed contemporary, well-built office spaces and DLF had that ready for them in Gurgaon. Companies like GE were ready to ferry employees from their residences and drop them back as Gurgaon had no public transport in those days. That was the constant drawback. While the city grew in leaps and bounds, the government development agencies could not keep pace and provide the supporting infrastructure. In most cases, this was due to frequent change in the political leadership in the state and its effect on the bureaucracy's functioning.

Rajiv and Arun Singh had envisioned Gurgaon as a city with abundant green spaces and wide roads, one without unauthorized construction. They wanted the city to be developed based on the lessons learnt from the failures of urban development policies in India. This called for a pragmatic relook at town planning and land-related regulations of Haryana. Despite such political backing, successive politicians, town planners and bureaucrats were not very enthusiastic about ushering in bold reforms in the urban housing and infrastructure sector. This is precisely why private sector development in Haryana went far ahead of the offsite infrastructure development that HUDA was meant to create. Had the state government worked side by side with the private sector to create offsite roads, water supply, drainage, parking spaces and green open spaces, Gurgaon would have been a world-class city. Unfortunately, despite all our efforts, this cooperation remained a dream.

Yet, Gurgaon's development and Rajiv Gandhi's role in it show what politicians with no ideological baggage and modern minds can envision and achieve. Being young, Rajiv was passionate about doing something new. He brought a new hope to people who were disillusioned with the direction of politics in India. I have pleasant memories of meeting him numerous times when he was the prime minister between 31 October 1984 and 2 December 1989. India's urban development story took off only because of Rajiv Gandhi's vision. DLF is what it is today because of the change in the government perspective towards housing and urban development that he brought in. I found Rajiv's biggest strength was that he was a patient listener and tried to understand the nuances of every issue, negative or positive. Arun Singh too had a good understanding of the issues involved and he and Rajiv were a great positive influence on Indira Gandhi while she faced opposition on the issue of allowing the private sector into urban development.

Unfortunately, not everyone shared that view. The dream of building Gurgaon started thirty years ago. What really excited me was that if it succeeded, it would change the look and pace of urban development in India. I am proud to have been a pacesetter. It was unimaginable to think of something like the Golf Course Road three decades ago. Today, it is lined with buildings that speak of a new class of living for urban Indians. Buildings like

Aralias and Magnolias are a statement in superior living comparable to the best anywhere in the world. Looking back at the battle I had fought, I wonder where the strength came to carry on. When DLF restarted in 1981, we wanted to set up a highrise group housing project called Silver Oaks on a plot of eleven acres in Phase I.

At that time, such an idea was unheard of as town planning regulations did not permit tall buildings. As in Delhi, there were restrictions on the height of a building in Haryana too. Only eight floors were allowed. It made a mockery of our plans to build a new age city! I requested a meeting with Bhajan Lal to discuss the need for changing the norms on height restrictions. I argued that a new city could not be built horizontally. Tall buildings were inevitable if one needed to have enhanced quality of life and create spaces for wider roads, parks, parking and recreational areas. Bhajan Lal was open to new ideas. He wanted Haryana to be the harbinger of change.

He asked Khurshid Ahmed to bring along town planners and bureaucrats for our meeting. Ahmed had progressive views on urban development. The meeting was held in a huge room on the fourth floor, where the chief minister had his office. Bhajan Lal and his senior functionaries sat on one side of the large table. I was alone on the other side. But, I had a strange sense of confidence. The tone of the meeting was set by the chief town planner, B.P. Sinha, who was doggedly opposed to the construction of buildings that went beyond eight floors. Bhajan Lal asked him to spell out his reasons. Sinha tried to create a false sense of alarm by saying that there could be an earthquake.

'Apart from earthquakes, firefighting would be difficult with taller buildings.' he cautioned. 'Moreover, people would die if they fell off taller buildings,' he concluded.

Bhajan Lal listened patiently before asking, 'Tell me, Mr Sinha, how are tall buildings all over the world surviving?'

Instead of answering the question, Sinha said it would be unwise to grant permission for taller buildings by changing the existing town planning and building norms.

'Am I then to understand from your arguments that up to eight floors is safe and all floors beyond that would be dangerous?' Bhajan Lal asked sarcastically.

The chief minister's stand was clear. He looked towards the big window to his right and said, 'We are sitting on the fourth floor and what Mr Sinha is saying is that up to eight floors are safe. Will he or any one of you who are now opposing tall buildings jump out of this window as the fourth floor according to you is safe? If any of you get injured, then the fourth is also dangerous. Will you then shift your norm from eight to less than four?'

There was silence. The point had been driven home.

'What we need to do is to come out with structural and safety norms for taller buildings like they have done in all foreign countries. If tall buildings have survived abroad, they can survive in Gurgaon too,' he added.

It was Bhajan Lal's pragmatism that convinced those in that meeting that what was required was to think logically for the future and not worry about building norms that were created several decades ago. The way forward, he said, was to ensure earthquake-resistant structures, better firefighting methods, safer construction methods and safeguards to be followed before granting approvals for highrises. It was music to my ears though Sinha looked distinctly unhappy.

The real credit should go to Khurshid Ahmed. He was able to visualize way back then what the scene would be like after fifty or sixty years. After numerous sittings, he along with Bhajan Lal realized the need to permit highrises to speed up urban development. In fact, it was Ahmed who brought in the Haryana Ownership Apartment Act which ensured that future township development would incorporate a percentage of vertical growth in the form of group housing. It was a step I was able to pioneer in the face of stiff opposition. Town planning norms were changed to enable developers to make intensive use of land by constructing taller buildings with prescribed safety and structural norms. It was only then that other developers started building highrises. Bhajan Lal always retained the town planning portfolio with himself as he was keen that urban growth in Haryana should happen fast. He took personal interest in ensuring that it took place. This kind of push from the top is of crucial importance in a political culture like the one in India where such decisions are often taken on personal whim or for dubious reasons.

Development always suffers when it is caught in the pincer of politics. The main problem in Haryana and many other northern states was the culture of vindictive politics where settling scores, and not change or development, was the priority. Mistakes made in industrial growth can be corrected with technology but in urban growth such mistakes can set us back for generations. Urban growth is all about vision.

It is an area in which consistency in political direction is essential. Bansi Lal invariably reversed key urban-related decisions particularly if these were taken by a predecessor who was his political rival. His unfortunate attitude towards predecessors like Bhajan Lal and Om Prakash Chautala ended up retarding urban growth in Haryana. But when Bhupinder Singh Hooda took office in April 2005, it was like a breath of fresh air. He came in with a futuristic vision for Haryana and was widely respected by the trade and business community and society at large because of his genial ways and forward-looking attitude. He was sophisticated and imaginative. Hooda inherited an ailing urban infrastructure in Gurgaon. The private sector had grown rapidly but HUDA could not keep pace with matching offsite infrastructure. Though the money collected from private developers as EDC to finance offsite urban infrastructure ran into millions of rupees, HUDA had not been able to utilize the money fully to improve the crumbling infrastructure due to its organizational and procedural limitations. This mismatch between the pace of the private sector and the public sector in Gurgaon continues. What Hooda needs to do is surround himself with a few visionary and development-oriented bureaucrats and town planners who will deliver what he wants. Just the way Chandrababu Naidu in Andhra Pradesh, Sheila Dikshit in Delhi and Nitish Kumar in Bihar did by motivating their bureaucracy to deliver and bring in good governance.

I have not really had the opportunity to work with Hooda but my son Rajiv tells me that he wants to make Haryana the number one state in India and bring about a paradigm shift in the state's infrastructure. His intentions are obviously good. Gurgaon is exploding and what it needs is a unified development authority covering all aspects of planning and growth. The need for such an authority was felt as far back as 1990. In fact, during the regime of Devi Lal in the late 1980s a bill was drafted to establish it but it was torpedoed by self-seeking senior political leaders and bureaucrats who wanted to keep decision-making powers with them in Chandigarh. Noida in Uttar Pradesh, which is also in the NCR, has grown more systematically as it can take independent decisions without referring to Lucknow, the state capital. If Gurgaon had copied the Noida model, it would have moved ahead with greater speed.

Unfortunately, due to the political reluctance of Devi Lal and thereafter Bansi Lal's open opposition, this was never achieved. Even today, one has to travel to Chandigarh for minor permissions. Senior bureaucrats and town planners are not ready to abandon their petty powers by delegating these to officials in Gurgaon. In today's age and time, this sounds almost primitive. In any state, a chief minister has to create an environment for bureaucrats to take bold pro-development initiatives. Only then will they be able to get away from negative and rule-bound decisions. This was brought home to me when I tried to sell to town planners the idea of transplanting the Florida model to Gurgaon. Whenever I went abroad, I made it a point to visit residential areas that were being developed to get ideas. On one such visit to Florida, I saw scores of residential areas where both low- and highrise buildings coexisted, built around sprawling green spaces generally in the form of golf courses.

In India, most residential developments were essentially in the form of plot-based development with a very small percentage of group housing to ensure that such developments remained within the prescribed density norms of a particular sector of the master plan area. However, the Florida-type developments were all a mix of such housing. The idea of creating something like that in India kept me up at nights. When I suggested to the chief town planner and the director, town planning, that we could do the same in Gurgaon, they immediately said it could not be done under existing master plan norms.

Undeterred, I took up the issue with Bhajan Lal. I gave him an idea of my vision and strongly advocated that if such development were permitted, it would accelerate the flow of investment into Gurgaon and create avenues for new jobs and prosperity. Bhajan Lal seemed amenable to the idea and asked Dhanendra Kumar, his principal secretary, Pradeep Kumar, commissioner of town and country planning, and Bhaskar Chatterji, director, town and country planning, to examine the idea with open minds. He told them that if it benefited the state and provided more jobs to the young, the government should have no hesitation in amending the master plan. A key feature of the plan was the creation of a proper golf course and substantially more green and open spaces than were permissible under the prevailing norms.

It took almost three years of sustained persuasion. Along with architect Hafeez Contractor, I made scores of presentations on why the idea was innovative and how it would change the image of Gurgaon as a prime international business destination. Haryana, we argued, would be seen as a pacesetter in India.

Eventually, after several meetings, the officials were convinced that the creation of Phase V could be a magnet for encouraging more investment into Gurgaon, paving the way for accelerated growth and employment for the youth. Dhanendra Kumar, Pradeep Kumar and Bhaskar Chatterji asked us dozens of questions, but once they were convinced that we were offering something worthwhile, they ensured that government approvals were speedily given. The master plan was amended to enable development of a mix of low- and highrise buildings in the form of group housing spread over the entire land area of DLF Phase V, located around central open spaces and golf courses. I contacted the famous golf course architect Arnold Palmer to help us in establishing an international championship course, which he did at a substantial cost. We were going to create history. Today, twenty years later, Phase V is on its way to becoming a prime example of environment-friendly urban development in the country.

Building Gurgaon was not easy. It was not that it was such a gigantic challenge but I was constantly cautioned that I was chasing an impossible dream. Deep within, something told me it could work. I persevered, fuelled by the belief that this was written in my destiny. While engaging with multiple hurdles, I visualized how Gurgaon would eventually become and how it would contribute not only to the development of Haryana but the whole country. This is what fired my enthusiasm while arguing with the government of Haryana on why private developers have to be permitted into urban development. Bhajan

Lal was appreciative of the arguments and saw reason in them, but the town planners were rigid and did not want to give away their authority. However, Bhajan Lal and his minister Khurshid Ahmed put their foot down saying policies needed to be changed if that would bring prosperity to the state and the people. This is why they ultimately took the courageous decision of allowing private developers into Haryana. The results are there for all to see. Today, Haryana is one of the best-performing states. Leadership matters.

When the *New York Times* wanted to interview me in the summer of 2011, I dug up some statistics on the growth parameters of Haryana. When I looked at where Haryana was and where it is today, a deep sense of satisfaction and pride enveloped me. I am proud of having been a catalyst in the creation of Gurgaon. When I started expanding DLF in 1980, there was hardly any economic or commercial activity there. Thirty years later, the city is one of the fastest growing commercial hubs in the country and a shining symbol of emerging India. It is now a thriving industrial city with over 435 large- and medium-sized enterprises that cover the corporate spectrum – information technology, automobiles, sewing machines, sports goods, hosiery and the hospitality sector, creating thousands of jobs.

According to the Haryana government's statistical abstract of 2009-10, as much as 31 per cent of the state's 741,411 factory workers were based in Gurgaon alone. Today, Gurgaon produces 99 per cent of the automobiles produced in Haryana, 96 per cent of sewing machines, 92 per cent of sports goods and 86 per cent of all hosiery products. Moreover, according to Haryana's Department of Industries and Commerce, nearly 71 per cent of the total exports from Haryana in 2009-10 worth Rs. 30,608 million originated from Gurgaon. Now, Gurgaon rivals Bangalore and Chennai for its contribution to software exports from India.

In fact, I believe it was this boom in the IT and BPO sector that spurred the overall growth of Gurgaon. Large-scale projects in the commercial, retail and residential space dominate the skyline of Gurgaon, which many people have compared to Singapore. For the young, upwardly mobile Indian who found a well-paying job in the city, it also came with a superior quality of life. Gurgaon's cosmopolitan character has attracted professionals from all across India in search of better prospects. The city's population doubled in just twenty years, from 100,877 in 1981 to 228,820 in 2001 and is probably double that now. Provisional results of the 2011 Census indicate that the population in Gurgaon district has increased by 74 per cent in the last decade, from 870,539 in 2001 to 1,514,085 in 2011.

Another indicator of the growing business profile of Gurgaon is the nature and scale of foreign direct investment (FDI) inflows it has attracted over the years, hugely benefiting the state's exchequer. Gurgaon accounts for nearly 50 per cent of Haryana's contribution of direct taxes to the Central government. It may come as a surprise to many, but Haryana's direct tax collections of Rs. 8,358 crore (Rs. 83,580 million) in 2010-11 is more than the combined collection of states like Punjab, Jammu and Kashmir, Himachal Pradesh and the Union Territory of Chandigarh which amounted to Rs. 8,017 crore (Rs. 80,170 million). Much of that distinction is because of Gurgaon. It is now the number one district in terms of tax revenue collections in Haryana and has played a pivotal role in helping the state become one of the fastest growing in India.

Due to the encouraging atmosphere prevailing in Haryana that respected and lauded entrepreneurship, it was possible to think big. Although DLF City Phase V is still in the early stages of completion, it has already become the most sought-after residential area in the NCR. I am proud to have pioneered the Gurgaon form of development where the entire financing of both onsite and offsite infrastructure is done by the private sector, thereby ensuring there is no financial burden on the government exchequer. This is now being replicated elsewhere in the country.

My vision for Gurgaon would never have been complete without a golf course. I kept thinking of the beautiful golf courses in Florida and Mauritius with residents living all around who could enjoy the view throughout the year. While conceptualizing our golf course, I had only one goal: it should be the best eighteen-hole championship course in India. Secondly, it must change the look of Gurgaon. As golf courses age, they add to the environment. Flowering trees and flower beds change colour every season. I planned everything, the grass, trees, shrubs, the fairways, the water bodies, down to every minute detail. It was originally a dry, rocky area. I got incredulous looks when I said I would build India's most beautiful golf course there.

On a visit to Mauritius, I had once played on a golf course which had well-shaped fairways with scattered rolled ribs. I graphically described this to Ranjit Nanda, who was executing the work at the golf course. He worked hard on the idea and ultimately the shaping of fairways became comparable with the best international standards. Ranjit remembers how I always insisted on finding new and better ways of doing even small things. I was fussy about everything, the shape of every boulder, the kind of pebbles in the streams, the sound and flow of water as it flowed over the stones and so on. Seeing how it looks today, most people say it is awesome. I think that nature joined hands with us to create it.

I also brushed aside objections from my managers who said that it was costing too much. I knew if I did it well, the market would pay back the investment. The Aralias, which is a highrise apartment complex in front of the golf course, was initially marketed at Rs. 1,800 a square foot. Today it commands over Rs. 30,000 a square foot. There are two things that distinguish a golf course. One is the name of the designer and the other how well the fairways and greens are sculpted. Both had to be outstanding. We opted for Arnold Palmer who was then one of the best course architects in the world. We got the Singapore-based landscape designer firm Belt Collins International who were also among the best in the world. Then we chose Rainbird, a reputed firm of irrigation system providers from the United States, to set up an irrigation system controlled by computers to operate the sprinklers. We built five lakes to collect rainwater. It also helps store water to irrigate such a large area.

Colleagues like J.K. Chandra, director, Golf Resorts, must have been irritated with my attention to detail which extended to the club house construction and quality of material. Today, all of them agree that it is the attention to detail by the team that helped us create such a magnificent golf course. The work began in late 1996. Till then, no developer had built a golf course in India with highrise buildings around it. We were determined to show that it could be done.

However, excellence came at a price. I spent endless hours, days, weeks and months at the site when it was being designed and constructed. Hard work always pays. It felt great when we sent Akash Ohri, who now heads the golf business of DLF and is the director of DLF Golf Resorts Ltd, to pick up an international award for the best golf course in India. That apart, it is a green lung in the heart of the city. The nature-friendly environment attracts numerous species of birds that fly in during the migratory season.

Our biggest challenge today is to create green spaces. Anything we do must enhance the environment, not degrade it. Satellite pictures of Gurgaon show that the DLF golf course and country club with over 20,000 trees is now one of the greenest areas of Gurgaon.

What is the legacy I would like to leave behind is a question a lot of people have often asked me. I wish I could have developed Gurgaon into a world-class city. Because of frequent political changes and bureaucratic hurdles, supporting offsite urban infrastructure continues to be inadequate. Gurgaon has not taken off the way I visualized. There is so much that needs to be done to make it a city that India would be proud of. But when the idea of creating Phase V struck me, I knew I had found my dream. If we built it well, it would be a place where people would love to spend the rest of their lives as comfort and beauty would be their constant companions. I did not rest after conceptualizing Phase V.

For three years, in the 1990s, I must have gone to Chandigarh hundreds of times to meet senior political leaders, bureaucrats and town planners to convince them of the idea of creating a showpiece for Haryana. There was always stiff opposition and on most days I felt that I had been talking to a wall. Given that the political direction was clear about encouraging such urban development the opposition was quite flabbergasting. Fortunately, a different kind of bureaucrat, R.S. Gujral, was appointed as director, town and country planning. He was a pro-development officer who had the capability of taking bold decisions if they were in the interests of the state. After he was convinced that Phase V could become a magnet for accelerating investment in Haryana, he approved the zonal plan of Phase V on 6 May 1996. It was around the time when elections to the state assembly were ordered. One day when I went to thank him, he said there was no need to do so as he had only done his duty. 'I am only doing my dharma and will continue doing what needs to be done,' he said. If we had more bureaucrats like this, India would have overtaken China many years ago instead of the other way around.

Rajiv's mission is to develop Phase V into a state-of-the-art residential complex and he is engaging the best architects of the world to make this happen. His daughter Anushka is an extremely bright girl and is immersed in the project. We were chatting one day and I casually asked her how she was doing. I was happy to hear that she had formed a team of young professionals to go around buildings that DLF had built to get feedback from residents on what they thought of the places they lived in and how DLF could improve its services.

She said, 'I am trying to first observe and learn about developments in Phase V. I then want to create those buildings and facilities that would make residents and consumers feel that they got more than what they had bargained for. Each one must feel they got more than their money's worth.'

I am now convinced more than ever that once completed, Phase V would become one of the most sought-after residential addresses, not just in India, but in the world. Phase V will eventually encompass two eighteen-hole championship courses and one nine-hole golf course. It will be surrounded by a mix of high- and low-rise group housing buildings and scattered villas with all required amenities and facilities. It will have a constructed area of about 50 million square feet. I may not live to see it completed, but it will be a dream fulfilled.

In January 2000 when my wife Indira came close to death in a helicopter crash, it was clear that I would have to be by her side till she recovered. I called my son Rajiv.

'If I continue with active management of DLF, I will not be able to look after your mother. I need to be with her. We have to save her. You have to take over the reins till she gets back on her feet,' I told him.

As fate would have it, she contracted cancer after she recovered from the accident and for seven years I spent most of my time nursing her back to health. In those trying years, Rajiv rose to the occasion and put DLF into a new growth trajectory. Rajiv has aggressively steered a new path for DLF by taking it outside the National Capital Region and giving it a pan-Indian presence.

Rajiv convinced me that DLF had to get out of plotted development as land was scarce and the business would peter off. It was his idea to go in for highrises. To ensure intensive use of scarce land, he created a larger basket of business activities for DLF dealing with shopping malls, cyber parks, hotels and so on. Pia Singh, my daughter, spearheaded the retail and mall operations of DLF and gave these a new spin. When Om Prakash Chautala took over as chief minister in July 1999, he brought in new policies for the industrial development of the state. One policy related to development of IT and cyber parks. He saw that by encouraging development of IT-related business more investment would flow into Haryana, and with it, more jobs.

Rajiv moved in immediately to benefit from this policy and obtained approval for development of the DLF Cyber Park in Gurgaon. Spread over an area of 13 million square feet, it has changed the skyline of Gurgaon. International companies were attracted to it due to the ideal environment – different types of housing amenities for its employees, a golf course, good schools, hospitals, and shopping arcades. It is a combination of all these that have made Gurgaon an international destination. If DLF has become the undisputed market leader in the realty sector, it is largely due to several bold, imaginative and well-planned initiatives taken by Rajiv. DLF's rise was not easy: thanks to the synergy of the entire team, and its dedication, DLF kept raising its own bar from time to time to achieve excellence in whatever it did. It redefined luxury, quality and aesthetics. It has not compromised on its commitment to customer satisfaction and social responsibilities.

As Rajiv had charted an ambitious new growth plan, it was only logical for DLF to go in for an initial public offering (IPO). Till

2007 DLF was a closely held company with my family holding 98.5 per cent of the paid-up capital. The IPO in July 2007 was necessary to help DLF go to the next level. We therefore decided to bring a large issue of equity shares aggregating 175 million shares of Rs. 2 each. Of these, one million shares were to be reserved for subscription by employees so that they also could become part owners of the company. As expected, it was oversubscribed. DLF was welcomed by both the Bombay Stock Exchange (BSE) and the National Stock Exchange (NSE) as the real estate sector in India was finally emerging on the stock market.

After DLF got listed on BSE, the exchange created a separate realty index to show share price movements in the sector to help investors make informed decisions. The IPO was the first step towards realizing DLF's motto of 'Building India'. The IPO which raised the equivalent of nearly two billion US dollars came at the right time when real estate was booming. There was a shortfall of over 20 million housing units. In another few years, the IT sector itself would require at least 75 million square feet of office space. As foreign direct investment was being allowed into real estate, there was great promise for growth. The IPO brought in a lot of capital as too pressures.

Leaders with experience in their respective fields always make a difference. I, therefore, handpicked directors to take advantage of their range of experience to help DLF grow. The directors had a record of excellence in their fields. M.M. Sabharwal had received the Padma Shri for his sterling work as an industry leader as also a UK honour, the OBE. Kashi Nath Memani was a former chairman of Ernst and Young. Ravinder Narain, an eminent lawyer, was involved in the review of India's central excise and custom laws. Dr D.V. Kapoor was a former chairman and managing director of the National Thermal Power Corporation. G.S. Talwar was former group chief executive, Standard Chartered

Bank. B. Bhushan had thirty years of experience in company law and finance. Brigadier N.P. Singh was an associate member in the British Institute of Management. Rajiv Singh, vice chairman, DLF Ltd, had received the Udyog Ratna Award for his contribution to the economic development of Haryana. Pia Singh had been instrumental in driving the company's retail experience. T.C. Goel, managing director, DLF Ltd, had decades of rich experience building the company, and Kamreshwar Swarup, executive director, DLF Ltd, had forty-four years of management experience in legal affairs.

Added to all this wealth of accumulated experience was what I had learnt in my struggle over the years in an extremely challenging environment aggravated by lack of adequate financial resources. It taught me the value of money. Struggling to start a business, then establishing it, fighting market forces, taking over DLF when it was virtually shutting down, acquiring land, plot by plot, without any banking support, lobbying to change outdated laws, borrowing short-term finance to push ahead the real estate business, battling to win life back for my wife . . . all this gave me an inner strength, a fighting spirit, and, above all, humility and the need to be always ready for a lean period.

Rajiv wanted to use the IPO money to make DLF expand rapidly and diversify into numerous areas. His priority was to inject a new dynamism into DLF. He moved away from plotted development to a mix of high- and low-rise buildings. He also ventured into SEZs (special economic zones) and several other new areas – hotels, insurance, shopping malls, retail businesses, entertainment and wind farms. By early 2007, DLF had become a pan-Indian company and its construction activities were spread over nearly 45 million square feet.

When the markets went down during the recession of 2008, DLF could have faced insurmountable problems, but Rajiv's resilience came to the rescue. He quickly moved in to restructure, disinvest non-core ventures, and refocus the businesses of DLF to come out virtually unscathed. After a difficult period of two years while the recession was on, he ensured that the company emerged leaner and with increased creditworthiness by meeting all financial obligations. He learnt fast and the company is back in better health and form. The recession, which forced us to reshape DLF, actually ended up as a blessing.

Rajiv's two daughters, Savitri, 26, and Anushka, 24, have now joined him. They have quick grasp of issues and have learnt from the challenges we faced. They are not intimidated by the problems that business often throws up. Youngsters today are obsessed with rapid growth; they must be realistic and careful not to pile up unhealthy debt. During the recession, the most affected businesses of DLF were those relating to retail and shopping malls. After graduating from Wharton, Rajiv's elder daughter, Savitri, quickly moved in to support Pia in running the day-to-day operations of the shopping malls. She also had the benefit of guidance from Pua Sackquan, a renowned mall management expert from Singapore. In the short span of two years, she is now virtually supervising all mall operations. I was happy to see that she believes in micro-managing and has been able to demonstrate a visible change in the functioning of the malls.

Real estate was one of the worst affected sectors during the recession of 2008-09. Real estate stocks plunged by as much as 50 per cent. Property prices collapsed. Indian builders were in a bad way. To make matters worse, SEBI, the Securities and Exchange Board of India, tightened regulations on foreigners investing in real estate firms ahead of public listings. All this made it harder and more expensive for Indian builders to raise money, but there were lessons to be learnt too. Rajiv puts his experience this way: 'Hubris can set in in the best of companies. We tightened our belts, brought in new systems, cut flab and saw that it was actually an opportunity to re-programme the way we worked.

The financial prudence we brought in helped us learn a lot about running a business in the worst of times. It was a painful transition. But, it taught us a lot of lessons, maybe something we would not have learnt in twenty years! It was a crash course in doing business the right way.'

We told ourselves that we would not default or ask our customers for an extension. Some of them demanded their money back during the recession and we paid up. Banks reposed tremendous trust and confidence as we never walked away from our obligations. We were one real estate company in India that dealt with clients as if we did not know what recession meant.

I always told myself not to give up, to be persistent, never to compromise even in adverse times, to honour commitments and be fair with customers. They, in turn, would respond positively. If we do things the right way, there are plenty of chances to profit. It is much wiser to do that than to make a disproportionate amount of money in one project and then pay the price for the rest of one's lifetime. Overleveraging in real estate is a recipe for disaster.

Spearheading the rapid rise of DLF in recent years, Rajiv has emerged as one of India's finest young entrepreneurs. He loves his low-profile image and it helps him focus on growth plans and play with innovative ideas. It feels good to finally see a hard-boiled and visionary professional like Rajiv at the helm of DLF as vice chairman. With the reins of the company firmly in his hands, I have no worry about its future. DLF is destined to make even greater strides in the years ahead. It has been a fascinating journey.

It gives me great satisfaction to look back and recall the pioneering efforts I made to push Haryana to alter town planning and real estate norms so that urban development could happen and change the living standards of millions of people. It is equally gratifying to see other states re-examining their laws with a view to doing what Haryana did years ago. Other than Maharashtra, where Mumbai has many highrises, Haryana was the first state in India where skyscrapers entered the housing sector.

Gurgaon is now a showcase for India. Had it not been developed the way it was, none of the scores of multinational companies would have moved there. India's real estate market is constantly growing as the country liberalizes and globalizes creating millions of opportunities and dreams. DLF has a major role to play in setting new standards and bringing in an ethical framework into the real estate sector so that both the government and customers start viewing us in a more positive light. The growth of DLF into one of the world's top real estate companies is an inspirational story of how hard work, strategy, determination and perseverance can catapult a relatively unknown company to the top. We must have the courage to dream. It ultimately motivates us to achieve what seems impossible.

I often look back to those days when both the manufacturing business ventures I was involved with had suffered setbacks. American Universal and Willard India had not taken off the way I had wanted. I never believed that failure meant closure: I took my setbacks and failures as challenges, even as guides to new endeavours and future success.

In a venture like DLF leadership is important, for if the leader falters, the battalion of employees will be paralysed with nervousness and indecision. I learnt this lesson in numerous field exercises during my days in the army. But a venture thrives due to the collective effort of all, high and low, who are involved in it. DLF is what it is today because of the dedicated efforts of Rajiv along with his over 4,000 employees who worked very hard to help me realize my dream of making DLF one of the best real estate companies in India. They often attribute all credit for our success to what they call 'my passion and commitment', but the fact is that many of them sacrificed a lot, working round the clock, struggling against great odds, as if the future of the company was no less their responsibility than it was mine. It created a very strong bond between us which I will cherish till the end of my days. I want to record here my deep personal gratitude and appreciation for their hard work and above all their loyalty and trust in DLF's destiny.

12

IGNITING INDIA THE WELCH WAY

IN EVERY AGE there are some business leaders who possess the gift of seeing beyond the curtain of time and whose vision and philosophy rub off on those who come into contact with them. It has been my good fortune to have been influenced by some extraordinary personalities who not only had a profound influence on my way of doing business but gave me the chance to play a role in two nationally important developments – the HBJ pipeline project and the birth of India as a global outsourcing hub.

When I look back and take stock of all that has gone into the making of the DLF story, I often think how vastly different my life as a businessman and my approach to business might have been had I not met Sheikh Diraar Alghanim, a member of the powerful ruling family of Kuwait, and Jack Welch, the legendary CEO who made GE one of the world's most admired companies.

Some time early in 1984 I had gone to the Delhi airport to receive Sheikh Dirarr Alghanim whom I had invited on the occasion of my son Rajiv's wedding.

Senior customs officials courteously received him and requested that a routine declaration form be filled in. After Alghanim handed in the form, custom officers noticed that he had declared a solid gold box stacked with perfumes, a wedding gift for Rajiv and the bride. He had also put down the real value of the gift. He knew that gold was not allowed to be brought into India without paying heavy custom duty and an equally heavy penalty in case you were caught trying to smuggle it in. Seeing the surprise of the customs officials, he remarked, 'This is a practice I follow all over the world. I follow rules and will pay whatever I have to pay.' That was the kind of man he was and his business practices were equally ethical.

About six months later, Alghanim called me from London asking if he could bring along a close friend who had the potential to contribute to the economic development of India.

A few days later, I received him along with his friends, Fred Hatfield, chairman of Ingersoll-Rand, and Tom Englesman, vice president, marketing, of the UK arm of the company, which was a leading supplier of compressors and turbines for gas pipeline applications. They invited me for a lunch meeting at the Chambers, a private business club of the Taj Mahal Hotel in Delhi. At lunch, Alghanim asked me if I knew anything about the HBJ (Hazira–Bijapur–Jagdishpur) pipeline.

'I have no idea as I am in a totally different business. While I know all about water and drainage pipelines of a township, I know nothing about gas pipelines,' I replied.

They looked disappointed. It must have been embarrassing for Alghanim who had got these senior management executives all the way from England to meet me. Patiently, Englesman drew a map of India and showed the location of Hazira, Bijapur,

Jagdishpur and other places on the pipeline's projected route. They explained the logistics in detail. The massive HBJ project needed gas turbines and compressors for transporting gas through the pipeline.

'We are interested in the project and want your help to get started in India,' they said. 'Our company is among the world's leading manufacturers of high-quality, efficient and economical gas turbines and compressors. It puzzles us that despite our reputation, we are not able to get an appointment with A.S. Gill, the secretary in the Ministry of Petroleum and Gas.'

Alghanim had remembered meeting Gill at Rajiv's wedding reception, which is why he had asked me for the meeting with Ingersoll-Rand. He asked me if I could arrange a meeting with Gill so that they could present their case. All they wanted was an opportunity to familiarize him with the high-end products they had to offer.

'We do not want any favours. We just want a fair hearing,' Englesman said.

It seemed a pretty straightforward issue so I called Gill's secretary to confirm if he was in office. He was, and knowing him well, I decided to barge in with the team from Ingersoll-Rand.

Gill was taken aback when I walked into his room without even informing him beforehand. I wanted to demonstrate that this was an urgent situation where the Indian government was not even considering the best option.

'I am sorry for barging in on you unannounced,' I apologized. 'But, I need your attention for five minutes or India might lose out on a good option for the HBJ project.'

He immediately showed interest. I started by saying that Ingersoll-Rand's high-quality turbines and compressors were fuel efficient and competitively priced and it might help to look at them seriously. I added that the company's case was being ignored and that is why I had taken the unusual step of bringing the two top executives to meet him.

Gill informed us that the HBJ issue was coming up for consideration of the cabinet later that day and we were just too late.

'I wish you had brought this to my notice earlier. It is going to be decided in a few hours,' he concluded.

I remember remarking that the heavens would not fall if the issue were re-examined. I emphasized once again that the country might suffer if a wrong decision was made. Being the professional he was, Gill managed to get the decision deferred at the meeting so that Ingersoll-Rand's offer of equipment for the project could also be evaluated. The issue was re-opened in August 1984.

Incidentally, the rival bidder, indeed the leading bidder, at that time for the project was Snamprogetti, the Italian giant represented in India by Ottavio Quattrocchi. That the cabinet agreed to defer the decision and include a late bidder shows how wrong the media reports were, and still are, about Quattrocchi's supposed ability to swing any deal in his favour.

Once the decision was deferred, I spent long hours studying the details of the HBJ pipeline. I had been embarrassed by my ignorance earlier but it would not happen again. Hoddy had repeatedly advised me to research and examine every project in minute detail to devise the right business strategy. The more I examined the project, the more I was convinced of the viability of what Hatfield and Englesman had told me about their products and their suitability for the HBJ pipeline. The HBJ pipeline was to transport gas from Hazira in Gujarat via Bijapur in Madhya Pradesh to Jagdishpur in Uttar Pradesh and then on to various other parts of India for use in fertilizer and thermal plants. The ambitious venture was the outcome of a study by Gas Authority of India Limited (GAIL), one of India's leading public sector enterprises. During the weeks following our meeting with Gill, the Ingersoll-Rand case was examined by senior secretaries of various ministries since the turbines would have multiple applications in other sectors like defence, power and energy. The project also required getting public sector companies like Bharat Heavy Electricals Limited (BHEL) and Hindustan Aeronautics Limited (HAL) to be involved in manufacturing operations and product-support services in India.

Various studies were carried out by several expert committees to determine the best suppliers of turbines for applications in power, industry and defence. No single company in the world could supply equipment for the entire range. The best consortium, therefore, would be the one which could supply what is called aeroderative gas turbines of the smaller range of up to 3 MW. For a higher range, heavy-duty turbines would be the obvious choice knowing that the industrial and power sectors would be the main users. After exhaustive studies by experts, GE's heavy-duty turbines were found to be the best option for manufacturing by BHEL for use in the industrial and power sectors.

Since I had got inadvertently dragged into the project, I was following every development keenly and with personal interest. I was not intimidated by the fact that Snamprogetti and Quattrocchi were in the race. He was close to the family of Prime Minister Rajiv Gandhi and had great government connections. His consortium included Nouvo-Pignone (NP) of Italy as the supplier of gas-turbine-driven compressors. In those days, the general perception in bureaucratic and political circles was that eventually Quattrocchi would get any deal he wanted because of his proximity to the Gandhi family.

My personal experience proved the contrary. In fact, when Rajiv Gandhi's attention was drawn to the result of evaluations by various expert bodies, he did not show any favour to Quattrocchi. Instead, he insisted that the best bid be approved. He asked an additional secretary in the Ministry of External Affairs to re-examine the issue and see what was in the national interest of the country. Not once did Rajiv Gandhi show any preference for Quattrocchi.

Both the lead consortiums had a strong case. Allison Gas Turbines, a division of General Motors, USA, was the manufacturer of a major component of Ingersoll-Rand Gas Turbines. Their agreement was that Ingersoll-Rand and Allison Gas Turbines would transfer manufacturing technology to HAL, Bangalore. Obviously, it would help India gain from technology as well as ensure that product support services for the gas turbines were available locally. The Ingersoll-Rand bid was part of a consortium led by Spie-Capag of France.

The transfer-of-technology agreement made it an attractive proposition for India. Both BHEL and HAL were key participants in the Indian side's strategy. However, Quattrocchi had an ace up his sleeve. He introduced the idea that the Nouvo-Pignone gas turbines could also be manufactured by BHEL if they got selected. The government had two options. One was Snamprogetti represented by Quattrocchi with Nouvo-Pignone gas turbines. The other one was Spie-Capag with Ingersoll-Rand gas turbines. Exhaustive evaluations were carried out at different stages. Subsequently, another high-powered committee was formed to make a de novo evaluation and thereafter take the final decision. It included P.K. Kaul, cabinet secretary; G.V. Ramakrishnan, secretary, petroleum; S. Ganapathy, secretary, expenditure; H.S. Cheema, chairman, GAIL; S. Bhatnagar, defence secretary; and D.V. Kapoor, secretary, heavy industry.

The Ingersoll-Rand bid led by the Spie-Capag consortium of France, along with Nippon KK and Toyo Engineering of Japan as consortium partners, which I helped to put together, was finally selected as it was the best option. I was elated that finally Ingersoll-Rand's turbine was approved for the HBJ pipeline. Here I was, in a quite different business of real estate, managing

DLF, and at the same time getting involved in what had become a very complex high-technology project.

By 1987, the HBJ pipeline stretching across 2,300 km had become the largest such network in the country. The success of Ingersoll-Rand in the HBJ pipeline project also resulted in the merger of the gas turbine and compressor businesses of Ingersoll-Rand and Dresser Inc. The joint venture company formed was named Dresser-Rand. Ironically, the companies were fierce competitors for the HBJ pipeline project.

The success of this venture, in which I was now directly involved, also brought me close to Paolo Fresco, head of GE's international business, and Jack Welch, the chairman of GE. At that time, I had no idea of the influence Jack would have on my life.

While interacting with BHEL officials in connection with the pipeline deal, I understood that they were keen on getting GE to partner them in manufacturing heavy-duty turbines. At that time, GE was not well represented in India and was also not really looking at the Indian market. That changed when Paolo Fresco visited India. Gradually, I got Paolo to see the logic of GE seriously getting into business in India.

Paolo had completed his law degree from the University of Genoa and practised for a while in Rome before he joined General Electric's Italian subsidiary, Compagnia Generale di Elettricita, as corporate counsel in 1962. He ended up being a GE stalwart and rose to be its executive vice chairman. Paolo ensured that GE's activities in manufacturing and sales were expanded to cover every important country in the world. Paolo was constantly bubbling with plans for the company. He had also developed a close friendship with Jack Welch. Paolo and Jack globe-trotted together and met policy makers of different committees which made a significant impact on the expansion of GE's worldwide business activities.

In the mid-1980s, numerous multinational corporations were trying to set up projects in India, which was just starting to open up its economy. At that time, India was not an easy country to do business in. Corporations were, therefore, looking for businessmen who could advise them on India's investment environment and the complicated processes of securing government approvals. I was totally immersed in the real estate business. A project such as the HBJ pipeline was outside my area of expertise but personal connections and the desire to see India get ahead with the best technology had got me involved.

Paolo introduced me to Jack Welch. Jack had a deep and lasting influence on my life with his extraordinary business sense, insight and ethics. My association with him changed the way I did business at DLF.

Jack started at GE in 1960 as an engineer. He rose to become its chairman and CEO and transformed it into a global giant. Having got involved with GE through Paolo, I decided to get Jack to India to see for himself our country's emerging business potential. He flew down here but I could sense he was not very enthusiastic about doing business in India. Since I was his host, I felt I could convince him that India was at a take-off stage and this was the right time to move in. I felt the best strategy was to get him to meet Prime Minister Rajiv Gandhi, who was into technology and computers. I thought it would send positive signals to Jack about the new, emerging India led by a savvy young leader who was trying to do things differently.

I threw a big party for Jack. We had two bands playing and a distinguished guest list. I had arranged pools of water on which flower petals floated and an exotic, elaborate dinner menu. Jack was impressed with the reception. On the final lap of his tour, I got Jack to visit Jaipur.

Rajasthan has a magical effect on foreigners. Once he reached the Rambagh Palace Hotel, the former palace of Maharaja Jai

Singh of Jaipur, Jack was stunned at the reception. There were colourfully dressed riders in traditional Rajasthani attire on horses and elephants. The entire front lawn of the hotel was done up in fresh flowers forming the logo of GE! Dinner at the palace was hosted by the maharaja. In the end, there was a grand display of fireworks in honour of the visitors from GE. Jack was quite overwhelmed by the way he was treated here. He interpreted it as a sign that India was going all out to get GE to invest in the country.

I also showed him the other side of India, at Agra, where the streets were dusty and chaotic and crowded with animals jostling for space with vehicles. In his book, *Jack: Straight from the Gut*, he wrote: 'The efforts of KP and his friends worked. They showed us an India and people that we loved. We saw all kinds of opportunities there. After that trip, I became the champion for India.'

Since his visit had the blessings of the PMO, the three persons who handled his visit in India were Sam Pitroda, chief technology advisor to Rajiv Gandhi, Jairam Ramesh, who was in the Planning Commission, and Montek Singh Ahluwalia, who was a special secretary to the prime minister. They were astute enough to see the importance of Jack's visit. Jack also called on the defence minister, K.C. Pant, and the commerce minister, Dinesh Singh.

A significant turning point was a breakfast meeting I arranged at the Taj in New Delhi between Jack and Sam, Jairam and Montek. Sam made a forceful presentation showing how India was potentially a great destination for business process outsourcing (BPO) as it had such tremendous young talent. At that time, such outsourcing was non-existent in India. Many did not even know what the term meant.

That meeting would lead to the first BPO in Indian corporate history and open the doors for the creation of an industry worth over $14 billion today. I was equally privileged to be a facilitator for numerous other business deals at a time when the Indian economy, under Rajiv Gandhi, was just starting to liberalize and open up to the world. It was like having a front-row seat to an extraordinary event.

I also organized some back-to-back meetings for Jack with business leaders. Jack was a livewire, highly energetic and a sharp, precise and clear thinker. For him, productivity was the key. He hated to waste time and abhorred long-winded presentations. He was interested in meeting Indian business leaders between the ages of 25 and 35. He was not really interested in meeting elderly political and business leaders, as most other businessmen did. Jack wanted to feel the pulse of young India. I recall a meeting he had with the commerce minister, Dinesh Singh. He bluntly asked the minister: 'Why is your foreign trade so low when you have so many bright people in India?' That was his approach with most Indian ministers he met during that visit. His eyes really lit up only at the breakfast meeting with Sam, Jairam and Montek.

All three were extremely bright, articulate professionals and technocrats brimming with ideas and they told him what he needed to hear about India's future and the growth path they had in mind for it. Pitroda's BPO presentation was the icing on the cake and Jack announced that GE would place an order of $10 million to get part of its outsourcing done in India.

It was a landmark moment. History will record that India's outsourcing revolution started with that meeting. GE's first outsourcing order became a pacesetter for the growth of the IT industry in India. Subsequently, GE's outsourcing business grew exponentially in India. After GE, other international companies followed with their outsourcing businesses and IT ventures. Sam and Montek acknowledged that and said they were glad that I had got Jack to India.

Back home, Jack looked seriously at the India opportunity. He felt it was worthwhile to gamble on India as it had a strong legal system, a huge potential market and an enormous number of young entrepreneurs with great technical skills. He wrote in his book, 'The real benefit of India turned out to be its vast intellectual capability and the enthusiasm of its people. We found terrific scientific, engineering and administrative talent that today serves almost every business at GE.' Looking back, I am glad that I invested so much time and effort in convincing Jack about the India opportunity. Had Jack and GE not made their foray into India, the outsourcing story of India would have been altogether different. Once the economy opened up in 1991, outsourcing and IT defined the new growth mantra for scores of entrepreneurs in India.

In the early 1990s, GE started to ship software work to India. As its operations expanded, it opened a separate unit in 1997 in a DLF building in Gurgaon. This unit is now called Genpact. In 2005, it had revenues of $419 million. By 2010, Genpact revenues had crossed $1.12 billion. India's outsourcing industry is expected to earn around $50 billion annually by 2012 and employ around two million people. It was a phenomenon clearly stoked by Jack Welch who had the vision to see India's potential. This was crucial for India, which was just starting to open up its economy. The early investments by GE in India gave its technology and business service sectors crucial credibility. Till then, other countries and companies were hesitant to invest as they viewed India as a risky proposition. But Jack had his ear to the ground and knew what he was doing. He said that wherever he looked, he saw potential as India was full of young talent.

During one of his meetings with important business and political leaders, this is how he defined India: 'India is a developing democracy with a highly developed intellectual infrastructure. Some of the best profitable ventures in the world are being driven by Indian managers as we know how to respect and tap their talents. The day India starts doing this to its own manpower, it will become an economic superpower in the world.'

Soon after his visit to India in September 1989, Jack called me to Paris to attend a board meeting of GE. It was there that I saw him in his element, laying out his vision of what he saw as the new India. I felt a surge of pride listening to him talk so positively about India to people who had earlier been sceptical.

Paolo Fresco also played a great role in bringing GE to India. I am proud to have been the catalyst that triggered their new perception of India. Frankly, at that time, I did not visualize that it would grow into such a giant and benefit so many people over the years. Fresco asked me if I would accept the position of being the first national advisor to GE. I hesitated and said that I would help in every way without taking up the position. Paolo kept persuading me till I finally accepted. After that, every venture of GE in India went through me.

It was another great learning experience in my life as it was such a different field from real estate. It was not easy handling both the real estate business of DLF and the new responsibilities at GE. The two were totally different entities requiring separate business skills and strategies. It was also exhausting. There were days when I would get up before dawn to drive for more than four hours to Chandigarh for a meeting with bureaucrats and top political leaders. Then I would drive back to Gurgaon and be there by sunset so that I could meet the farmers with whom I was negotiating purchase of land. By evening, I was engaged with sophisticated technocrats and business leaders like Jack, Paolo and other executives. It was a huge challenge and I still do not know how I managed it all.

But what I did have in me to fall back on were the lessons I had learnt from Jack. One of them was the importance of focusing on essentials to increase productivity. He turned GE into one of the most profitable companies in the world by taking bold decisions and encouraging its associates to innovate. Over time, every organization gets flabby with a lot of systems being added. Before one realizes it, time-consuming procedures and bureaucracy eat into the profits. To avoid this, he encouraged all levels of management to come forward with ideas where unnecessary business processes could be eliminated without sacrificing quality. He called these workouts. In short, remove what was not required. The more one identified workouts, the more was the increase in productivity. He had the concept of workouts implemented in GE to make it one of the most profitable corporations in the world.

I tried to implement workouts at DLF but it did not happen the way I wanted. As land-related development was an evolving business, highly complex and government regulated, it became difficult to implement these workouts. But I did manage to implement the concept in some areas with fairly good results. More than anything, I used the platform of industry associations and chambers of commerce to underline to other businessmen how workouts could increase their profits and productivity. If we avoid non-essentials, it naturally gives us more time to concentrate on the main activity. Jack's toughness in dealing with matters in GE taught me how I could rework my game plan for DLF by thinking big and emerging as number one. He also indicated how a leader should walk the talk and be a role model. Leaders must demonstrate the behaviour that their company wants and expects from others.

Being with Jack was an education. He convinced me that experimentation pays. A leader must fearlessly explore new markets, ideas and products to emerge successful. He was always focused and ready for a challenge. He also had the capacity to energize anyone around him. You became proactive just by seeing him work. His decision-making style and his ability to execute what he decided on were lessons I have absorbed. One of the things that struck me most about GE was its commitment to values. GE would not get involved in any activity that would require bribes to be paid. Nor would it indulge in any other form of influence peddling. They had a clear value system and every employee strictly followed it.

One of the reasons why Rajiv Gandhi respected GE was because of their unambiguous stand of not compromising on values. They had a policy called 20.4 which specified that employees could not be involved in payment directly or indirectly to any private or government organization while soliciting for GE's business. It was one of the most important influences GE had on me. It was amazing that GE operated with those values at a time when the business environment was geared towards some kind of underhand payment to politicians or bureaucrats. It was the accepted thing.

Initially, GE found it difficult to operate because of this policy, but Jack and Paolo emphatically declared that regardless of the benefit or loss to the company, any GE employee involved in payoffs would be dealt with very sternly. Because of such a policy, GE lost out on many businesses that could have been secured had they greased palms. I am glad they did not do that since ethics and values were deeply ingrained in my DNA as well as in DLF. Jack was truly committed to this policy.

Here is just one example that is difficult to believe today. GE was to supply locomotives to the Indian Railways. It was a worldwide tender. After an intensive selection process, GE's locomotives were found to be not only the most competitively priced, but also technologically superior. The Indian Railways was to buy a large number of locomotives in a deal which involved progressive indigenization. After all the procedures were completed, the file was sent for formal approval to the railway minister, Madhavrao Scindia.

Just before he was about to sign, he got a telex message from the GE Headquarters in Connecticut asking him to hold it in abeyance. It also said that if the Indian government was in a hurry, it could go ahead and consider another company. It was extremely unusual for a minister to get such a request from a company that was about to bag such a huge business deal. As it turned out, GE had discovered that an Indian based in Washington who was working as an agent of Canadian Locomotive, GE's associated company that was supplying locomotives, had done something they considered unethical. Apparently, this agent had thrown a dinner party for the wedding of a daughter of the general manager of a locomotive workshop in Varanasi that was under the Indian Railways.

Since the technical recommendation was to be made by this organization, GE felt it was tantamount to influencing the decision. GE appointed Fairfax to conduct an inquiry. It turned out that the agent happened to be a classmate and old friend of the Varanasi workshop head. Since both were childhood friends, the dinner issue could have easily been overlooked, but GE maintained that it was an unethical business practice. They lost the huge contract for locomotives, but did not regret it one bit.

Their example had a special relevance for me. In India, the real estate sector is regulated with archaic laws. Over the years this has created a lot of unauthorized developers who have flourished under the direct patronage of politicians and bureaucrats. I had to deal with this reality. Based on what I learnt at GE, I tried changing the culture and lobbied to get the laws changed instead of circumventing them and bribing regulating agencies. I succeeded in Gurgaon only because I managed to convince the government to change the laws. I am glad that the Haryana example and the growth of Gurgaon opened the door for a new kind of urban development in India.

I will be forever grateful to Jack Welch for being a friend, guide and mentor. Together, we kick-started India's BPO revolution, but more than that, he was the perfect role model any entrepreneur could hope to have. The greatest lesson he taught me in his own words was this: A company should be either number one or number two in a particular industry or else leave it completely. It was this philosophy that fired my imagination and ambition to make DLF the number one player in the real estate business.

13

WINNING LIFE BACK

FROM THE VERY first day I set eyes on Lynndale Estate in the hills of Mussoorie, I dreamt of making it my family's country home and a retreat. Spread out over 110 acres, with a thick cover of pine trees, it has a charm that I found simply irresistible. The grandeur of the natural surroundings, the bracing air, the early morning chirping of birds and the gentle gurgling of streams that ran through it were enough to make me want to acquire it. I had no money at that time, but knew that some day I would earn enough to acquire an estate as entrancing as this. I fell in love with the estate in June 1980 while I was visiting my friend Rudy Singh and his endearing wife, Odette. Rudy was the former raja of Bansi and a cavalry officer. The first brewery in India was set up in this estate by an enterprising Scottish businessman some 120 years back because of the marvellous taste of the water that ran through the property. The palatial house had been built by the Scotsman in 1889. It was in a state of disrepair, but with its gabled roofs, tall porches supported on grand columns and breathtaking views of the mountains and the valley, it was beautiful all the same. Because of its colonial structure, it reminded me of Scotland and my days in England. Rudy and Odette had renovated only a part of it. While chatting with them, I kept visualizing how it would look after completion of the renovation work.

Before I left, I pleaded with Rudy that if he ever wanted to sell his estate, I should be given the first right of refusal. I told him that I would not negotiate or bargain with him and all that he needed was to give me his demand in an envelope and that it would be respected. Rudy laughed at that time, thinking I was joking. But the estate never went out of my mind. I saw it as one of the special rainbows I had been chasing all my life.

Years later, in 1988, Rudy and Odette landed up in Delhi one sunny morning and sprang a surprise. Rudy had decided to sell the estate and handed over an envelope to me. I opened the envelope and read the contents. We looked at each other and smiled. I kept my promise and the deal was done. No questions were asked and I paid him what he had asked for. Fortunately, by that time, I had acquired sufficient money to enable the pursuit of such luxuries. Soon after acquiring this property I visited Mussoorie again with Brig. (Retd) Krishan Chand, who was the head of our engineering department. He assured me that he would organize the entire renovation work with military efficiency. He mobilized around eight hundred men from the adjoining hills and completed the entire work in just six winter months.

Curiously, at around the time when work at the estate had started, rumours began flying around Mussoorie that DLF had massive real estate plans in the hill station. Prices rose overnight as they thought we were going to develop the 110 acres and rake in millions of rupees. But I had no such plans. Many of my friends have often asked me why I did not commercially exploit it and build a huge housing complex as there were 110 acres of land to play with. But I could never even think of commercially exploiting a place of such natural beauty. For my wife and me, the Lynndale Estate was not just a property, but a gift of nature that we could call our home.

It became a passion for Indira and me to visit Mussoorie every fortnight over a period of six months to ensure that the renovation work was being done the way we wanted, without in any way spoiling the pristine beauty and majesty of the place by adding modern architectural features. Brig. Krishan Chand did a remarkable job. My dream of owning a home in the hills had finally come true. I was so grateful to Rudy and Odette that I told them they were free to stay there whenever they wanted, and they often did, which gave me much pleasure. Sadly, Odette has passed away, but Rudy still goes there once in a while, perhaps to revive memories of his happiest days.

The brigadier exercised overall supervision of the property for the next ten years and ensured that not even a single tree was cut. On the contrary, thousands of saplings were planted every year to further improve the environment. This practice still continues. Out of all my family members, my daughter Renuka is most fascinated with Lynndale and makes regular visits to the estate with her friends. As time went by and the family grew, we found ourselves being drawn to the place more and more often. Holidays at the estate with close friends from India and abroad soon became an annual ritual, especially on year-ends, when the snow-clad hills around were at their most enchanting.

Occasionally, we used to set off with our friends to Mussoorie for around three days. This was a fantastic getaway for all of us who lived a hectic life in Delhi. No wonder they were all very excited. Normally, we would start the first day with a performance by a specially selected pipers band from Dehra Dun. They would enthral the guests coming in from different directions with their melodious tunes. The pipers – dressed in their eyecatching bright uniforms of kilt, tunic and spats – would gently mill around them. It naturally took me back to memories of the Scottish trip in my student days. The energetic pipers would then get the guests to dance to Kumaon hill songs. We would enjoy the merrymaking that followed.

The next day, we would take off on a hiking expedition to the hills and thereafter converge at Everest House that was steeped in history. This house is just about an hour's walk away from Lynndale. This was the residence of the celebrated Col. Sir George Everest, the Welsh surveyor and geographer after whom Mt. Everest is named. He was surveyor general of India from 1830 to 1843. He used to do his research here as the house was his laboratory. Though the trek was exacting, we loved it as Everest House was a picturesque place from where one could catch a panoramic view of the Doon Valley, the Aglar river valley and the snowbound Himalayan ranges. It was a perfect spot to have a good picnic.

Many of us would then pursue the sports we loved at the estate like tennis, badminton and golf. As this eighteen-hole chip-and-putt golf course was cleverly designed on the hill slopes, the golfers found that they burnt more calories as it involved walking up and down numerous times. Some would try their hand at clay pigeon shooting.

After a siesta in the afternoon, some would play cards, dumb charades and treasure hunts. We would again get together around a huge campfire in the evening, and as musicians played everyone would be persuaded to join in the singing.

All in all, our days at the estate were packed with lots of fun and activity. The days would fly past as we de-stressed ourselves.

It became our special way of greeting every New Year at Lynndale in the company of our dearest friends. In December 2000, we looked forward to a very special holiday at our picturesque retreat wanting to welcome the new year. I had even hired two Bell 404 helicopters to give our guests a close-up aerial view of the Himalayan range.

Our holiday in the hills started off with excitement and high expectations when we arrived a few days after Christmas. The weather was especially wonderful that year as we ushered in the year 2001. Our hearts and minds refreshed and at peace with the world, we got ready to depart. Before flying back to Delhi, we decided to take one last look at the majestic peaks. In one of the helicopters was my wife Indira with her close friends Indira Dhody and Veena Mehra. Veena's husband was Maj. Pradeep Mehra, the former commandant of the President's Bodyguard and one of Delhi's best-known horse breeders, who was running Usha Stud Farm in Gurgaon. He had bred some of the finest young bloodstock in Indian racing history at his stud farm.

At first I climbed into the helicopter in which my wife was sitting, while Pradeep walked towards the other one in which our friends Kamal Nath, Laxmi Walia and Vanilla Jain were to fly. Since I was eager to get the final panoramic view of the Himalayas, I occupied the co-pilot's seat in the helicopter and had just fastened my seat belt when Pradeep came over, saying that he wanted to swap places with me as he wanted to sit in the co-pilot's seat. I was unsure about what to do since I had fastened my seat belt and the chopper rotors were already turning. From the other chopper, I could see Kamal Nath gesticulating with his hands and urging me in sign language to let Pradeep have the co-pilot's seat. Had Kamal Nath not done that, I would probably not have given in. On such throws of the dice of life are destinies decided. I unfastened my seat belt, gave up my seat to Pradeep and moved over to the other helicopter. That one decision was to impact my life in ways no one could have imagined. We were in the Himalayas, the lap of the gods, and amidst all that beauty and spiritual serenity, my life was about to descend into the darkest depths of despair.

The two helicopters lifted off, one after the other, around midday on 2 January 2001. It was the last sightseeing trip of the vacation. I had no premonition it would be the very last day for some of us, surrounded as we were by such majesty and tranquillity.

The two choppers had separated, taking different routes to reach Dehra Dun airport where we were to land. As soon as we touched down, our pilot informed me that he had lost contact with the second helicopter. We scanned the skies, but there was no sign of it and we were unable to re-establish contact. I panicked. I used to pride myself at my ability to find inner strength and courage in the most intimidating moments of my life, but it had deserted me now. My mind was a blizzard of negative images. I tried my best to stay positive but it was impossible not to imagine the worst.

Kamal Nath, being a close friend, sensed my apprehensions and asked me to get off the chopper and wait inside the airport. He said that he would take off again with the pilot and retrace the route we had taken from Mussoorie to find the other chopper. He suggested that it might have developed some technical hitch and been forced to land. He was trying to keep my hopes up, but I was filled with dread.

I immediately rushed to the air traffic control tower to inquire if they had heard anything. They said they had no communication at all. Just then, a call came from the Dehra Dun police to the air traffic control that a helicopter had crashed in the gorges near Mussoorie. The police said that everyone on board had died. My hands turned to ice and my legs began to shake uncontrollably. I went numb. It almost seemed as if my life had come to an end. The silence was overpowering. No one wanted to say anything or even knew what to say.

I thought of my wife and the wonderful years we had spent together flashed before my eyes. Images of our first meeting at the cricket match, the months of courtship, Indira proudly watching me taking part as a tank commander in the Republic Day Parade, our wedding, our jaunts together while I was in the army, our family of three lovely children, the most difficult years when she stood by me . . . we had grown together for almost fifty years! Suddenly, in one blinding moment, life had no meaning any more.

In the midst of despair and darkness, a faint glimmer of hope appeared on the horizon. I received a phone call from my colleague V.K. Bhatia from Delhi. He said that Kamal Nath had called him asking him to inform me that Indira was alive. She was, however, in a critical condition and had been rushed to the military hospital in Dehra Dun. The hospital is about an hour's drive from the airport. It was easily the longest hour of my life. When panic strikes and your life starts to unravel, every minute seems like an eternity. I was desperate for a miracle. Indira has to live, I kept repeating to myself again and again. It was one of the most harrowing experiences I have gone through. It seemed unbelievable that just hours earlier, Indira, Pradeep, Veena and Indira Dhody had been together, enjoying the mountains and grateful to be in each others' company. What had they done to deserve such a cruel fate? And in the prime of their lives?

Reaching the hospital, I learnt what had probably led to the crash. The helicopter was at the final high altitude point on the flight, but for some reason, the pilot had deviated from the flight plan. The aircraft hit an air pocket, brushed against a tree and spun out of control, crashing into a gorge. Some villagers saw the crash and ran to help. They heard one person crying asking to be pulled out. It was Indira. The others were dead. The helicopter door was jammed and the aircraft had turned upside down. As they could not open the door, the villagers broke the window pane and pulled Indira out. They got her out just seconds before the helicopter caught fire and exploded. Someone who had arrived at once with a jeep quickly removed her from the accident site and rushed to the closest helipad, from where she was immediately flown to the military hospital in Dehra Dun. It was a miracle she had survived the crash but it needed another, bigger miracle for her to pull through. She was battling for life with serious internal injuries.

Kamal Nath had alerted the doctors at the military hospital and they were ready with emergency treatment when Indira reached there. She was unconscious and required massive blood transfusion. Her blood pressure was dropping alarmingly. The doctors said she was critical and should be rushed to Delhi immediately. Kamal Nath, who was a member of parliament, took charge. Fortunately, a fixed-wing plane belonging to his aviation company was at Dehra Dun airport, waiting to take us back. He had it converted into an air ambulance and Indira was flown to Delhi accompanied by army nurses and doctors. In Delhi, she was rushed to Aashlok Nursing Home, where she was immediately given emergency care by Dr Alok Chopra and Dr Ashwani Chopra, who ran the hospital. Dr Naresh Trehan, who was then heading Escorts Heart Institute and Research Centre, had heard the news and he arrived at Aashlok to lend a helping hand.

Though Dr Trehan headed Escorts, a heart-care hospital, he created a special unit to provide her emergency orthopaedic treatment there. Rajan Nanda, chairman, Escorts, ensured that everything happened on an emergency footing. He even gave up part of his office to me to monitor her medical needs. Every minute was vital as her life was hanging by a thread. I chose to move her to Escorts because it was a state-of-the-art hospital with the latest facilities for complex surgeries.

Indira had suffered multiple injuries, which included a broken back and hip, leg and other complicated fractures. I flew in Dr Nandu Laud from Bombay. He was the orthopaedic surgeon who assisted Dr C.S. Ranawat of the United States who had performed knee replacement surgery on Atal Behari Vajpayee when he was prime minister. Dr Laud was of the opinion that Indira needed a super specialist as she had complicated bone injuries. He suggested Dr Ulrich Holz, from Katharinen Hospital in Stuttgart, Germany, who he felt was the best person in the world for the job. I immediately called Dr Holz and requested him to fly down to Delhi. He took the next flight and operated on my wife. Attending doctors said the operation was successful.

My family and I were ecstatic. We thought the worst was over.

Three days after the operation, Dr Holz returned to Germany. Soon after, Indira developed high fever. Despite continuous medical care and support, she was in agony from the pain. I tried calling Dr Holz, only to be told that he was not reachable for ten days as he was on a sailing vacation. Panic set in again as Indira's condition was deteriorating. As Indira had multiple injuries and other related complications, it was obvious to me that one specialist doctor's treatment would not work. Her condition demanded special attention from a battery of specialists. Also, she needed one person who could coordinate all the aspects of her treatment.

Looking at the medical complexities involved and the need for one central coordination point, I decided to take over that responsibility myself. The situation needed micro-management and I was good at that. I got down to conducting detailed research on her medical condition and the possible treatment. I did this by gathering together all the doctors who were treating her. I asked them questions on every aspect of her injuries and the treatment she needed. I then asked them to arrive at a consensus so we could move forward. Dr Naresh Trehan and Dr Alok Chopra were cardiologists, Dr Ashwani Chopra was a gastroenterologist, while Dr P.S. Maini, Dr Nandu Laud and Dr J.S. Arora were orthopaedic surgeons. Chest specialist Dr Neeraj Jain and general surgeon Dr K.C. Mahajan had also joined the team which now included specialists for every injured part of her body and every medical condition she was suffering from. Blood tests and scans were conducted which showed she had developed two serious infections, staphylococcus, a hospital-acquired bone infection, and a fungal infection caused by an excess of antibiotics. Both were life-threatening. To make matters worse, the infections had been detected late. Doctors were puzzled how she had contracted a hospital-acquired infection in Escorts, reputed for its clean and sterile environment.

Meanwhile, Dr Trehan mentioned that Dr T.D. Chugh, a senior microbiologist in Kuwait who was working on heart valves, could be helpful. For a drowning man, any straw is to be clutched. I immediately called people I knew in Kuwait and discovered that Dr Chugh was already in India to attend a wedding at Bhiwani. I requested the Haryana chief minister, Om Prakash Chautala, for help. He put a deputy commissioner on the job and Dr Chugh was quickly located. I spoke to him on the phone and explained Indira's condition and requested him to rush to Delhi.

Being a true professional, he abandoned his vacation plans and arrived in Delhi with his wife. He was a fine microbiologist with an analytical mind. He examined the case in detail and took over all the testing. He changed the medication and closely monitored all other aspects of her treatment. Since the infections were spreading fast and proving immune to drugs, he arrived at a consensus with the other doctors to use Amphotericin B and Vancomycin. These are extremely powerful drugs which could have severe side effects on her renal system. Indira's kidney tests had also indicated that her creatinine level was double the permissible level.

Some specialists felt that if a high dose of these injections was given it might damage her kidneys. However, Dr Chugh was convinced that the core issue was to stop the fungal infection as it would otherwise prove fatal. He insisted that both these injections should be given to her without further delay. After listening carefully to all the doctors, I told Dr Chugh to go ahead despite the risk of damaging her kidneys. I took the decision as there were divergent opinions and it was leading to delays.

Though Dr Chugh was scheduled to return to Kuwait, he chose to stay back for another five weeks. It was crucial that he stay and monitor her reaction to the drugs. If he had not stayed back, Indira would probably not have survived. I am deeply grateful to both Dr Chugh and his wife who changed their plans to return to Kuwait just for one patient. The best doctors get emotionally and personally involved in their cases, and I was touched by their commitment to Indira's condition. I was even more touched when I asked for his bill at the end of his treatment and he refused, saying my gratitude and appreciation were enough. He did not accept a single rupee. The bond we had formed and the relationship were more valuable.

Similarly, Dr Trehan also refused to take any money. They were so involved with saving Indira that money had no meaning. They were also dedicated professionals apart from being outstanding doctors. For them, the ebb and flow of her life had involved them so deeply that when she was recovering, it was almost like their own family member had survived.

The battle, however, was far from over. The fungal infection had been tamed but Indira's bone infection was causing a lot of concern. Doctors were not sure how to deal with it. An earlier operation had been unsuccessful and the infection had started spreading after the surgery. The specialists in India could not control the infection which was now starting to threaten her life. The pain was also becoming unbearable and once again, her life hung by a thread. Dr Laud told me that the best specialist for the treatment of such a complicated trauma case was Dr David

Helfet, who was director of the Orthopaedic Trauma Services Hospital for Special Surgery in New York.

I tried to contact Dr Helfet, but somehow could not get through. In desperation, I turned to Jack Welch for help. Welch assured me he would make sure Dr Helfet contacted me as soon as possible. Welch immediately asked Ken Grossman, the medical head of GE in Connecticut, to track down the doctor. He found him and I was informed that he was available for telephonic consultation. I got together the concerned doctors, Dr Maini, Dr Laud, Dr Arora, Dr Mahajan, Dr Chugh and Dr Alok Chopra and put Dr Helfet and Ken Grossman on a conference call. After the discussion, Dr Helfet suggested that the way out was to operate on her again, clean up the affected area and put in Vancomycin beads close to the affected bone. After that, she would need to be closely monitored for six weeks. Then, he suggested, she should be operated upon again to check if the infection had been contained. This was an option that the doctors treating her in Delhi had not even considered. After an hour of discussion, Dr Helfet said as he was sitting thousands of miles away, the doctors in Delhi should do what they thought was best. Before signing off, he stressed that Indira's infection had to be removed fast as she could lose her life.

Listening in, I noticed that the doctors in Delhi were still undecided. The case was just too complicated. I was holding on to the phone after the conference had ended and by chance, I overheard Dr Helfet asking Grossman, 'Who is this K.P. Singh?'

'He is a close friend of Jack Welch and is also on the advisory board of GE,' Grossman replied.

Helfet then said, 'I feel sorry for him. I do not think she is going to live.'

It was shattering news.

Dr Helfet was the world's leading authority and his words should have destroyed any hope we harboured of Indira coming out of the crisis alive. Yet, it is always darkest just before dawn. I decided I was not going to let her slip away so easily. She had survived a helicopter crash, battled multiple complications and a deadly infection. She had beaten all the odds. These were good signs, and I decided that instead of going into depression, I would summon every last bit of strength and all the resources at my command to give her every possible chance of survival. After half a century of togetherness, we had become almost as one. Without her, life would not be worth living. I pulled myself together and objectively analysed the options. It was clear to me that the treatment suggested by Dr Helfet was the right choice.

I tried to call him back but he had left to attend a conference in Switzerland. I kept trying to reach him. Finally, I managed to trace him at an international orthopaedic conference in Davos. It was 3 a.m. his time when I called. Dr Helfet was fast asleep. He picked up the phone and groggily muttered a hello. He was surprised to hear who was calling.

'Could you please come to India to operate on Indira?' I asked him.

I wanted him to come immediately as he was the only doctor who could handle the emergency and she was in a critical condition.

'I do not fly across the world operating on patients,' he said and added, 'Moreover, I am scheduled to leave for Zurich in a few hours to take a flight to New York.'

I kept pleading with him. He said that he had already advised the Indian team of doctors how to handle the infection and the steps to be taken. The conversation went on for almost thirty minutes. Though it was early morning, Dr Helfet did not hang up. He listened to every word and then made a suggestion.

'Why don't you get in touch with Swiss Air Rescue which could fly into Delhi in an air ambulance and transport your wife to New York where I can take up the case?'

I realized this was impossible as Indira was in a very precarious condition and was in no position to travel.

'Indira is septic and is likely to have a renal failure. She needs immediate surgery. My wife is dying,' I told him.

'I do not have a solution,' Dr Helfet replied.

I then asked him, 'Dr Helfet, what would you do if your wife was dying?'

There was silence for maybe three to four seconds.

He then said, 'Okay, how quickly can I get to Delhi?'

I was relieved but also frustrated. He did not have a visa to travel to India and getting one would take time. I took a chance and told him all he needed to do was to drive to Zurich and everything would be taken care of, including his visa and arrangements to fly to Delhi. I quickly called Ronen Sen, the ambassador to Germany, for help in issuing a visa to Dr Helfet. I also asked my friend, Paolo Fresco, to arrange a special aircraft. He had recently retired from GE and had become the chairman of Fiat, based in Turin. They both responded magnificently. Within a few hours, Helfet had taken off from Zurich. I was waiting for him at Delhi airport when his plane landed. I drove him straight to a hotel where some of Indira's doctors were waiting to have a meeting with him.

After examining her reports, charts and X-rays, Dr Helfet said he would operate on Indira at 8 a.m. at Escorts the same day. Appropriate arrangements were made to enable him to perform the operation. He even made the antibiotic beads of medicine with his own hands. After the operation and having impregnated the beads, he said that Indira would have to be brought to New York for further treatment. He left, giving us all some hope. He was a doctor but also a man of compassion. Like Dr Chugh, he too refused to accept any payment.

Indira's condition improved considerably after the operation. Yet, it was not safe to keep her in Escorts as the fear of her catching hospital-induced infections was still real. I decided to take her home. I had our entire house at 14 Aurangzeb Road sanitized. In Indira's room, I had the carpets removed as floor coverings are a potential nesting place for bacteria and laid on wooden flooring.

Before she was shifted home on 21 February 2000, the bedroom was converted into an intensive care unit. At that time, GE was the largest supplier of medical equipment in the world. I requested Scott Bayman, president of GE in India, to have his company instal the required equipment at home. Indira was constantly monitored at her bedside not only by her family, but by a host of doctors, nurses and machines. This arrangement was to prove invaluable. As we had installed an ultrasound machine, we immediately detected some internal bleeding in her right leg. There was a fracture in the tibia where a plate had been fixed for support. Dr Trehan brought in Dr Samir Srivastava from Escorts who was an expert in a technique whereby he could stop bleeding by using the pressure of his thumbs.

Despite all this, Indira's condition remained precarious. The complexities of her case were so immense that I started acting and thinking like a doctor. In fact, doctors often wondered how a real estate developer knew so much about medicines, their properties and after effects, and lines of treatment. I had got in touch with Carol Farkas, a close friend based in New York, and she used to get various specialists to talk to me every day. The daily inputs from the New York doctors coupled with the care given by doctors in Delhi proved decisive. Dr Helfet had already advised that I take her to New York for further treatment.

In Delhi, Dr Rupa Salwan, a cardiologist and family friend, also strongly urged that Indira needed to be taken abroad for specialized treatment. I had looked at that option but hesitated out of fear that she might not be able to take the strain of a long flight. After three months at home under careful monitoring, I felt she had recovered enough to manage a journey by air. I decided to take her to New York as Dr Helfet was already familiar with her case and treatment. There was still the problem of how to get her to New York. A chartered aircraft would require refuelling at various stops on the way. I wanted to avoid putting that extra strain on Indira. We ultimately opted for Air France as it had the fastest route to reach New York. They were also willing to convert the entire first-class area into an airborne ICU.

In September 2001, we landed in New York and took Indira straight to the Hospital for Special Surgery, where Dr David Helfet was director and senior surgeon. In view of her multiple injuries, I had received varying opinions from doctors on what needed to be done. There were as many opinions as there were doctors. Besides her hip injuries, the D4 and D5, two upper vertebrae, had also been fractured in the accident but luckily the fractures had not yet impaired her neurological system.

As it was a very delicate injury, I tried to secure opinions from the best spine surgeons of the world. The Mayo Clinic specialists strongly felt that they should operate on her to set the vertebrae right. But Dr Frank Cammisa, neurosurgeon at the Hospital of Special Surgery, felt that instead of a surgical intervention, the natural healing process should be allowed with support of braces. I decided to probe deeper and found that the suggested operation was an extremely complicated one as it would have to be done through an incision in the chest as intervention from the back was ruled out.

'What do I lose and what do I gain?' I asked the doctors.

The Mayo Clinic specialists said that if she was operated, she would not later develop a hunchback and could stand straight. Moreover, she would also not lose any height.

'And the risk?' I queried.

'She may not be able to survive the operation,' they said.

Indira's looks did not matter, her life did. The doctors agreed that it was a wise decision.

Likewise, some doctors suggested that Indira should undergo only a partial hip replacement but Dr Helfet felt that she needed a full replacement. I went with his opinion. Eventually, a full hip replacement was done. Dr Helfet got Dr Barry Brause, an infectious disease specialist, to deal with the bone infection and Dr Paul Pellicci, an orthopaedic surgeon, for the complicated hip surgery.

Indira was kept on suppressive antibiotics till she was healed. As things turned out, Dr Helfet's line of treatment turned out to be the right one. When they removed the hip, it needed to be tested to assess the state of infection. Dr Manjula Bansal, chief of pathology at the hospital, carried out a special investigation as there was some fear that tuberculosis might have set in.

As a special case, some samples were allowed to be sent to another lab. While all this was going on, I was sitting in the visitor's lounge. Looking out of the large glass windows, I could see the Hudson and the city of Manhattan. A television in the lounge suddenly came to life with live coverage of the terrorist attack on the World Trade Centre. It was an appalling sight, and it was hard to grasp that just some distance away from where I sat, thousands lay dead or dying.

It was also a reminder of how lucky Indira had been. Hers was the last major surgery at the hospital before the trauma centre suspended all scheduled operations to handle the emergencies caused by the 9/11 attacks. Despite the shock and horror of one of the most defining events in human history, it was amazing to see how every American came forward and the nation banded together at that moment, regardless of race, creed or social status.

Panic had spread all over New York and the streets were deserted. I was staying with Carol Farkas and her husband Robin at 730 Park Avenue, a fifteen-minute walk from the hospital. As I walked to their home, I could see air force fighter aircraft patrolling the skies. American flags were fluttering all over the city. It was one nation together in grief and unity that day. India has much to learn from the United States in dealing with terrorist forces which have inflicted enormous damage on our country during the last two decades.

Days later, I brought Indira to Carol's home. Here again, we got her room converted into an ICU as Indira's immune system was still weak. She had to be in a sterile environment.

Being in the warmth of Carol's home was more healing than being in a hospital. In a couple of weeks, as Indira's condition started improving, all her post-trauma rehabilitation and physiotherapy took place at Carol's house. Carol and Robin went out of their way to ensure the best possible post-operative care for Indira. They have been our closest friends for over three decades. It is only in situations like this that one realizes the importance of having good friends.

Soon, we fell into a new routine. Indira would be put in a wheelchair and her nurse, Manjit Kaur, would take her to the nearby Central Park. Then, with the help of a walker, Indira would try to walk. After a few weeks, she got rid of the walker and started using a stick for support. A few weeks later, she started walking without help. Dr Helfet told us that in his career of thirty-two years, he had seen few patients who could match Indira's courage. I was grateful enough for his treatment and the care that had given her, and me, a new lease of life.

Soon, Indira was well enough to fly back to India. There is nothing like being home. The thought itself was healing. I watched her progress with relief and happiness. I wanted her to feel as normal as possible. But the trauma of her accident and the operations had taken a toll: just how much emerged only after some time. One fine day, in an attempt to convince her she was back to normal, I walked her to the front lawn of our house in Delhi and suggested she try to hit some golf balls. Indira loved golf and I thought chipping a few balls would make her feel she was fully recovered and back to her old self. She feebly hit three or four balls before she started coughing and saying that she was feeling very weak and could not hit any more. She wanted to get back into the house.

We had gone back to our earlier lives, albeit in a less strenuous way and with less socializing, but I had no idea that fate was waiting in the shadows to deliver another blow. By afternoon, Indira developed a fever. As she was coughing intermittently, it appeared to be an upper respiratory tract infection. Dr Jain was called and he examined her at home. He suggested a chest X-ray. When the radiologist, Dr Sudharshan Aggarwal, examined the X-ray, he recommended a CT scan. The scan showed a shadow on the left lung. Dr Mahajan, a close friend and senior surgeon at Sir Gangaram Hospital, looked at the results and recommended a biopsy. When the biopsy report came, it was like a death warrant. It showed that Indira was suffering from small cell lung cancer. It is a type of cancer that grows vigorously and spreads fast.

For the second time, I flew to the United States on account of a medical emergency. I consulted a range of oncology specialists, including Dr Manjit Bains and Dr Henry Miller at the Sloan-Kettering Cancer Centre in New York, one of the best in the world. I also called on Dr Philippe Chahainian, professor of medical oncology at the Mount Sinai School of Medicine. They concluded that since it was small cell lung cancer, the best treatment was a combination of chemotherapy and radiation. They ruled out surgery. The crucial issue was to determine what kind of radiation could be given. As usual, I got down to finding out more about the subject.

I found that there was a new radiation technique called Intensive Modulated Radio Therapy (IMRT). However, research on its effectiveness was ongoing. Doctors were hesitant to use it on the left lung as it was close to the heart and was not in a static location. I asked Dr Manjit Bains for advice. He advised me to contact Dr Dattatreyudu Nori, professor and chairman, Department of Radiation Oncology at the New York Presbyterian Hospital. He had a great reputation. However, when I approached him, he was hesitant to take up the treatment. I kept pleading with him till he agreed. Simultaneously, I was also in touch with a noted oncologist, Dr S.H. Advani, who was then with the Tata Memorial Hospital, a specialized hospital for treating cancer in Mumbai, and Dr Harsh Dua of Apollo Hospital in Delhi.

The purpose of getting together a group of internationally respected doctors was to find the best possible treatment. Meanwhile, I started researching the most suitable doctors in England. Carol contacted a research organization in Boston and found that the best person would be Dr Peter Harper in London. He was a highly regarded lung cancer specialist in the United Kingdom at that time. He was later appointed advisor to the French president. He is one of the finest oncologists I have met.

I flew to London to meet Dr Harper and elicit his views on the treatment. He ran a large National Health Service centre at Guy's Hospital in London, apart from a very busy private practice. In the last thirty years, he has published over 400 papers on cancer. Dr Harper realized that I already knew a lot about the type of cancer that Indira had. Every time he spoke, I would have a series of questions to ask. He was an extremely busy doctor and told me upfront that he did not mind my asking so many questions, but he would not be able to find so much time every day as he had many other patients to be attended to. We made a deal that I would get fifteen minutes a day to ask questions. On most days, it would extend beyond that but Dr Harper graciously tolerated my persistence. He said he respected me for being so thorough with my research on the treatment that Indira was being given. He also realized I was pestering him as I had almost lost her once and did not want to go through the same hell as before. A few doctors had already told me that Indira's cancer was fatal. Dr Harper gave me the statistics. The figure showed that no more than 8 per cent of patients suffering from small cell lung cancer survived beyond two years.

I was desperate enough to take the bull by the horns.

'What you are currently doing in terms of treatment may not be enough, so how about doing something different?' I asked him.

Dr Harper said that there was no medical evidence available for him to attempt anything different. I kept the pressure on Dr Harper each time we met, begging him to think out of the box. He is not sure what finally worked in Indira's case. Was it the chemotherapy or radiation therapy or a combination of both? Was it Indira's strong will to fight the disease? Was it my determination to leave no stone unturned? Maybe it was a combination of all of these and, of course, God's grace.

I remember Dr Harper told a friend: 'Indira was amazing. She cooperated in fighting the battle and was very brave and determined like her husband. I do not know of anyone who has fought the disease like Indira. Small cell lung cancer is seen universally as a lethal disease. Without her husband beside her, she would not have been able to fight.'

Typically, in cases like Indira's, doctors are extra careful because of the serious side effects of chemotherapy. They cut down on the radiation doses so as to make the therapy tolerable. I insisted that the doses be given despite the discomfort they caused her. The only thing that mattered to me was Indira's survival. After the third chemo cycle, Indira started experiencing the side effects. At least four cycles had to be completed before the radiation dose could be administered. Indira was brave and was willing to fight the battle. She had already gone through so much after the helicopter crash that almost killed her, but she somehow found the courage to carry on fighting.

Looking back, I think what worked was the fact that both of us fought it together. One doctor told me that I could not buy outcomes just by spending money.

I shot back, saying, 'I am not buying it, I am determined to make it happen.'

I left nothing to chance. We were looking at every incremental benefit. We treated her for a year in London. We did unconventional things. At one stage, Dr Harper suggested that some studies indicated that the game of bridge would be helpful during the period of radiation treatment. I was determined not to let any opportunity slip away. I immediately called Kiran Khurana and Madhvi Bery, two of Indira's closest friends, from Delhi, to come to New York to play bridge with her along with Padma Devgan, another friend who was already in New York. Believe me, it was worth it. There was a let-up in the side effects and Indira showed signs of recovery. We created an environment in the hotel to accommodate bridge as if it was the most normal thing to do while she underwent treatment. I could see how it helped as she was able to successfully complete the radiation treatment of six weeks. I later learnt that research had shown that if the brain was kept occupied, it helped the immune system recover faster.

Her nursing attendant, Manjit Kaur, was exemplary. She was always around and her caring attitude was invaluable. She became her companion and friend. For the last ten years, she has been with Indira taking care of her. She is now part of our inner family and takes care of everything concerning Indira's health and happiness.

After the chemotherapy, we gave Indira top-up radiation where the cancer had spread in the abdomen. This was not routinely done. Since IMRT treatment had just been introduced and experiments were still going on, it took great skill to administer it without damaging adjoining areas of the body. It was this fact that was worrying Dr Nori. But, he involved himself completely and ensured that he supervised every detail of her radiation therapy. He even radiated those areas where he had a faint suspicion the cancer might have spread. The careful handling by Dr Nori and his personal interest made a major contribution to Indira's survival.

In an interview, Dr Nori recently said, 'Indira's positive attitude to life was amazing. It was her inner strength that helped in her ultimate survival. Every day, KP used to come with her for over two long months, and when we saw their determination to fight the disease, it charged up all of us. Every doctor worked to go that extra mile. KP asked us tough questions that were really challenging to doctors like me. I loved this couple as I had not ever met one like them in my forty years of practice. KP reviewed every move that doctors made as he wanted to ensure that she got the best treatment and survived a type of cancer which is very difficult to treat.'

Eventually, Indira was back on her feet after the cancer treatment. We now ensure regular checks to keep recurrence at bay. Over a decade has gone by since the accident and I am truly grateful to God that my soulmate is healthy and by my side. Numerous times in those crucial years when Indira was battling for life, I realized that it was such tragedies that make you retrospect, mature and learn the larger truths of life. I think we succeeded only because of the approach we took. I studied her ailments thoroughly. I paid great attention to every detail. We put the best team of specialists together, each one handling a different aspect, and so delegation was perfect. We got them to brainstorm and arrive at a consensus on the best treatment possible. We applied common sense wherever it was possible. We provided leadership when it was needed and inspired all to work towards a common goal: Indira's cure.

Above all else, we stayed positive and told ourselves that we were going to win her life back. We did not do it alone. There are any number of people, friends, doctors and specialists, here and abroad, who helped us achieve that goal. To them, I will always be deeply grateful, more than words can say. When someone you love is close to death and, by some miracle, recovers, the meaning of life changes. We start to see everything in a new light, cherish every moment together and appreciate every little aspect of our existence. There's a quote I read somewhere which sums it up: 'Unless you have waited in the darkness, you cannot appreciate the miracle of a sunrise.'

14

RELATIONSHIPS ARE MAGICAL

FROM MY EARLIEST days, I have always treasured my relationships more than my possessions. When I look back on the eight decades of my life, half-forgotten memories come flooding back – of the voices and faces of the people I have known over the years, of those who mattered the most to me and always will. Relationships have made my life more meaningful and made me what I am today.

Had it not been for the wonderful people who have played an important part in my life, steering it in the right direction, things would almost certainly have been altogether different. Had my college friend Bopal Singh not got me admitted to the Air Service Training course in England, I would never have left India at such a young age nor met Julie. Had my father not taught me tennis and my uncle Raghubir Singh given me a love for horses, perhaps I would never have been accepted so spontaneously by the British aristocracy. And had it not been for my uncle Kanwar Surendra Pal Singh and Lt. Gen. Wadalia, I might never have returned to

India to become a soldier. Without their advice and influence, I might have stayed on and my life and career would have turned out very differently.

Then there was Lt. Col. Baljit Singh, who so cleverly thwarted my secret plans to quit the IMA and return to England. It was because of him that I stayed on in the army and met and married Indira. It was her father, Chaudhry Raghvendra Singh, who convinced me to quit the armed forces and to step into the world of business.

Once I got into business, I surely would not have succeeded to the extent I did without the inspirational advice and enduring friendship of George Warren Hoddy. Another legendary American business leader, Jack Welch, also exerted an enormous influence on my career and ignited an ambition to become the number one real estate player in India.

In each phase of my life, it was relationships that got me there and propelled me to the next stage. I would probably not have met Jack Welch and got to know him so well had it not been for my friendship with Paolo Fresco, through whom I got involved with GE. Had I not built a relationship with John Davenport, head of ESB Inc., I would never have been able to acquire the shares of Universal Electric, which I desperately needed to secure majority control of DLF.

And had it not been for a chance encounter with Rajiv Gandhi in a deserted part of rural Haryana, when his vehicle broke down and I offered help and that meeting led to further interaction, my plans to develop Gurgaon into a modern city might well have remained just another unfulfilled dream. Who can tell what destiny has in store for us? But as it turned out, it was the relationship that blossomed between Rajiv Gandhi and me that almost magically transformed my own life, as well as the lives of thousands who make Gurgaon their home.

I sometimes marvel at the ease with which I have been able to interact and build relationships with people at opposite ends of the social and economic spectrum. On that fateful day, I was sitting on a charpoy in the blazing heat of summer talking to farmers in the local dialect to persuade them to sell their land to me. All of a sudden I found myself conversing with the son of Indira Gandhi with the same ease. It is perhaps this very duality of personality which eventually led to the rise of DLF. As much as I valued my meetings with Rajiv Gandhi even after he became prime minister. I equally cherished the relationship I shared with the villagers who helped DLF become a real estate success story. The only explanation I can offer is that perhaps my rural roots combined with my early exposure to the inner circles of British high society and my training as a cavalry officer gave me the ability to adapt to whatever situation I happen to be in. There have been days in my life when in the morning, I would be in the dingy office of a low-level revenue official, then a few hours later sharing a meal with villagers, and later in the same afternoon, playing golf with some of Delhi's social elite, having tea with the chief minister of Haryana trying to convince him to change antiquated laws, and finally dressing up for dinner with a globally admired CEO like Jack Welch.

At one end were the hundreds of farmers without whose friendship and trust I would not be the chairman of India's biggest real estate company today. It took months and years of painstaking effort to build a relationship of mutual affection and respect with each one of those families who backed my dream, risked their money, and gave me the greatest opportunities of my life.

At another level, it has often been my own business rivals and competitors who have proved to be my greatest strength. When DLF's licences were cancelled in Haryana by a chief minister, it was my friendship with fellow developers like Sushil Ansal of Ansal Builders and Ramesh Chandra of Unitech that enabled us to stand shoulder-to-shoulder to weather the storm. Thanks to their support, we survived and triumphed in the end. A visible phenomenon in urban India today is that most of us try to build 'relationships' that we can benefit from. In the bargain, we also end up with fair-weather friends who invariably dump one when the dark clouds gather. It is only when we start giving without expecting anything in return that relationships grow and add meaning to life.

This was brought home to me most forcefully just a few years ago when my wife was at death's door. I was deeply touched when some of the world's best medical professionals like Dr Naresh Trehan and Dr David Helfet refused to be paid for treating Indira after her accident. The emotional journey we had been on together in battling to save her life had formed a bond that was stronger than mere commerce. It was the same bond that inspired the combined efforts of Dr Helfet, Dr Harper, Dr Nori and many other doctors who joined me in the fight to help her recover, first from the helicopter crash, and later, from a deadly cancer. In fact, Indira's brushes with death forced me to wonder what it was that brought so many people together to help me so selflessly. It was simple; the relationships which we formed made the difference.

Life provides us with thousands of opportunities to reach out to each other. It is just that most of us do not convert them into relationships. I have been fortunate to turn even casual meetings into lifelong relationships that have brought me immense joy and fulfilment. One such story of which there is a brief account in an earlier chapter needs to be told in some detail. Part of the dome in the DLF Centre in Delhi is a vibrant, gigantic painting. It traces the history of Delhi and how it has grown. It is a modern masterpiece, the work of India's most famous artist, and it is the result of a casual encounter I had in the 1960s.

I was travelling by train from Hyderabad to Delhi where I was posted in the Army Headquarters. The train was packed. I was standing at the door of my air-conditioned coupe when a man with an unkempt beard and dressed in pyjama-kurta rushed up, looking harassed. He was finding it difficult to board the train because of the crowds and pleaded to be let into my compartment as he had urgent work in Delhi. His appearance made me hesitate but as the whistle had blown, I reluctantly let him in. He told me he painted hoardings for a living in Hyderabad. He started sketching me while we were chatting. He handed the sketch to me but I was not impressed with it. Before reaching Delhi, he took my address. I never expected to see him again but there was something about him that had intrigued me, a vibrancy and zest for life that belied his bedraggled appearance.

A few years later, a young Indian Foreign Service officer, K. Natwar Singh, was my house guest. He had a visitor and it turned out to be the same bearded painter. A few days later, the painter returned and asked if I could loan him Rs. 600. I gave him the money. A few months later, he was back, asking for another loan. At this point, I offered him a job at DLF to do some paintings. He agreed. We would provide him the paint and materials he wanted and he could paint when he felt like.

He had simple tastes and was happy with the monthly salary of Rs. 800. He lived in a small barsati in Jangpura in New Delhi where I used to often visit him as I had started to admire his work. He created some of his finest paintings in that barsati. He produced some stunning, priceless works for me from the 1960s to the '80s. The testimonies to his genius are all over my home and office. One is an exquisite portrait of Indira.

In the late 1980s, when DLF Centre was being built, I wanted a piece of art that would complement the building. He agreed but took several months to think of an appropriate theme. He arrived at the building, saying he needed a huge canvas and paint and wanted loud music playing in the background. His other demand was naan and chicken for lunch. When we offered him Earl Grey tea, he scoffed at the suggestion and asked for ready mixed tea from a roadside stall. He put a lot of love and involvement into the project, painting with energy and passion.

It took him four days to finish the painting. He called it *The Enchanting Damsel of Delhi*. I get to look at it every day when I enter my office So does everyone else who visits or works in the building.

Our relationship went beyond patron and artist. He was an unaffected person who loved the basic things of life. Food from roadside dhabas was preferable any day to a five-star hotel meal. He was also delightfully disorganized. I once asked him if he wanted help from the DLF office to file his tax returns. 'What is a tax return?' he asked innocently. When I told him, he laughed saying that the taxman would never come calling as he did not make that kind of money.

I got him a small residential apartment in the Gole Market area of New Delhi so that he was more comfortable. In May 1986, we elevated him to the position of art advisor at DLF at a salary of Rs. 2,500 a month plus accommodation. He had not asked for a raise but I felt he deserved it since he was producing such wonderful paintings. He remained with DLF till September 1993.

Well before that, he had become an international name and was travelling all over the world as a celebrated artist. His name, of course, is M.F. Husain, who is, alas, no more. Incidentally, it is not Husain who inspired my interest in painting. I have always admired works of art. It was just a chance encounter that brought me close to Husain. I will always remember the wonderful times I had with him and his paintings which are very dear to me.

Just an occasional phone call would illuminate the memories of the time we spent together. Towards the end of 2010, I was lucky to meet him in Dubai. He came all the way from Qatar just to meet me, picked me up from my hotel in his Bentley and drove me to his museum in Dubai that housed some of his recent works, which are truly magnificent and worth all the millions of dollars his work commands.

He turned 100 on 7 December 2010, according to the lunar calendar, and we spent an entire afternoon talking of how we had first met, his days at DLF and how he had become an international celebrity. I kidded him about his wealth, asking who kept track of it. He laughed and replied that he recorded all transactions in a pocket diary and somewhere in his head. Fate takes care of everything, summed up his philosophy of life. He was as animated as ever and full of life and passion. 'What is the secret of your youthfulness?' I was tempted to ask. He said that for many years now, he only ate half of what he felt like eating. I had not the least idea that our meeting in Dubai would be our last. Husain passed away on 9 June 2011.

Decades earlier, Husain was known to sleep in his battered Fiat car on days when he felt like it. Nothing much had changed. Though he had a garage full of the world's most expensive cars, even in the last years of his life he would usually drive to the house of any of his grandchildren, relative or friend to spend the night there sleeping on a sofa or on a mattress spread out on the floor. It was remarkable that despite his enormous wealth, he remained till the end the unassuming Husain I had known several decades ago.

Great art has always been a source of inspiration for me. Just having Husain's works around me adds a sense of vibrancy. That is why there are so many paintings all over my home and office. My love of art often takes me to the Delhi College of Arts to spot talented students and buy their paintings. Over a period of time, I have become a discerning collector and am glad to have works by such masters as Satish Gujral, Paresh Maity, Jehangir Sabavala, Sanjay Bhattacharya, Paramjit Singh and, of course, M.F. Husain. I collect art not because I can afford it but because it just adds so much vitality to a room, a house, an office, and to life itself.

Often, in the race for material prosperity, we lose sight of the intrinsic values that make our lives complete. The closeness of families, care for children and the aged and even marriages are increasingly under threat in some societies. We have forgotten the part they play in bringing us true happiness and fulfilment. As India prospers, one of the first casualties of the new affluence would be the extended family, which has already been replaced by nuclear families in urban India. The challenge before our young generation today is to ensure that while we accept the inevitability of nuclear families, we also need to keep the spirit of the extended family alive. We need a blend of the two. It is only then that our children will learn the value of relationships and draw benefit from them.

I have greatly benefited from a joint family and it has instilled values that have helped me throughout my life. No school can teach the values that a family does. When I met Indira, she was just seventeen. Although she came from an affluent background, she adjusted well. After my broken relationship in England, Indira filled the vacuum in my life in the most rewarding manner. We got to understand and accept each other's idiosyncrasies, strengths and weaknesses. We grew together. Indira has this extraordinary gift of getting on with everybody which helped both of us to build relationships together. She complemented me in every way. Today, if something happens to her, I panic; such is my love for and dependence on her. I do not know how I would have managed without her. Life with Indira has been a fulfilling and beautiful journey for over fifty-five years. Our relationship has evolved every day and there is not a moment of regret. To have remained together with mutual understanding and love has been the essence of our happiness.

I was lucky to have my in-laws around when my children were growing up. They were the emotional anchor the children needed while growing up, compensating for the lack of my being around as I was busy trying to revive DLF and build up the business. I was working long hours, sometimes as much as nineteen hours a day. There were days when I never even saw Rajiv or Renuka as they would be sleeping when I left early in the morning and when I returned late at night. It is only the elderly who can give the much-needed care, attention and emotional support to children when they most need it.

One of my greatest joys is seeing how my children have bonded with my grandchildren. My son Rajiv's two daughters, Savitri and Anushka, are now getting down to steering the business to a new level, while Renuka's son Rahul has recently joined DLF after completing his graduation studies and is fast learning the business. His initial few months in the company showed good promise. Pia's daughter, Tara, 5, and son, Jai, 4, are bundles of joy and cheer that they spread all around.

As age caught on, Chaudhry Saheb battled loneliness, especially after Indira's mother, Savitri Devi, passed away in 1970. Both Indira and myself decided to make it a practice to visit him every week and spend an evening with him. We often shared a drink and talked about everything including business. We saw what it meant to him as he eagerly looked forward to our visits. I followed this up by organizing a family lunch every Sunday. That made him even more happy as he could meet all of us. It also enabled our children and grandchildren to bond well with all of us. I sincerely believe that we must look out to create such occasions so that relationships within the family can get stronger. Children benefit the most as they learn a lot, learn to respect elders and in the longer run, develop strong ties apart from such occasions sparking happiness and a sense of well-being. In a day and time when hectic schedules regulate our lives, this makes even more sense. It touched me when Chaudhry Saheb one day told me that our weekly lunches gave him much pleasure and a sense of belonging; he felt that the quality of his life had been enhanced substantially.

Towards the early 1980s, he had developed plaques in his carotid arteries that could affect blood supply to his brain. I contacted the best surgeons in the United States and eventually took him to Winston, Salem, in North Carolina where Dr Jim Toole operated on him successfully. On his return, he was like a new person. He started playing golf, a game he enjoyed immensely. Indira and I were thrilled to see him back to his old self. When we do things for others without selfish motives, great relationships evolve. Parents have a great role to play in teaching their children these essential values.

Indira and I embraced and nurtured not only our children but also our extended family. My wife was very close to her sister, Prem, and so was I. She was part of our immediate family. That relationship would bring us to a very traumatic phase of our lives.

Prem was married to Major Shamsher Singh, with whom I had a warm relationship from my army days. He quit the army to join the family business. They did not have any children. Prem loved children and would have made an excellent mother. One day, Savitri Singh, my mother-in-law, called Indira and me and said that only we could fulfil her deepest desire. We both were very close to her and said we would do anything to make her happy.

In a faltering voice she said, 'You have two lovely children. Why don't you have the third for Prem? Only you can give her happiness with this small gift of life. I want to see a child in her lap.'

Indira was expecting our third child but this came like a bolt from the blue. We did not know how to react to this unusual proposal. We both loved Prem, but how could we give her our baby? It was also difficult to ignore the only request my mother-in-law had made. We had grown up in families where the wishes of the elders were respected. The coming weeks were emotional torture. My mother-in-law kept begging us to agree to an adoption.

Finally, with heavy hearts, we agreed. We were blessed with a beautiful daughter on 26 December 1970. We named her Pia. She was a bubbly, good-looking girl and Prem immediately adopted her. The first few months were wrenching for Indira and me. How could we forget that Pia was our child? I could imagine the turmoil that Indira was going through. We were distraught at the thought that our daughter would not be with us in the way our other children were. Eventually, we accepted the reality of the situation.

In subsequent years, Shamsher and Prem drifted apart. I had developed a close relationship with Shamsher and told him numerous times to try and patch up but it was not destined to be. One day, a tearful Prem told us that she had decided finally to split with Shamsher.

Despite that, Pia got all the love and affection any child could have hoped for. Prem's life revolved around Pia. Seeing Pia with Prem lessened the pain of losing her as Prem was such a doting and caring mother. After completing her schooling at Modern School in New Delhi, Pia went to Wharton Business School in the United States to complete her undergraduate studies.

I was in Bangkok in September 1992 with Indira when I got a call from India saying that Prem was in acute pain. We rushed back. Prem had developed a nasty cough and had a severe pain in her throat. We rushed her to the clinic for a CT scan. It showed a shadow over her lungs. There was panic in the family. In the next twenty-four hours, we made plans to take her to Sloan-Kettering. We got in touch with Carol Farkas asking for help. She put us in touch with Manjeet Bains, an excellent oncology surgeon at Sloan. Every test showed that it was not a case of lung cancer. Dr Bains kept trying to determine the ailment but could not succeed. Her condition kept deteriorating.

By the time he found out that she was suffering from Wagner's granulomatosis, a very rare immune disorder, Prem had slipped into a coma. She was so full of life, and suddenly she was unable to move. Indira was deeply affected as the two sisters were very close. Prem passed away in the hospital in New York on 6 December 1992. It was a terrible loss for all of us. She was a caring soul and her passing created a vacuum in all our lives. The shock drove Pia to skip her final year at Wharton. The trauma she was going through also hurt us very deeply. We decided to bring Pia to Delhi. It took her several years to return to her normal self and come back into our lives once again. What helped was that we have always loved Pia as dearly as our other two children, Rajiv and Renuka.

After graduating from Wharton, Pia took a film-making course at New York University. For a while, she joined the National Broadcasting Corporation, a film production division of General Electric. On her return to India, she set up DT Cinemas. She then joined her brother Rajiv to steer the retail business of DLF. She is doing a great job there and the two make a great team.

Pia and her husband, Timmy Sarna, had known each other for years before they got married. Timmy is from a well-known business family of Delhi. His relationship with Pia reminds me of mine with Indira. He is now heading a retail and brand business.

After a brief stint at DLF, my eldest daughter, Renuka, married prominent banker Rana Talwar who was Citibank's executive vice president responsible for development of retail businesses worldwide. He rose to become the worldwide CEO of Standard Chartered Bank based in London. He later resigned and created an organization called Sabre Capital Worldwide that acquires troubled banks and helps them turn around. In India he acquired Centurion Bank, Punjab Bank and Lord Krishna Bank and amalgamated them with HDFC Bank. Rana operates from London and Renuka lives there most of the time. I get to see her when she comes to India during the winter months. Her son, Rahul, after having graduated in liberal arts from McGill University in Canada, has recently joined DLF. He is extremely focused and has a great ability to build relationships. He is certain to do well.

Rajiv's two daughters, Savitri and Anushka, who recently graduated from the Wharton School of Business, have also joined DLF. Grandchildren today are made of different mettle, and both girls are turning out to be extremely competent and appear determined to outdo Rajiv and me in the years ahead. Savitri, the elder daughter, is now the business head of the company's mall division. The younger one, Anushka, has been chosen by her father to head the ambitious DLF Phase V Project. This is a venture close to my heart as in my own days I had worked very hard to build a showpiece for the country. I may not be around when it is completed, but I can rest in peace knowing that Anushka and her father will do full justice to my dream.

When I ponder over the past, one of my greatest regrets is that I could not devote as much time as I wanted to my children. I missed seeing them grow, playing with them, catering to their curiosity and taking them to school or the park to play. I have some consolation in the fact that they grew up in an extended family environment and adopted the right values.

I am happy to see that Rajiv and his wife, Kavita, were able to spend time with Savitri and Anushka and ensured that she grew up with a respect for principles. In today's age, it is unusual to see children from affluent families grow up with that awareness. Pia now devotes most of her time tending to her two kids and I am sure she and Timmy will see the benefits of their efforts in the years to come. Likewise, Renuka and Rana have spent considerable time all these years in instilling the right values in Rahul.

Another relationship I valued tremendously was with Uncle Surendra. Whenever he read about my achievements in the media, he would call to congratulate me or even come over, despite his advancing age. I used to visit him often to hear him reminisce about the past. There was a strong emotional bond between us. The last time I met him was a week before he passed away on 10 December 2009.

At his funeral at Unchagaon, thousands attended. I can never forget the role that he played in my life. He had helped my father financially to enable him to send me abroad to study, then persuaded me to return to India, join the army, marry Indira and had been my emotional anchor till he died. With his passing, a major influence in my life and a highly rewarding relationship ended, leaving a deep sense of loss which is still with me.

Often, my relationships went beyond the confines of business. George Hoddy, for instance, got so close to the family that he decided to take Rajiv under his wing and admitted him in a Michigan school so that it would be easier for him to get admission into MIT. He realized that my long hours at work trying to build a business was resulting in Rajiv not getting the attention he deserved and decided to step in. That is what great relationships are all about.

Sometimes, first meetings can create an instant rapport and long-lasting relationships. Such was the case in my meeting Preston Madden, a famous thoroughbred horse breeder based in Lexington, Kentucky. Ever since he and his wife Anita first visited India during the 1960s, we have remained close friends and are in constant touch.

In the mid-1970s, we were invited by James Gourley and his wife Gilda for a pheasant shoot with Lord Devonshire. In the following years, we went on several such shoots in England where we met a number of interesting people, mostly from the United States. Among them were Robin and Carol Farkas, who were then prominent mall operators in New York. As I have mentioned, I can never forget how they went out of their way to ensure that Indira not only got the best medical treatment but whatever else that would make her feel comfortable. Robin and Carol opened their home to us and installed the required medical equipment. Carol was always at her bedside. Similarly, in a touching gesture, Sant and Daman Chatwal would send specially cooked Indian food for Indira every day.

Over three decades ago we met Leonard and Evelyn Lauder, owners of Estee Lauder, the renowned global cosmetics brand, on their first trip to India. We made a trip to Jaipur together and have remained good friends ever since. They have a beautiful home in New York adorned with the work of some of the world's most renowned artists.

We also have happy memories of Norman and Suzanne Cohn, a reputed business family of Philadelphia. Another couple, Madge and Martin Miller, have always been our hosts during our visits to New York. We never miss an opportunity to meet them. These relationships are so special because of the warm memories they have left us with.

Another close couple is Tom Spiegel and his wife Marilyn. I well remember a holiday Indira and I spent a few years ago on the West Coast of the United States. The Spiegels have an extraordinarily wide circle of interesting friends all over the world. Through them we have met a variety of people like Mike and Lowell Milken, American business magnates.

We also met Steve Wynn from Las Vegas, globally acknowledged as the creator of the finest luxury entertainment destinations in the world. I was impressed with his philosophy of how when one developed a real estate product, one should not look for immediate gains but create something that posterity would judge. This is something that I would have liked to create in India had it not been for the rigid town planning norms and archaic laws.

Indira's accident also brought me in touch with Ken Langone, chairman of the NYU Medical Centre in New York, who went out of his way to ensure the best medical support for her. Whenever we visit New York we make it a point to meet Ken and his thoughtful wife, Elaine. During one of our recent visits, we spoke of how all our friends were ageing. Elaine then remarked that she and Ken had developed a philosophy of life which they called Quality Time Remaining, or QTR. They now spend their remaining time pursuing only those activities that they love the most. Both of them lose no opportunity to travel to places where they have developed good friends. It reinforced the thought that came to me years ago while Indira was recuperating. Being blessed with a good family and with Rajiv taking DLF to new heights, Indira and I could take it easy and pursue our hobbies. That has added a new dimension in our lives as we have now resolved to enjoy life in the time that remains.

During my younger days, it was riding and tennis, but with advancing age I switched to golf, which I could hardly play for decades as I was so deeply involved with building the business. I went back to golf and Indira went back to a game she loved, bridge.

As we age, it is very important to have hobbies. I believe that people without active hobbies tend to age faster. I had time in London during Indira's rehabilitation so I started playing golf at different courses near the city.

In the months that followed, I developed a new set of friends, Indians mainly, who were as enthusiastic about the game as I was. They included Moni and Shobha Varma, Hira and Barbara Sehgal, Peter and Mona Thukral, Mohan and Manjit Chadha, Vijay and Shama Bhardwaj, Surendar and Sunita Arora, Satya and Veena Tohani. Another couple, Chiku and Biri Piplani, organized some very enjoyable trips to Switzerland for us. We started going on golfing trips as a group. These trips were organized by London-based Jeet Bedi and his wife Kusum, who have tremendous energy and enthusiasm. In the last few years, Jeet has organized several trips to Austria, Germany, Italy, Portugal, Ireland, France, Russia and elsewhere. He also arranged a golfing cruise during May 2007 in the Mediterranean region. We would party till late in the night while the luxury liner sailed. When we woke up in the morning, we would find ourselves at a golf resort where we would play all day and then board the liner again to head for the next destination. All these activities have added sparkle to our lives.

During our short vacations in England, we forged new friendships. Notable among them were Evelyn Rothschild and his glamorous wife, Lynn. They are from a renowned family in England. Inspired by India's economic growth, they formed a company with Sunil Mittal called Fieldfresh which grows a variety of agricultural products that are mostly exported. While Lynn and Evelyn were in India, they made a remarkable contribution in convincing the government to bring in reforms in the agro sector. It is always a pleasure to meet them as they are great admirers of India's growth story. We always looked forward to meeting Edouard de Boisgelin and his wife Sheena, as they are so full of life. Being with them has always been great fun.

Renewing an old friendship with Jaquine Arnold, who now mostly shuttles between New York, Nassau and Paris, has been equally rewarding. In recent years, we have met her often at Harry's Bar and Annabel's in London and reminisced about a relationship stretching back almost thirty years!

In India, too, golf has broadened my circle of friends and we often go on short golfing trips with many of them – Nikky and Kumkum Talwar, Ashi Burman, Guddu and Cristina Patnaik, Arvind and Ritu Chowdhry, Duke and Laxmi Walia, Tiny and Mani Thapar. Farooq Abdullah joins us occasionally on our golfing expeditions to Switzerland and England. On numerous occasions, he has invited us to play in Srinagar and we have always taken the opportunity to do so as it has one of the finest golf courses in India. It overlooks Dal Lake and was laid out with great care during his chief ministership of Jammu and Kashmir.

One cruise among the many we have done stays in memory for a sad reason. In July 2007, Indira and I had gone on a cruise from Vancouver to Alaska with Tiny and Mani Thapar, and Laxmi and Duke Walia. The cruise would stop at different ports where we would board seaplanes and see Alaska's stunning landscape from the air.

When I boarded the ship at Vancouver, I had a strange premonition. Yet, since everybody was in a party mood, I did not want to play spoilsport. After four days, we docked at a scenic place surrounded by mountains and thick forest. The seaplanes could seat about eight passengers. We were a party of six and decided to charter a plane for ourselves and not wait for two more passengers. We were then told that there was just one plane available for charter and that had already been taken by a family of four from Philadelphia. I walked up to the family and politely asked them if they would mind giving us their seaplane as there were six of us and we were in a bit of a hurry and wanted to travel together. While the family were considering our request, Tiny Thapar came across to tell us that she had managed to find another eight-seater plane which we could charter and pay for the two extra seats. The Philadelphia family had almost agreed to allow us the plane, but I thanked them saying we had made alternative arrangements.

I sat in the cockpit next to the pilot and as the plane was about to take off, I noticed a brass plate on which was etched, 'De Havilland–Manufactured in 1945'. Sitting in an ancient, rickety single-engine plane made me extremely nervous because of Indira's accident. I told the pilot that we were not going to fly in a plane that was sixty-two years old. The pilot was a happy-go-lucky kind of person. He patted me on the shoulder saying, 'Relax, old man,' and took off. He kept chatting incessantly instead of concentrating on the flying. A heavy fog was building. We were looking down at the scenery while the pilot was swinging the plane from side to side to give us a better view. As we cleared a misty patch, I suddenly saw to my horror that he was heading straight for a cliff. He saw it too and yanked the plane into such a steep climb that we would have fallen out had it not been for our seat belts. My heart sank and I kept asking him to be more careful. He finally landed on a lake and asked us to look out for wildlife. I told the pilot that we had seen enough and wanted to return. All of us were relieved when we got back to our ship.

We had just settled down after the nightmarish ride when we saw a CNN newsflash that a seaplane carrying a family of four from Philadelphia had crashed killing all on board. We were shocked into silence. That was the plane we were planning to hire. None of us were in a mood to complete the cruise after that. Memories of Indira's accident came rushing back. I remembered Pradeep Mehra who had forced me out of my helicopter as he wanted to take my seat. In the process, he saved my life as that helicopter crashed, killing him and his wife, Veena. It was eerie, thinking how fate had once again intervened. I had cheated death for the fifth time in my life.

Pradeep was a very dear friend from my cavalry days. While I was involved in developing Qutab Stud Farm, he said he was thinking of resigning and establishing his own stud farm near Delhi but did not have adequate funds or land. I asked him to look for land to start the venture. He came back very excited, saying he had found a plot on the Gurgaon–Delhi border adjacent to the famous Bijwasan farms. I laughed and told him that the farm he was eyeing was jointly owned by Indira and Prem. Pradeep almost fell out of his chair on hearing this. I told him he was welcome to the land. When he said he had no money to buy it, I patted him on the back and told him it was 'payable when able'.

I knew he would succeed in the stud farm business. As soon as the first profits came in he started repaying me. My gesture was something that Pradeep always acknowledged with deep gratitude. In the bargain, we developed a great personal relationship. Pradeep established the famous Usha Stud Farm and produced some of the finest thoroughbred bloodstock in the country.

Another dear friend who is no more is K.K. Mehra. He was a cavalry officer who later joined Oberoi Hotels. Whenever I meet his wife Prem, I remember his sense of humour and how he enjoyed poking fun at us. He was a great orator and it was always a pleasure to hear him speak. I miss him very much. My cavalry connections also brought me close to Bubbles, the maharaja of Jaipur. As he loved horses, we often played polo and had great times together.

Life is all about building relationships. Our grandparents were full of stories of the people who defined, enriched and gave new meaning to their lives. Our parents had fewer such stories to narrate. We will have fewer still for our children and our children will have only Facebook to talk about! No wonder so many young people these days, despite affluence and opportunity, do not have a proper sense of identity, happiness and fulfilment. You cannot have faceless relationships. It is important for the young to learn from the experiences of their elders instead of having to learn from their own mistakes.

Relationships grow only if we have the time and patience to nurture them. I enjoy being in touch with most friends who helped and influenced me all these years. Many of them are no more, but their memories will last forever. Whatever I am today is because of the wonderful people I have met. I learnt from them the importance of dreaming big and that riches do not come from money but from the right values and the right companionship. Indira's near brush with death taught me the greatest truth – life is short and one must make the most of it. If we were told we had just ten minutes to live, what would we think about? Would we spend the remaining minutes in worry or sorrow, or thinking of the petty fights and squabbles we had or some of the beautiful moments we enjoyed? Being with people has given me some of the most magical moments of my life.

15

BUILDING LIVES

A HOLIDAY WITH friends suddenly turns into a nightmare, a tragedy of unimaginable proportions, and everything you have achieved in life counts for nothing. Often, a tragedy or a setback can have that effect, when you start to re-examine your life with a different measure from the one you have used all along. Ancient Indian texts and mystics have delved deep into the process of self-awakening, the realization of one's fundamental nature, but one does not have to be deeply religious to arrive at this defining, or re-defining moment. In every person's life, there comes a time or an incident which brings about a re-awakening. In my case, it came on 2 January 2001, when a helicopter crash near Mussoorie killed several of my dearest friends and almost extinguished the light of my life, my wife Indira. The emotional turbulence was something I had never experienced before. There was shock, grief and the guilt that the helicopter in which I had been travelling had landed safely but the other one carrying my wife and closest friends had crashed. I was given a glimmer of hope when I discovered that my wife, through some miracle, was still alive, even though she was in a critical condition with multiple fractures and internal injuries. The accident roused in me an inner strength that I did not know I had, and a fierce determination to get her back on her feet with the best medical care that modern science could provide. For several years, I was focused on this mission to the virtual exclusion of all else, leaving it almost entirely to my son Rajiv to take care of DLF.

All through those tumultuous days, at the back of my mind I could sense the stirring of a new awareness. During the long hours spent in hospital corridors and waiting rooms in India and abroad, while Indira was recovering, I started to ask myself some hard questions about the meaning of life and destiny and one's place in the larger scheme of things. Till now, such thoughts had been quite alien to me, and I had never really had the time or inclination to address these questions seriously. The helicopter crash brutally brought home the uncertainty of human existence. It prompted me to examine the value of my worldly success and personal achievements. What dominated my thoughts was one niggling question: had I adequately repaid society for all the fame and fortune I had been blessed with? Pacing up and down outside my wife's hospital room, praying for her recovery, I could sense a re-setting of my inner moral compass. For the first time in my frenetic career, I had the time and the motivation to think about the importance of giving rather than accumulating.

Money does have value, but I realized that it would have much more value if it were used to help a greater number of the less fortunate realize their dreams. Often, we get so caught up in the pace and promise of our lives, we forget about everything else.

Perhaps, this was nature's way of giving me a wake-up call. One day, while waiting for Indira to be wheeled out of an operation theatre in a New York hospital, it struck me that I was indeed fortunate to be able to afford such treatment for my wife whereas so many of my countrymen did not even have the most basic of medical facilities within their reach. At that moment, I made a promise to myself: from now on I would devote a portion of my money, time and energy to provide healthcare and education to the poor and underprivileged.

Soon after my return to Delhi, I decided to discuss my resolve with my son and suggest that we allocate a percentage of our earnings to help our fellow citizens lead a better life. I was elated when he told me that during the period when I was preoccupied with his mother's treatment he had already initiated a series of major programmes as part of DLF's corporate social responsibility (CSR). His education at MIT in Boston, he told me, wasn't just about learning how to run a major corporate enterprise: an awareness of wider social responsibility was part of it. The programmes were already beginning to make a difference to thousands of poor people who lived around DLF sites. Both of us realized that as this involved the DLF brand, we had to reach out on a scale that no other builder in India had done before. I was happy to see the visible change in so many lives that DLF's first few CSR initiatives had already produced. I could see it in the faces of semi-skilled labourers and children who were being given free education. Learning to read and write was giving them a new confidence. I felt a greater satisfaction at that moment than I did while inaugurating a new DLF building. It brought home another stark truth: sometimes, simple things can bring a great deal of happiness and satisfaction.

The more time I devoted to expanding DLF's outreach programmes, the more I realized that, subliminally, I had always practised and enjoyed the act of helping others. Even when I was accumulating land to build Gurgaon years ago, I was intuitively practising my own version of social welfare. But, quite frankly, CSR as a corporate agenda was never on my radar when I first plunged into the business world. I was too busy concentrating on consolidating my business and overcoming the numerous problems that plagued the real estate sector to think of such deep and varied issues. My instinct was to survive and succeed and there was not enough time even to think of my family, let alone others' families.

Yet, looking back now, I can see that I was practising CSR in a way by investing a great deal of my time and energy to rehabilitate farmers who had sold their land to us. In those days, CSR as a concept was alien to the Indian corporate jargon. I did whatever I did as part of a natural inclination. Back then, my logic was that it was my duty to help the farmers who were, in turn, helping me build my real estate business. I was grateful to them for parting with their land and so I assisted them to find and acquire land that was much larger and more productive, to help them buy appropriate equipment and construct wells so that they could continue the life and livelihood they were used to and, one hoped, move ahead to a better future. I often also arranged medical help whenever needed, secured school admissions for their children, gave jobs to the needy and even tried to settle protracted family disputes.

Looking back, it is apparent that helping them actually helped my business grow. By giving them my time and effort and help, I had won their trust. They became my biggest well-wishers and brand ambassadors for DLF. Above all, they invested their money in DLF, helping it to grow into the giant it eventually became. Today, when there is so much news about farmers protesting against acquisition of their land for development, I feel great pride in the fact that in Gurgaon, DLF was able to assemble 3,500 acres of land without resistance or legal disputes. There's a valuable lesson in this. In my case, credit must go to George Hoddy, who had taught me that if one wants to progress, it is essential to treat the people around you with empathy and compassion. Genuinely well-intentioned CSR will not only increase your profits but will reward you in time with goodwill and credibility.

What I have described as my 'awakening' may, in a sense, be nothing more than my conscious mind giving form and substance to the intuitive approach that has always been a part of my way of working. Now that it had come to the surface and become a priority agenda, I decided to explore the best ways of taking the social outreach programme forward. I came to the conclusion that confining it within the ambit of conventional CSR practices would not suffice. In order to carry out effective empowerment in a big way, it was necessary to create a separate vehicle with a distinct identity, one which had committed and dedicated staff and clearly defined social welfare goals. This was how the idea of establishing the DLF Foundation was conceived. The corporate credo of DLF Limited is 'Building India', while the DLF Foundation, established in 2008, was entrusted with 'Building Lives', by empowering communities and creating opportunities for the underprivileged in education, livelihood training, health and environment.

In January 2011, I attended the annual conclave in Davos where the India-related theme was 'inclusive growth'. Listening to the debates combined with my own experience over the years made me realize just how gigantic and difficult the task is. Achieving the ideal of 'inclusive growth' in India is not the responsibility of governments alone. The gap between the haves and the have-nots is so wide, and the sheer number of the people below the poverty line, or just above it, is so huge, that unless every major business house, and indeed every responsible citizen, makes a conscious contribution to the mission to harness the country's vast human and social capital to build healthy, educated, enterprising and sustainable communities, there is no way any meaningful change can be brought about. I strongly believe that the business community in particular should never forget that they are not only part of society, but thrive only because of the socio-economic environment they function in. They have, therefore, an added duty to think big, not just in terms of making money for themselves, but also in looking for remedies to the problems and imbalances in society. I have also veered around to the view that such contributions should be in the form of targeted programmes and not just charity. Charity creates a relationship of dependence between the giver and the receiver. Philanthropy seeks to empower and enable sustainability. Charity is band-aid, philanthropy is medicine and, eventually, the cure.

That formed the basis of the DLF Foundation. Its agenda is to help the weaker and disadvantaged sections by empowering them – through education, jobs, training, and other methods. The idea is to help them stand on their feet and emerge as earning members in their families. Our task was to first identify the problems they face and then find practical ways to empower chosen communities and individuals to improve their lot by virtue of their own efforts and newly acquired skills. I am delighted to find that this approach has already started to show beneficial results and I, personally, am finding it deeply satisfying to monitor the projects we have initiated and to see the impact that is beginning to be made in building lives.

What adds to my belief that we are on the right track is that we have on board the foundation some truly dedicated, talented and creative mission managers and executives. I'll provide one example of the innovative approach of the team we have built in the context of the rural education project we started. I discussed the matter with the CEO of DLF Foundation, Lt. Gen. Rajendar Singh. We both agreed that many existing village schools were not being run the way they should be. Some had no regular teachers, others had staff for whom teaching was just a side job. He suggested a quick survey of schools in rural Gurgaon. We sent Gayatri Paul, a committed executive, to check out schools in villages close to existing DLF sites. She returned with the predictable feedback: there were schools without properly trained teachers and schools where children just wasted their time because there were no teachers at all. DLF Foundation then worked out an arrangement with Pratham, an NGO specializing in education, to initiate a teacher-training programme to cover as many as forty-four schools in Gurgaon district. Within a few months, dramatic improvements were visible – dropout rates fell and more and more children started attending classes regularly and getting interested in the learning process. This inspired Lt. Gen. Singh to raise the bar even higher. As a former director general of infantry commanding 300,000 troops, who was also force commander of UN troops from forty-three countries in Ethiopia, he had seen how difficult it was to rebuild lives destroyed by conflict. This was a different experience, but with the same objective, and here he was able to see what building lives really meant.

These are early days and there is still a long way to go, but there are several other areas in which we have begun to make a difference. The appalling lack of basic healthcare, for instance. I remember seventy-five years ago, I lost my elder brother Rajendar to pneumonia because there were no medical facilities in our village. Shockingly, even today, one has to travel only a few kilometres outside Gurgaon city to realize that the situation is still virtually the same for those living in the rural interiors. There are several primary health centres in rural areas, but, like rural schools, they exist only in name and on government records. The buildings are there, but without trained doctors or even medicines, as a field trip by Gayatri and Vijay Kumar Singh, now associate directors, at DLF Foundation, revealed. I was horrified by their report. I looked at the statistics on medical facilities in the country and realized just how pathetic India's healthcare infrastructure was in relation to the growing economy. The country has just seven hospital beds for a population of 10,000. The world average is about forty beds.

Another report by PricewaterhouseCoopers showed how much needs to be done: India needs 74,150 community health centres for a population of one million. It has less than half that number. Nearly one million Indians die every year due to inadequate healthcare facilities. As many as 700 million have no access to specialist care (80 per cent of specialists live in urban areas). Kerala is the only state in India which stands out with the spread and reach of its healthcare services. No wonder it has the distinction of reaching an average life expectancy of close to seventy-four years because of its healthcare model. The other, bigger states will take decades to achieve that level of healthcare, and by then will be catering to a larger population. It's a depressing, no-win situation.

The huge shortfalls in healthcare in rural India, like education and employment, can only be made up by private sector involvement. In Gurgaon, Gayatri and Vijay worked hard to bring together experienced doctors to provide quality healthcare in primary health centres close to DLF sites. It made an immediate difference for the women, who generally ignored health and reproductive issues out of ignorance and lack of medical advice or facilities. The hygiene standards also improved as doctors started to counsel them on the advantages and benefits of cleanliness. I remembered how as an eight-year-old I had to travel with my uncle for nearly eight hours from my village to Bulandshahr city when I was struck by diphtheria. There were no medical facilities anywhere near my village. I am lucky to have survived. Not many are that fortunate. It prompted me to introduce ambulance services for the villages.

We also established the CGS Hospital to deliver top-class veterinary services in Gurgaon after we discovered that livestock in the rural areas was dying because of inadequate care. For many villagers, these animals were an important source of income. Brig. A.P. Singh, general manager, DLF Foundation, says that the hospital is unique as it has the kind of sophisticated equipment for animals that major hospitals in India do not. My philosophy is when we do things we must do them perfectly or not do them at all. Periodic camps help treat animals at the village itself. The veterinary hospital even has an ambulance service for animals. I felt strongly about this as animals are generally neglected in our society.

Another discernible change at DLF was how Rajiv had integrated many initiatives that were directed at preserving the environment. Global warming and ecological disasters are burning issues these days. I feel that while we must continue to progress, we must do everything we can to minimize the ecological damage caused by development. After seeing what DLF has managed to do, I am convinced we can. One of my mantras in corporate life is that we must not wait for the government to enforce regulatory measures but must show responsibility by self-regulating. Even before environment-related measures were enforced on industry by the government, DLF had launched various initiatives to address these concerns by using eco-friendly building materials, recycling sewage and opting for piped natural gas to generate power instead of highly polluting diesel. These are basic norms that anyone can follow. Just one initiative to use natural gas as an alternative fuel in Infinity Towers at Gurgaon resulted in an annual reduction of 22,000 tonnes of carbon dioxide emissions. Because of those results, DLF has installed and commissioned 122 MW of gas-based generation in its commercial and retail complexes in the National Capital Region. Once such initiatives became an established part of our corporate identity, executives were enthused to come up with innovative ideas. One such idea was feeding the exhaust gases produced by the generators into vapour absorption machines to produce chilled water for the air-conditioning requirement of a building complex. These measures have resulted in the reduction of approximately 160,000 tonnes of carbon emissions every year. Since we started utilizing the waste heat for air-conditioning, there has been an annual power saving of 132 million units. To top it all, there is no ozone depletion as refrigerant gases are not used. There is also no waste water discharge and no carbon soot emission.

DLF today is the largest owner of this type of gas-based co-generation power plants and also of wind power (228 MW). Together, they reduce approximately 400,000 tonnes of carbon emission every year. That is why I believe there is no need to be overawed by the challenges of the future. We just have to put our heads together, allow space for new ideas to emerge and then implement them. Just as we did at DLF for energy management. K.K. Bhattacharya, senior executive director, DLF, and his team were rewarded for these initiatives with the 'National Award for Excellence in Energy Management' in 2008 by the Confederation of Indian Industry.

Every year, DLF earns substantial carbon credits from the United Nations Framework Convention on Climate Change. Such distinctions only make me feel more optimistic about our future. In isolation, our contribution may seem a drop in the ocean. Yet, if it could motivate fellow builders and developers across the country to take similar steps, it would make a sizeable contribution towards reducing the fallout from climate change. The construction industry in India is huge and will continue to grow as the country progresses. The construction industry is also one of the major contributors to global warming and a collective effort can go a long way towards reducing ecological damage.

Conservation of water is another issue that gives me sleepless nights. It doesn't need rocket science to figure out that water shortage will be one of the major crises facing India in the near future. I remember when the master plan of Gurgaon was being conceived, Khurshid Ahmed, then minister of finance and town planning in Haryana, visualized that if planned development was to take place, availability of water would become a major issue. As he was also the finance minister, his worry was how to generate the resources to counter the problem. I suggested that the funding could come from the external development charges levied on builders. It was an idea I had conceived and got builders and developers paying EDC interested in so that offsite infrastructure could be built by cash-strapped state agencies. Ahmed adopted the idea and used the money to bring in water from the Yamuna through a specially constructed canal to Gurgaon. The canal today is working at its full capacity but can only meet part of Gurgaon's requirements as the population has almost doubled since then. Invariably, these shortages are being met by builders, developers and even individuals by digging bore wells. This has resulted in groundwater levels in Gurgaon dropping to below 530 feet, an alarming figure.

Rajiv foresaw the disaster in the making. As a responsible developer, and something of a visionary, he took far-reaching measures to save as much water as possible. He came up with the idea of setting up DLF's captive sewage treatment plant with a capacity of 14 million litres a day so that the treated water could be used for non-domestic purposes like construction, gardening, air-conditioning and flushing toilets. DLF is now setting up dual pipelines to every residence in our new buildings as one will carry fresh treated water for drinking and cooking while the other will carry treated sewage for other purposes. It will reduce the potable water usage by over 50 per cent, a substantial figure. If such measures were to be adopted all across India, I am sure we would be able to stave off a water crisis that threatens our future as a country.

At first, when I created the DLF Golf and Country Club in October 1999, I relied on tubewells to create a green oasis. These were the only source of water at that time. Fortunately, the population was much less and water requirements were comparatively small. Today, the situation has dramatically changed. Now, there is an urgent need to conserve groundwater. The golf course has over the years become a green lung for Gurgaon with over 20,000 trees planted by DLF. Every year, we plant around 3,000 trees. Today, all the water required to maintain the golf course comes out of DLF's water treatment plants, which have a capacity of nine million litres a day. All future golf courses that DLF now creates will use water that has been recycled from sewage. Apart from saving precious water, we have been able to cut down on the use of chemical fertilizers as the treated water is rich in nutrients. Using bio-fertilizers has also greatly helped in maintaining the ecological balance. It is a unique golf course. In the migratory season, hundreds of thousands of birds fly in from various parts of the world. They do not nest and breed in an area that they do not find comfortable. More than sixty species of birds come in every year. The golf course has changed the ecology of Gurgaon.

In any well-planned city, such green spaces are vital. If more such golf courses are developed, they will add to the green spaces but also require more water for irrigation. Rajiv has taken steps to ensure that the sewage treatment plant has enough capacity to meet the needs of the present as well as future golf courses. It will enhance the quality of life without depleting groundwater and also not rely on the external water supply. Golf courses developed in the manner DLF has done are a model which has not been attempted on such a scale by other developers in India. I am planning to get the DLF Foundation to propagate this model of development elsewhere in the country.

All these initiatives have been taken in the short span of four years and have produced encouraging results. The success of the DLF model in areas like education, healthcare, vocational guidance and eco-friendly practices has shown me the future. I am convinced that the time has come when we need to replicate the

DLF model in various parts of the country and motivate other builders and developers to adopt these practices on a voluntary basis. To create the ambience for this to happen, we need a national movement. The DLF Foundation is well placed to lead such a movement. It is clear to me that a huge national initiative of this kind would require careful handling and the coordinated efforts of groups like the apex chambers of commerce, the real estate industry, National Real Estate Development Council, Confederation of Real Estate Associations of India and other like-minded organizations.

I am determined to use the DLF Foundation to kick-start this movement. Everyone at the foundation is charged up as they have seen the results of their initiatives. I want them to channelize their energy into igniting a national movement on issues like education, employment-oriented learning, education for poor but meritorious students, and healthcare for the underprivileged. They could also help create an awareness in the urban development sector in India about the importance of moving ahead in an environment-friendly and sustainable manner. This may seem like an impossible dream, but if done systematically, I am sure it will produce results that will benefit us all in the long run.

My own experience at the DLF Foundation showed that the task might seem huge and insurmountable, but with the requisite organizing capacity and availability of finance, it is possible to focus on specific initiatives as catalysts for change. We took up a few flagship programmes that would concentrate on areas like vocational training centres, scholarships for meritorious students and multi-specialty healthcare facilities. While millions graduate every year, they do not find jobs as they lack the skills required. This creates frustration among the educated unemployed. What really fired my enthusiasm was that all those whom we put through vocational training got jobs.

As our current education system is not designed to ensure jobs, it is only such focused initiatives that will help graduates find suitable employment. Brig. A.P. Singh, Vijay Singh and Gayatri did extensive research by travelling to various parts of the country to study the issue. They interacted with other institutions and organizations working in the field. They also looked at initiatives of GMR Foundation and L & T and various other NGOs that were doing similar work. They worked on their research for over a year and made numerous presentations to enable us to finally draw up a blueprint of a vocational training programme.

I believe that securing jobs for the educated should be a national priority. Literacy has meaning only if it leads to employment. We have developed a model that I consider is the right one for our country. The DLF Foundation will put educated youngsters from vulnerable sections of society through skill-development training programmes that will make them readily employable. To achieve this, executives of the foundation are constantly coordinating with industries and relevant organizations to assess their needs so that all our students can be gainfully employed. Such initiatives if done on a larger scale should also fuel the India growth story as there is presently a huge shortfall of skilled manpower to sustain growth levels. We intend to first start the programme in Gurgaon and then extend it to other parts of the country in a systematic and planned manner.

As it is conceived as a national programme, Gayatri has put in place a DLF pan-India initiative of providing vocational and skill development training. The plan is to have a nodal centre with state-of-the-art training facilities and then link it with numerous smaller centres spread across the country. To make it truly effective and broadbased, we intend to impart the training in a variety of disciplines by specialized organizations working in this field who have partnered with us on this programme. Each centre will have different disciplines depending on the needs of local industry. The training will be provided at a minimal cost and will be free for vulnerable sections.

I feel such an initiative will see thousands of families step into a better future. Today, there are lots of good schools and institutions that give scholarships to meritorious students, but what happens to such students from vulnerable sections of society who will never have the opportunity to study at, say, the Indian Institute of Technology? Our scholarship programme for meritorious students from vulnerable sections is intended to break that vicious circle. In all such initiatives, without proper research and resource provision, the efforts can come to nought. It took over a year of hard work to plan our scholarship programme as Brig. Singh and Vijay travelled all over the country to collect feedback from numerous institutions and met with social activists, eminent academicians and scholars to arrive at a strategy that would work the best. This role has now been taken over by P.K. Joseph, who as head of special projects of the foundation is bringing an innovative approach to the scholarship project. After interacting with other specialists, he structured the scholarship programmes to suit the typical needs of the community to achieve best results. Disadvantaged but meritorious students will be identified and given free quality education from the sixth standard onwards up to a graduate programme in engineering, medicine, information technology, management, fine arts and sports. Some outstanding students will be given scholarships to pursue postgraduate studies. The beneficiaries will, I am sure, emerge as leaders of tomorrow.

My experience in securing the best possible treatment for Indira often made me think of how many lives could be saved if we had similar facilities open to the poor in our country. In India, quality medicare is now available, but it is prohibitively expensive and out of the reach of the poor. In our rural areas, quality medicare is virtually non-existent, often resulting in needless deaths. I wanted to do something about the problem. Healthcare in India is a basic right of every citizen but only on paper. The

DLF Foundation has entered into a joint venture with Medanta-the Medicity, one of the best medical institutes of the country, to set up medical facilities in Delhi to begin with. Those who can afford it, will pay for it but a certain percentage of the treatment will be given free to those from vulnerable sections of the society while others will be charged heavily subsidized rates. Once it takes off, I want to get it replicated in other parts of India close to DLF sites so that a large number of poor people benefit from free or affordable state-of-the-art medical care and facilities.

When I was invited to address the graduating class of 2008 at the Indian School of Business on 5 April 2008 at Hyderabad, I spoke about the fact that while a sector like telecom had taken off in India, one was embarrassed by the state of urban development in our country. One reason for this was archaic laws and the absence of new thinking on the subject. This could be, I pointed out, because urban development was not part of the curriculum in schools and colleges so no new perspectives were forthcoming. There was an urgent need to set up an institute that would exclusively cater to the real estate and urban development sector. It would be aimed at creating professionals who could bring in new thinking and changes in the way the sector operates today, which is ad hoc and somewhat chaotic. The McKinsey Global Institute in April 2010 had presented a comprehensive report, 'India's Urban Awakening: Building inclusive cities, sustaining economic growth', to the prime minister, Dr Manmohan Singh, which also recommended the setting up of such an institute. I was really taken with this idea as reforms and policy changes at the state and Central level are urgently required.

We also require trained professionals who have in-depth knowledge of urban development and real estate management. So far, there are no professional educational avenues from where such specialized knowledge and perspective can be obtained. This situation will only deteriorate further as growth will accelerate urbanization. Having steered DLF into the position of the country's leading developer I would be happy to participate with the government and other like-minded fellow business leaders to set up an urban development institute which could become the crucible of new ideas that form the basis for a future policy and regulatory framework.

Training and educational programmes designed for executives will infuse new thinking and energy into the real estate industry. My vision is to help establish an institute that will be able to use its research to influence formulation of policy and regulatory measures and enhance their capacity. It will support policy makers and help industry take the advantages of planned development in real estate management and urban planning to a constantly growing customer base. It will take time but developers like Rajiv and the generations after him will see the benefits and advantages some years down the line.

All these flagship programmes are small compared to the needs of India, which are gigantic. It is tempting to do more such philanthropic work as it is so satisfying and fulfilling. I am, however, convinced that only after we succeed with these initiatives will I take the next logical step to expand these programmes. I am wary of the fact that organizations can trip over their own feet when they take on too many tasks without considering internal capabilities and other constraints. The growth story of India is inspiring but it will be an unbalanced one if we do not bring the poor into the mainstream and ensure that they also benefit from the fruits of development. If this is not done, there will be a volatile mix of injustice, bitterness and frustration that could explode later on.

'India inclusive' is one of the greatest challenges the country faces today. It looks certain that as India progresses, there will be increased migration from rural to urban India in search of jobs and a new lifestyle. This is inevitable as aspirations rise. But if migrants feel marginalized, they will invariably take refuge in unlawful activities in their struggle to survive. That is why well-intentioned and well-focused flagship programmes like the ones that DLF Foundation has initiated are aimed solely at bringing in inclusiveness and empowering the disadvantaged. This is why I am so passionate about replicating the foundation's work on a national stage. I can see the tremendous potential that exists. In another three to four years we will be able to make a meaningful change in the lives of millions living in abject poverty across the country. We are going ahead with a missionary zeal so that the foundation's success inspires other developers in India. To me, the work at DLF Foundation has become as important as our grand buildings rising into the sky creating new lifestyles, new aspirations and new dreams. One hopes the foundation will do the same for the disadvantaged and marginalized.

One day I told Indira how the DLF Foundation was moving into a new trajectory of social consciousness and the kind of wonderful work it was doing and planning to do. She smiled wistfully and asked me if I remembered how her father once told me that he had always wanted to do socially productive work, a desire he could not fulfil in his working life. He said that there were too many limitations and money had become a problem. I well recollected the day. He was quite ill and his voice was faltering that day. 'I want you to do what I could not. We today have so much and life has been kind to us. We have to repay society. When we do good work, God will reciprocate. You are my son now and must carry on the dream I have always had.'

I hope I am able to fulfil his wishes. I am so glad that Rajiv got into socially productive work even before I brought up the idea. My grandchildren show the commitment to carry the torch and add new energy to the foundation. Few of us are given the opportunity to change the lives of millions. Even though it gives me a sense of great satisfaction whenever I hear people speak of DLF's role in the development of India, deep down I am conscious that our contribution so far amounts to little more than a drop in the ocean. The task of Building India calls for a colossal, collective effort and has to be a continuous, never-ending process. An even bigger challenge is the mission of helping to meet the rising aspirations of all sections of society for a better life. If we are able to make a contribution, howsoever small, towards Building Lives, that will be the most meaningful legacy I could ever leave behind.

16

THANK YOU, LIFE

ABRAHAM LINCOLN ONCE said: 'In the end, it's not the years in your life that count, it's the life in your years.' I am now more than eighty years old, and it is the life in my years that has given me the energy and experiences to be able to say that it's been an extraordinary journey packed with enough highs and lows to last several lifetimes. Not many people can look back and say 'Thank you, life,' but I genuinely can, and also say thank you to so many individuals who made it such an exciting and rewarding journey.

I hope I have some years left to enjoy, but so far, the highs have triumphed over the lows and given me opportunities to reach heights I never dreamt possible growing up in a nondescript village in Uttar Pradesh and learning to read and write in a madrasa. Fate, destiny, karma, kismet, they call it by many names. Yet, looking back through the prism of time, there have been so many people, opportunities and circumstances that guided the course of my life that karma and individual choice have merged into the same narrative.

It was certainly destiny that led to a chance encounter with the viceroy of India and a love for horses, a recurring theme in my life. Providence also took me to England, and a highly enjoyable and enriching period of my young, impressionable years during which I mixed with British aristocracy. It was a heady phase, a swirl of parties, high-society balls, polo, and a close relationship with an attractive young woman who taught me much about living life to the fullest. It could have ended in my staying on in England had fate not intervened to bring me back to India.

There are times in one's life when the heart does rule the head but, in retrospect, I am really glad I allowed my head to make what was at that time a painful and difficult decision, one that set me on the road to fame and good fortune and also introduced me to the woman who would become the fulcrum of my life. I came back to India to join the Indian Army and my experiences as a cavalry officer were tough and adventurous but also highly educative. The army taught me discipline, courage in adversity, ethics, gentlemanly attributes and the ability to take risks and face challenges. Above all, it instilled in me a fighting spirit. It was a character-building process that has served me exceedingly well throughout my life, given me the pleasure of lasting friendships, and shaped my personality. I can only salute the officers and colleagues who transformed my life and continue to ensure this country's security with selflessness, pride and honour.

Jack Welch once said: 'Control your own destiny or someone else will.' It brings back memories of my early years of struggle, having quit the army and trying to make it as a businessman, when a powerful politician attempted to thwart my career. The fighting spirit and self-belief inherited from my army training, the support of friends and family and the burning desire to succeed helped me overcome the obstacles and the relentless pressure I was under for almost two decades. That experience, like many others that were to follow, taught me that patience and perseverance are often more effective weapons than haste and a headlong rush to succeed. Success tastes much sweeter if it comes with challenges and life-changing moments. I have had my fair share of them all.

With most of us, every experience becomes an education and the stepping stone to the next phase of life. Not everyone, however, may have gone through the range of encounters and opportunities that have marked my career, like sharing simple meals in village huts. Persuading law makers to change obsolete land and town planning regulations. Interacting with a lower level revenue official in his musty office. Negotiating high technological business deals, and, later the same night, partying in the company of the international jet set. There were times when the imprint of fate was clearly visible. For example, the chance encounter with Rajiv Gandhi in the middle of nowhere, which later allowed me to plead my case before him when he became prime minister.

It was again a stroke of luck that elevated me to the head of an influential industries association when I was still finding my feet in the world of business. It gave me confidence and the rare opportunity to experience the interface between the government and the private sector. It gave me access to powerful people at a time when lobbying for change and reform was essential to lift the Indian economy out of the so-called Hindu rate of growth. Experiences like these are what have inspired me to write this book on my life. They gave me insights into how governments function, why politicians and bureaucrats act the way they do, how businesses are created and run, how challenges can be overcome, and how individuals impact one's life and career, as do circumstances, unplanned encounters and the invisible hand of fate.

There are so many people who see me today as an extremely successful individual, the builder of the country's biggest real estate company. Little do they know about the trials and tribulations that I have had to face and overcome. Equally, not many people know about the severe setbacks that have punctuated my business career and the early ventures that did not work out because of unforeseen technological setbacks. No businessman can claim to have all the right answers all the time. In my view, experience is the best teacher and the most valuable lessons I have learnt are from failures and setbacks rather than from success stories and profits alone. I sometimes come across some management books with titles such as, 'Ten Easy Steps to Success.' There are no easy steps. There are baby steps and there are giant steps but they are all governed by so many external factors that it is impossible to chalk out any single, static formula for success. Change is all around us and it takes place much faster now than during most of my career as an entrepreneur. The ones who win are the ones who adapt to change in a level-headed way and who always try to be one step ahead of their times.

Vision is all about the future; it acts as a source of inspiration for an organization and provides a road map. Its pursuit has to be flexible to negotiate twists and turns in the path to the goal, and requires the ability to adapt quickly to changes in the environment. A vision originates with a dream. In my case, the dream was to revive DLF after government-imposed regulations had almost crippled the company and, with it, ruined a reputation carefully constructed over the years. That dream became a single-minded obsession that allowed me to survive serious challenges and a relentless, personalized campaign. It was an obsession that had one objective: to create the biggest real estate company in India and with it, lay the foundation for a new, modern city on the outskirts of Delhi, the national capital. At that time, it may have seemed to many to be an utopian idea but I myself never gave up, never stopped believing in the ultimate objective and never lost faith in the people who were helping me achieve it. Most private sector corporations usually have an identifiable face and name behind the brand and DLF became synonymous with K.P. Singh, but there were numerous employees, especially in the early days, without whom it would have been impossible to achieve what I did. Some of them have been acknowledged by name in earlier chapters – the rest I would like to thank and salute for their unflinching loyalty in fulfilling our collective dream.

Often, dreams have a personal element in them. In the years ahead, my children will follow their own dreams and shape DLF in tune with their own visions. DLF's original corporate vision began with my father-in-law, Chaudhry Saheb, who founded the company. I entered the picture several decades later, in 1975, when it was virtually on the verge of shutting down. But my admiration for him as a business visionary ignited my resolve to revive the company. I shall never forget that moment when he asked me to choose between enjoying my social life or getting serious about business. This was the moment of introspection and I was forced to choose which road to take. I am so blessed that Chaudhry Saheb was around to steer me in the right direction, treat me as the son he never had and entrust me with the future of DLF.

When I say thank you, life, I really am thanking him. I also thank life for helping his daughter, my wife Indira, survive near-fatal injuries and then a deadly form of cancer. At the time, it was the darkest period of my life but I can now see how it made me a better human being, taught me to cherish every moment with those who are important to me, and made me think differently about wealth and existence. Indira was the pillar of strength I needed in the most challenging times when I was trying to revive DLF. One thing that constantly helped me was her remarkable positive streak. It rubbed off on me all the time, helping me to shore myself up during difficulty. It is difficult to talk of Indira without getting emotional. She knows I cannot ever thank her enough.

The greatest regret I have is not being able to thank others who played such a crucial role in my life and are no longer around. That list is headed by my father. He was a strict disciplinarian and a very private person, so I never got really close to him. I found out only later about the sacrifices he had made to send me to England to become an engineer. He did not earn much as a lawyer but he knew the importance of a good education. He had to sell a piece of land and borrow money from my uncle to pay for my fees and passage. I wish I had found out earlier so that I could have thanked him when he was alive, but I will forever be grateful. Family members often get taken for granted in the passage of life but the uncle my father borrowed money from played perhaps the most pivotal role in my life. Surendra Pal Singh gladly gave the money because he understood the value of a good education. He had studied at Cambridge and rose to be a minister in the cabinets of both Jawaharlal Nehru and Indira Gandhi. Fate brought him to England on a holiday at a time when I had to make the crucial decision to either stay on there or return to India. His wise counsel and persuasive power influenced me to make the right decision. I owe him a debt of gratitude that cannot ever be paid.

Writing about the journey of life one tends to look at the larger picture of the opportunities and impetus given by fate and coincidence, and of the personalities who shaped one's destiny. The negatives are buried in the joy of having lived a life of adventure and fulfilled ambition. I could not have wished for more. Advancing age offers more time for reflection and introspection. I sometimes sit back and ask myself what it was that made me succeed in the most challenging circumstances. Perhaps, it was my habit to always look for the silver lining behind every dark cloud I saw.

Indeed, I have always been curious about my own lineage and yearned to know more about my forefathers. I was fascinated when I learnt that a cousin of mine, living in the United States, had a similar urge to find out more about our family history. Such was his burning curiosity that he actually began to seriously research our family's roots. Inspired by his efforts, I took it upon myself to pursue the research by digging deeper into all available records in a bid to go as far back into the past as possible. The findings have been very interesting and to an extent startling – my team of researchers has been able to draw out a family tree dating back some 1,000 years! I am in no position to vouch for the authenticity of the findings; all I can say is that it gives one an indescribable feeling of deep humility and oneness with humanity to know, or to believe, that one belongs to a long line of ancestors whose blood still runs through one's veins. Age gives one the right to take certain liberties, especially when one is writing one's own autobiography! I may be pardoned for adding an appendix depicting my 'family tree' in some detail – with this caveat: I have no way to provide further authentication of the information other than to say the date is based on whatever archival records are available.

As I rose in stature and business profile, it brought the opportunity to meet many truly inspirational people who would prove so influential in shaping me as a person and business leader. One was Jack Welch, the greatest living corporate legend of the last century. I learnt so much from him, most importantly the value of developing a larger vision and constantly thinking big. It also gave me the valuable experience of being associated with GE, advising them on various aspects of doing business in India. It wasn't just a personal agenda. I was privileged to use GE's global vision and financial clout to contribute to India's economic growth. There are many who credit Jack and me for igniting India's outsourcing industry and being the first to tap the country's hidden potential. The greatest lesson I learnt from Jack was to strive to become the number one player in whatever business one got into. In hindsight, I believe it was his influence that helped me take daring entrepreneurial risks to make DLF the leading real estate player in the country. Thank you, Jack.

I also owe a huge debt of gratitude to my original mentor in the world of business, George W. Hoddy. How do I even begin to thank him for all that he gave me as teacher, role model and friend? Above all, he taught me that chasing dreams is an inherent ingredient of entrepreneurship. You cannot achieve incredible things without an incredible dream. Dreams are today's answers to tomorrow's questions. But your dream must be achievable and based on realism. All too often, many budding businessmen make the mistake of chasing irrational fantasies rather than setting attainable goals. That can lead only to frustration and failure, financial stress, strained relationships and even breakdown of health and self-confidence. From Hoddy I learnt the importance of setting goals which are road maps that guide us on what is possible and doable. He taught me that before embarking on any major venture, it is essential to equip oneself with in-depth knowledge of the field of activity that one gets engaged in and thereafter carefully evaluate the potential risks involved. One of the key insights that I gained from him was that every businessman should develop the ability to spot the difference between 'impulsive risk taking' and 'prudent risk taking'. I have applied this principle in my business career and have found that thorough analysis of the ground realities always led to my taking prudent risks which invariably resulted in success.

As life went by, Hoddy's mantra became my mantra. It helped me in whatever I did, whether in tackling the complex issues involved in acquisition and development of land for ambitious DLF projects, or even, at a very personal level, in providing the best possible medical care for Indira after her near-fatal helicopter crash. I also imbibed and internalized his business philosophy that there is no right way to do a wrong thing and that one should try to get the laws changed rather than circumvent them. It was from Hoddy that I also learnt the value of building relationships and of getting to know the people who work for you. It helped me get out of many tricky issues that could have affected my early business career which enabled me to transform my dreams into reality with a fair degree of success.

I do believe that some individuals come into your life for a reason, they help you to bring out the best in you and they leave behind a lifetime of learning. George Hoddy touched my life when I was an impressionable young man on the threshold of a business career, had a profound influence on my thinking and way of working and gave me the greatest gift of all – the secret of success. Thank you, George.

Indira and I often reminisce about our early days when we both struggled to adjust to whatever life had in store for us. She came from a privileged lifestyle. Yet, we happily adapted to the army environment, starting married life in a cramped, dingy room in the Jubilee Hotel in Jalandhar where I was posted as a junior officer. We were happy being together. We were as content then as we are today. Prosperity came in the years that followed, but our values never changed. Children of rich families born with the proverbial silver spoon may not know what it takes to build a reputation and achieve success. I am truly blessed to have children and grandchildren who do not take their wealth or position for granted. Having a close and loving family is one of the miracles of life.

The pursuit of my dreams have brought some singular honours. I was quite surprised to receive a call from B.L. Joshi, the governor of Uttarakhand, informing me that the Govind Ballabh Pant University at Pantnagar had decided to confer a doctorate on me in recognition of my contribution towards the economic development of the country. Moments like these make you realize the scale and larger value of what you have achieved.

Some twenty years ago, I was appointed as honorary consul general of Monaco in India. Again, it was totally unexpected and I wondered why they singled me out for the honour. However, it gave me the opportunity to play the role of a diplomat in promoting Monaco and improving its relations with India. It has been a rewarding experience, made more meaningful when Prince Albert II of the principality of Monaco came all the way to Delhi in October 2010 and conferred upon me the prestigious decoration of the Officer of the Order of Saint Charles.

One of the most humbling moments in my life was when the president of India, Pratibha Devisingh Patil, conferred on me the Padma Bhushan, one of the nation's highest civilian honours, in March 2010.

At a certain stage of your life, there occurs an awakening: in my case, it was the inescapable urge to give back to a society that had given me so much. That is why my focus these days is on the philanthropic initiatives that DLF has launched. Receiving the Padma Bhushan really spurred me to redouble my efforts to help millions of disadvantaged Indians. I have two dreams left to fulfil. One, help the disadvantaged achieve a better life and two, try and create a new climate for urban development.

I believe passionately in the concept of every Indian owning a home. It will change India's socio-economic matrix. Homeowners are more responsible, law-abiding and active stakeholders of society.

DLF's corporate credo of 'Building India' and the motto of our philanthropic mission of 'Building Lives' are not just rhetorical phrases. I want to live up to both these noble ideals and continue to contribute to the building of a better India. If I can succeed even partially, then the eighty years of my life would become more meaningful, and I shall be able to hold my head high and say with pride, Thank you, life.

Appendix

TRACING MY ROOTS

WRITING MY AUTOBIOGRAPHY has been a fascinating journey into the past, giving me the opportunity to revive cherished memories of the people who shaped my destiny and revisit the events and occurrences which have had such a profound impact on my life. At one level, the effort to share my innermost thoughts and to lay bare the motivations behind the momentous decisions I took at each crossroad of my life and career forced me to ask myself who I really was. This in turn triggered a chain of other questions at another unexpected level – it led me to wonder not just about my own personality but also about those who made me what I am, my parents, my grandparents and those who came before them . . .

Somewhere in my subconscious I have always been curious about my origins and the roots of my family history. But I never really had the time or inclination to indulge in any active inquiry into my lineage. It was only while gathering material about my early childhood and youth that I stumbled upon some intriguing information and clues pertaining to my roots. This whetted my appetite to find out more about my ancestors and forebears. Much to my surprise and growing excitement I discovered that the more I probed, the deeper into the past I was able to trace my family roots.

Quite by chance I came to know that one of my first cousins, Dr Satbir Tevatia, a distinguished cancer researcher, settled in Pennsylvania, in the United States, was already involved in a serious attempt to trace the family history. Satbir's deep interest in genealogy, and the progress he was evidently making in preparing a pedigree chart with the help of his brother Rajpal Singh, fuelled my own desire to create a credible family tree. I decided to pursue the project as methodically as possible by assigning the task to a team of volunteer researchers.

Almost immediately the project got off to a promising start. A virtual goldmine of reasonably reliable information was available in records and documents meticulously collected and maintained by an indigenous community of professional genealogists, known as the Bhats. For several generations, this unique community of upper-caste Brahmins has been keeping track of births, deaths and marriages in big families and clans of northern India. The Bhats, who are hereditary bards, are known for the dedication with which they have been tracking the male line in individual families and clans, updating and verifying their records by frequent personal visits to cross-check names, dates and other details. They are welcomed everywhere with families willingly hosting them and listening to anecdotes of their forefathers.

My team of researchers collected a wealth of primary and secondary data about the Tevatia Jat clan to which I belong. I asked Surendra Kumar, a research scholar of the Maharaja Suraj Mal Centre for Research and Publication, to study and verify the material. He, along with others, like my cousin Rajpal Singh and his grandson Dhananjay Tevatia, spoke to many chroniclers and visited numerous places where the Tevatias lived so as to authenticate the documents maintained by the Bhats.

Surendra Kumar met the head Bhat of the Tevatias at Ghaziabad, Rishi Pal Sharma, who is a repository of the records of the community. He also spent time with Kapil Malik, the grandson of Jal Singh Tevatia from Bhatona village in Uttar Pradesh, who authored a book on the life of Dagre Wale Baba. The Baba is worshiped by the Tevatias of Bhatona and Khandera villages. Other seniors like Mehtab Singh Tevatia, Jal Singh Tevatia and the elders of Khandera village were also contacted to cross-check details. The meetings were coordinated by Col. Prithvi Nath, S.K. Mukhi and K.C. Katoch.

In constructing the family tree, the researchers have exercised due caution and made necessary corrections based on the balance of probability. The picture that emerges is that my family lineage can, in all probability, be traced back to Madan Pal in the twelfth century. According to the documents provided by the Bhats, Madan Pal was an army chieftain of the Tomar dynasty founded by Anangpal I.

According to the Delhi Gazetteer, published by the Ministry of Information and Broadcasting, New Delhi, in April 1976, the city of Delhi was founded in 736 AD by the Tomars. It was probably the threat of Muhammadan invasions that made Anangpal build the Lal Kot fort near Qutab Minar in Delhi. It is seen to be the first known structure built to defend Delhi. Historian Alexander Cunnigham also mentions that there is an iron pillar in the Lal Kot fort which has an inscription saying that it was built in 1052 AD.

Broadly, the family tree traces the genealogy from militant warrior chieftains to farmer landlords with a few like me venturing into business.

Surendra Kumar's research indicated that my forefathers had a distinct cultural history dating back to the Tomar dynasty that ruled Indraprastha near Purana Qila in Delhi for around 500 years from the eighth century to the twelfth century. Madan Pal had only one son, Suraj Pal.

When Mohammad Ghauri, the Turkish sultan, invaded Delhi in 1191 AD, Suraj Pal's son, Yashpal, was the army chieftain in Delhi. According to legend, Yashpal fought shoulder to shoulder with Prithvi Raj Chauhan. Ghauri was defeated by the alliance army in that very year in the Battle of Tarain. Interviews with the Bhats in Ghaziabad established that one year later, in 1192, Ghauri again invaded Delhi with a larger force and defeated the confederation of Chauhan and Yashpal.

According to the records maintained by the Bhats, Yashpal's son, Basant Pal, and his grandson, Tevath Pal, migrated to Rajasthan and founded Tevath Nagar in Jaipur state in the thirteenth century after they lost control of Delhi. His son, Dhakmal Singh, and his grandson, Bhagat Singh, were also residents of Tevath Nagar.

In his book *The Jat Rulers of Upper Doab*, historian Jagbir Singh says the Jats survived all odds as they were very adaptable. They readily shed their royal trappings and evolved an interesting feudal system of governance that integrated social, political and economic aspects. This was primarily based on the acquisition of land and its management. The available evidence also points to the enterprising and adventurous spirit of the clan that helped them rule over a large cluster of people. Clearly, they were hardy survivors. They went around establishing villages like Tevath Nagar, Janauli and Alwalpur.

The Tevatias stayed there till the fourteenth century, when they were forced to migrate again due to severe drought. It was inadequate food supply that forced them to move from Rajasthan to Janauli near Palwal in Faridabad as the area was fertile. Bhagat Singh's son Bahariya Singh was one of the migrants. Soon, the Tevatias emerged as successful farmers and powerful landlords.

However, once again there was yet another migration in 1328 AD, when Poorn Mal Tevatia, the grandson of Bhagat Singh, went in search of more fertile lands and crossed the Yamuna to establish Bhatona village. After he got married, he decided to settle there as his in-laws were in Kulli village near Bhatona. However, Bhawani Singh, the elder brother of Poorn Mal Tevatia, chose to continue his journey to establish Bhawanipur, another village in Sambhal tehsil of Moradabad, after crossing the Ganga. Some villagers of this clan migrated to Sihi in Ballabhgarh. They were either landlords or agriculturists. Many gave away their land to peasants to farm giving them a part of the produce as wages.

Poring over numerous books at the National Archives in New Delhi and also at the Maharaja Suraj Mal Centre, Surendra Kumar discovered that it was the Tevatia clans of Jats who were largely responsible for the agrarian colonization in many parts of north India. Being proud, hardworking peasants, they moved from one place to another in their bullock-carts in search of fertile land. They lived in small cottages besides their farms.

Interestingly, the Tevatia Jats were designated by the British Empire as a martial race as they were by nature warlike and aggressive. They were known for their qualities like courage, loyalty, self-sufficiency, physical strength, tenacity in fighting, and military strategy. They emerged as staunch sons of the soil, with a long history of brave resistance to invaders seeking to ravage their motherland. In modern times, a large number of Tevatias have served in the Indian Army, including in the Jat Regiment, Sikh Regiment, Rajputana Rifles and the Grenadiers, winning numerous military awards for gallantry and bravery.

Historians have differing views of where the Tevatias originated from. One school of thought is that the Tevatia Jats were originally from Iran or what was then known as Persia. Ecbatana was an ancient city of Iran. Interestingly, the Tevatias used Persian names for most of their villages. They migrated to India mainly due to political disturbances in Iran around 600 BC. However, other historians like James Tod suggest that the Jats originated during the Indo-Scythian period of roughly 200 BC to 400 AD. Indian historian Dr Natthan Singh is of the opinion that they were pure Aryans and their original homeland was 'Saptasindhu'. They migrated from India, he said, for economic, social and political reasons but later returned. Though they migrated, they continued to be rooted to their language and cultural traditions. This was the principal reason why they did not have linguistic or physical similarities with Huns and Scythians. This view is also supported by Thakur Deshraj, a Rajasthan-based historian. He claims that due to political compulsions like battles, they had to migrate from India to places like Iran, Afghanistan, Arabia, Turkistan, Mongolia and Siberia. Historian Sir Herbert Risley declared the Tevatias to be the true representatives of Vedic Aryans.

History throws up fascinating details and different perspectives. In balance of probability, the research team was inclined to go with the records and interviews they conducted in the course of their inquiries.

The Tevatias settled down in hundreds of villages spread over north India in the course of a thousand years. Surendra Kumar says this was perhaps because of family expansion or confrontation with the reigning powers that eventually made them move around and spread out.

Today, the Tevatia Jats are mainly concentrated in Faridabad, Bulandshahr, Bharatpur, Mathura, Ghaziabad and Aligarh and are prospering in different fields.

According to a book by Jal Singh Tevatia on the life of Dagre Wale Baba, Poorn Mal had two sons, Sadanand and Pratap Singh. Sadanand had three sons, Chaubile Singh, Bihari Singh and Gokul Singh. Bihari had only one son, Nandlal, who in turn had five sons, Banwari, Dulichand, Amra, Bhagru and Jai Singh. Amra had four sons, Harlal, Ballu, Dina and Gagan Singh. Dina had five sons, Jawahar Singh, Majlas, Karan, Salga and Jalam Singh. Karan's successors were Saheb Singh, Vijay Singh and Badam Singh. They were landlords who wielded tremendous influence and commanded respect in society. Their interaction with other communities demonstrated a unity of purpose and unique qualities of leadership.

It was Vijay Singh who settled down in my ancestral village of Khandera after the revolt of 1857. Various Bhats and senior villagers of Bhatona and Khandera pointed out that Vijay Singh was not famous for his philanthropy. But his wife, Bunjiadevi, was a soft-hearted woman always wanting to help poor villagers and farmers.

The researchers told me an amusing story they had heard from numerous Bhats and elderly villagers: Once during a drought, some of them requested Vijay Singh for grain. He refused. They returned when Vijay Singh was not around to request Bunjiadevi for help. She readily removed her heavy gold kadas – bangles – asking the villagers to pawn them with Vijay Singh so that he would give them some grain that they could also use as seed. When they came with the bangles, Vijay Singh recognized that they belonged to his wife. Realizing that his wife wanted to help them, he pretended not to have seen through his wife's stratagem and readily parted with the grain.

The records of the Bhats show that Vijay Singh (1824) had four sons, Himmat Singh, Dharam Singh, Hardeo Singh (1848) and Hardayal. Hardeo Singh had only one son, Harprasad Singh (1872), who was my grandfather. He had four sons, Ramdas Singh, Mukhtar Singh, Giriraj Singh and Richpal Singh. Most of them were landlords and agriculturists but my father, Mukhtar Singh (1902-1985), chose to walk a different path. He emerged as a respected lawyer in Khandera and was then appointed as the public prosecutor of the Uttar Pradesh government in Bulandshahr.

This, then, is the outcome of our research so far. Usually family trees are constructed for around 200 years, whereas we have traced my family tree back to many centuries, although I cannot vouch for the historical authenticity of the findings. It needs to be noted that the dates of births and deaths of some of the members in the pedigree chart could not be ascertained and so have not been mentioned alongside their names. As there was no direct evidence, some dates were interpolated as the likely ones. Personally, I find the family tree that has emerged quite fascinating and intend to continue the research in the hope of filling in the gaps, finding out more about the lives that my ancestors led and uncovering more evidence to verify the links in the genealogical chain of my family.

Index